# SEED OF GOD
# JESUS CHRIST

KENNETH MCRAE

Copyright © 2021 by Behold Messiah.

ISBN:
978-0-473-57323-2 (Paperback).
978-0-473-57324-9 (Hardcover).
978-0-473-57325-6 (EPUB).
978-0-473-57326-3 (Kindle).

This work was published by Behold Messiah in Invercargill, New Zealand during 2021. All of our books and articles can be found at beholdmessiah.com.

Corrections, suggestions and all other feedback or criticism are greatly welcomed, and future revisions will take them into account. We can be contacted at beholdmessiah@gmail.com.

All rights reserved. No part of this publication may be reproduced, stored, or transmitted in any form or by any means, electronic, mechanical, photocopying, recording, scanning, or otherwise without written permission from the publisher. It is illegal to copy this book, post it to a website, or distribute it by any other means without permission.

Behold Messiah has no responsibility for the persistence or accuracy of URLs for external or third-party internet websites referred to in this publication and does not guarantee that any content on such websites is, or will remain, accurate or appropriate.

The Chicago Manual of Style 17th Edition has been followed for the footnotes and references.

Book edited and designed by Jordan McRae.

# Contents

ABBREVIATIONS ..................................................................... 5

ACKNOWLEDGEMENTS ........................................................... 6

INTRODUCTION ...................................................................... 7

BATTLEGROUND FOR TOTAL SUPREMACY ............................. 11
    THE GREAT DECEPTION ................................................................. 12
    THE REDEMPTIVE PROTOEVANGELIUM ............................................. 14
    THE BINARY CHOICE FOR MAN ...................................................... 17
    WATERMARKS OF AUTHENTICITY .................................................... 19
    CONCLUSION .............................................................................. 21

LIVING SHADOWS ................................................................. 22
    THE FIRST AGE OF MAN ............................................................... 22
    THE SECOND AGE OF MAN ........................................................... 27
    1. LIVING SHADOW OF ISAAC ........................................................ 36
    2. LIVING SHADOW OF JACOB ....................................................... 39
    3. LIVING SHADOW OF JOSEPH ...................................................... 51
    4. LIVING SHADOW OF JUDAH ....................................................... 55
    5. LIVING SHADOW OF MOSES ...................................................... 64
    6. LIVING SHADOW OF DAVID ....................................................... 83
    7. LIVING SHADOW OF DANIEL ...................................................... 92
    CONCLUSION ............................................................................ 100

MESSIAH ON THE THRONE OF DAVID ................................... 102
    JESUS' ROYAL LINEAGE VIA SOLOMON, SON OF DAVID ...................... 103
    JESUS' NATURAL LINEAGE VIA NATHAN, SON OF DAVID ..................... 113
    CONCLUSION ............................................................................ 117

GOD MANIFESTED IN THE FLESH .......................................... 118

- JESUS AND THE TRIUNE GOD .................................................................. 119
- DIVINE MINISTRY OF CHRIST .................................................................. 127
- MIRACLES OF THE MESSIAH .................................................................. 131
- CONCLUSION .................................................................................................. 140

## RIGHTEOUS ATONEMENT .................................................................. 142

- PREPARATION FOR DELIVERANCE ........................................................ 144
- GETHSEMANE TO GOLGOTHA ................................................................ 153
- SACRIFICIAL DEATH ON THE CROSS .................................................... 166

## NEW COVENANT FOR A NEW CREATION ........................................ 184

- FIRST FRUITS OF THE RESURRECTION ................................................ 184
- NEW CREATION ON THE EIGHTH DAY ................................................ 199
- SUCCESSION OF THE PRIESTHOOD ...................................................... 205
- THE MYSTERY OF APPEARANCES .......................................................... 211
- SERVANT IN THE SPRING, KING IN THE FALL .................................... 215
- CONCLUSION .................................................................................................. 219

## APPENDIX ........................................................................................................ 222

## REFERENCES .................................................................................................. 226

# Abbreviations

## Old Testament

Gen. Genesis | Exod. Exodus | Lev. Leviticus | Num. Numbers | Deut. Deuteronomy | Josh. Joshua | Judg. Judges | Ruth | 1-2 Sam. 1-2 Samuel | 1-2 Kgs. 1-2 Kings | 1-2 Chr. 1-2 Chronicles | Ezra | Neh. Nehemiah | Esth. Esther | Job | Psa. Psalm | Prov. Proverbs | Eccl. Ecclesiastes | Song. Song of Songs | Isa. Isaiah | Jer. Jeremiah | Lam. Lamentations | Ezek. Ezekiel | Dan. Daniel | Hos. Hosea | Joel | Amos | Obad. Obadiah | Jon. Jonah | Mic. Micah | Nah. Nahum | Hab. Habakkuk | Zeph. Zephaniah | Hag. Haggai | Zech. Zechariah | Mal. Malachi.

## New Testament

Matt. Matthew | Mark | Luke | John | Acts | Rom. Romans | 1-2 Cor. Corinthians | Gal. Galatians | Eph. Ephesians | Phil. Philippians | Col. Colossians | 1-2 Thess. 1-2 Thessalonians | 1-2 Tim. 1-2 Timothy | Titus | Phlm. Philemon | Heb. Hebrews | James | 1-2 Pet. 1-2 Peter | 1-2-3 John | Jude | Rev. Revelation.

## Extra-Biblical

Jash. Jasher | Jub. Jubilees | Eno. Enoch. | Mac. Maccabees.

## Bible Translations

KJV King James Version | NASB New American Standard Bible | NIV New International Version | NKJV New King James Version.

## References

Gen. 1-2 chapters 1 to 2 | Gen. 1:2 chapter 1, verse 2 | ch./chs. chapter/chapters | v./vv. verse/verses | OT Old Testament | NT New Testament | Comma for verses of same chapter, semi-colon for different chapter or book (Gen. 1:20-22, 27-31; 3:1; Col. 2:11-12).

# Acknowledgements

I must give thanks to those who have helped bring this book to fruition. First are two encouraging women who kindled my desire and confidence to write, Patricia McCullum and Evelyn Gilligan. Patricia was my schoolteacher at Nightcaps Primary School from ages 9-10 who recognised something within me worth encouraging and gave me the confidence to draw that out from within. Evelyn is my dear sister in the faith at St. Stephens Church in Invercargill, who after reading a short two-part summary of a couple sermons I shared, encouraged me to believe that I was to turn that into a book. Upon reflecting on her words, I decided to make good on her faith and Patricia McCullum's hard work fifty years earlier.

Next I thank my son Jordan for the invaluable help he provided as the editor and co-researcher of this ambitious project. Despite having no biblical background, he asked many important questions that pushed my thinking and understanding in a very positive way. I could not forget to thank my wife Jan for her patience over the last eighteen months as I have worked away at these two books.

My good friend Mike Ladbrook was another important link. He pushed me to complete the book after reading the initial draft.

A huge debt of gratitude goes to all the authors and teachers whose works I have cited for their hard work and insight. You cannot write a book like this without relying on the research of others who have tread this path before you.

Finally, and most importantly, I thank Jesus of Nazareth for not passing me by, but having the audacity to reveal himself to me as a living reality on the 20th of November in 1989. May this volume be a blessing to him, and to you.

*Kenny McRae, September 2021.*

# Introduction

*So, the LORD God said to the serpent: "Because you have done this, you are cursed more than all cattle, and more than every beast of the field; on your belly you shall go, and you shall eat dust all the days of your life. And I will put enmity between you and the woman, and between your seed and her Seed; he shall bruise your head, and you shall bruise His heel" (Gen. 3:14-15 NKJV).*

This book is based on the curse which God placed upon the serpent who deceived Eve in the garden of Eden. The prophetic picture therein served as the divine template for the unfolding of human history, concluding with the redemption of man by the seed of the woman. Opposing this seed or offspring is an ungodly seed of the serpent. Both are sons who seek the following of humanity to the close of the present age, but for entirely different ends. Both sons declare they are the one who brings forth the light and claim the right as king. We will see that the promise of enmity (hatred) is in fact the underlying nature between these two seeds and their descendants, the result of which will be a final conflict where the two are forever separated.

The focus of this book is in identifying the singular Seed from the seed or offspring of the woman. On the contrary, the companion book, "Seed of Satan: Antichrist" focuses on identifying the seed of the serpent, the Antichrist.

For two thousand years Christianity has declared Jesus of Nazareth to be the promised seed of the woman and Messiah of Israel. Christians picture Jesus to be the one to crush the head of the serpent and redeem man through atonement on the cross. The contemporary Jewish witnesses rejected the messiahship of Jesus and judged him a false prophet worthy of execution.[1]

For those among the Jews in first-century Israel who were expecting the Messiah, it took the form of a warrior-king from the line of David who would free them from oppression and restore full national sovereignty (DEUT. 28:13). The royal authority of the Messiah as a conquering Davidic king is indeed a biblical surety but the idea in their minds of the Messiah was fixed according to their own desires, even where scripture deviated from this ideal (PSA. 22; ISA. 53). Although clearly delineated in the scriptures, the Jews, and even the Jewish apostles of Jesus, were certainly not looking for a lowly suffering servant with no concern for political upheaval in Israel. They wanted a ruler who would grant them freedom from their oppressors and assert his authority over the nations.

Their estimation of Jesus throughout the centuries remained unchanged. In the *Mishneh Torah, Kings and Wars 11*, the massively influential Jewish scholar Maimonides purported that Jesus was a failed Messiah set up by God to refine or "try the masses" according to a prophecy by Daniel (DAN. 11:14, 35). Speaking of Jesus, Maimonides continued:

> *Was there ever a greater impediment than this one? All the Prophets spoke of the Messiah, Redeemer of Israel and Savior and Gatherer of the Exiles and Strengthener of the Commandments. But this one caused the ruin of Israel by the sword and the dispersal of its remnant and its humiliation and reversed the Torah, and caused most of the world to err and worship a god other than HaShem [Lord or Yahweh] (G-d).*[2]

Maimonides, and the Jews at large, were expecting a conquering

---

[1] B. Talmud Sanhedrin 43a:20-21; 107b:14; B. Talmud Sotah 47a:14 (ed. William Davidson Talmud).

[2] Maimonides, *Mishneh Torah: Kings and Wars*, 11:6.

king in the image of David:

> *Now, if a king should arise from the House of David who is versed in Torah and engages in Commandments, as did David his forefather, in accordance with both the Written and the Oral Torahs, and he enjoins all of Israel to follow in its ways and encourages them to repair its breaches, and he fights the Wars of G-d, then he may be presumed to be the Messiah. If he succeeds in his efforts and defeats the enemies around and builds the Sanctuary in its proper place and gathers the dispersed of Israel, he is definitely the Messiah. But, if he does not succeed in these matters or is killed, we will know that he was not the one Torah has promised.*[3]

But the Messiah was to be much more than a king, and the hint is in the meaning of the word Messiah. The Hebrew origin of the word Messiah is *mashiach*, which means *anointed one*. The *anointed ones* in the Old Testament were not just kings, but priests, and prophets (EXOD. 40:12–15; LEV. 4:3-5, 16; 6:15; NUM. 3:3; PSA. 105:15; 1 CHR. 16:22; ZECH. 7:12). God commissioned them for a specific task by anointing (*mashach*) them with oil or the Holy Spirit to be set apart as *mashiach*, an anointed one. They were all types of *the Anointed One* in the singular, Yeshua HaMashiach (Jesus the Messiah or Christ). As the heavenly reality behind these earthly representations, he is a prophet greater even than Moses, a priest greater than Melchisedech, and a king greater than David. The role of Messiah is threefold:

1. Messiah speaks as a prophet by boldly declaring the Word of God to his lost sheep that salvation will be through him.
2. Messiah mediates as high priest between God and man by offering himself as the sinless substitute capable of

---

[3] Ibid., 11:4-5.

> forgiving all sins before God.
>
> 3. Messiah reigns as king after defeating all forces of evil that have conspired against the throne of God and inaugurates the millennial kingdom and the new heaven and earth.

The content of this book will progressively outline how Jesus functioned perfectly in each of these God ordained roles for the salvation of mankind. The primary elements discussed include the prophetic qualities of the godly descendants, the biblical covenants which narrow down the context of his life and his identity, the divine nature of his being, and the spring feasts of the Lord which serve as rehearsals for his works of redemption. The messianic claims of Jesus Christ therefore must be put to the test. There must exist convincing evidence to defend the case that Jesus of Nazareth is the seed of the woman, the Messiah of Israel and of the world.

# 1

# Battleground for Total Supremacy

At the beginning of Genesis, we are told the story of the creation of the heavens and earth, of all life, including the pinnacle of life—man himself, and his fall from divine favour. In the garden of Eden, the subjects were given access to two trees: the tree of life, which related to their union with God; and the tree of the knowledge of good and evil. To eat from the latter tree was to incur the curse of death (Gen. 2:9-17). This forbidden tree was the one point of attack for the anointed archangel Lucifer in his rebellion against God.

Even in the most perfect of circumstances, Lucifer desired to lift his heart up in pride and rebel against God. In his lust for exaltation by his own means, he craved to "be like the Most High" and take dominion over all creation for himself (Isa. 14:12; Ezek. 28:12-19). To further his own selfish purposes, he disrupted the perfect and harmonious order of the heavenly realm by convincing a third of the angelic hosts to follow in his lawless ways (Rev. 12:1-9).[4]

---

[4] The question then is the following: what caused Lucifer to look not at God, but within himself for exaltation, and to rebel against Him, from whom all things were perfect? Was he simply dissatisfied with his place in the heavenly order? Perhaps this came into question after God created man and entered a special and direct relationship with them. In the pride of his own heart, Lucifer may have felt his place of honour, authority, and communion with God had been stolen by the inferior man (Gen. 1:28; 2:7). Out of jealousy, or perhaps seeing an opportunity to usurp God's rule, might he have strived henceforth to take authority over man in place of God by implicating them in his rebellion? Lucifer would have been emboldened by his successful rebellion in the

In response to the angelic rebellion, God set aside a place totally separate from Him and all His goodness, known to us as Hell. The angelic rebels are to be cast into Hell after—and only after—a final judgement by God is rendered that is fully righteous and beyond reproach. After this time, the reality of His greatness above all others will be unequivocally accepted by all and balance will be restored. God needs not to prove this to Himself—but by doing so, avoids a situation of loyalty to Him predicated on fear rather than true reverence. In a once-and-for-all act, God will righteously judge His enemies yet win the hearts of all who choose to be faithful. Love and truth united in justice are to be the motivating factors for loyalty. Judgement in wrath is God's final act after every other means has been exhausted (Exod. 34:6-7; Hab. 3:2; Matt. 5:7; James 2:12-13).

## The Great Deception

"You will not certainly die," the serpent (Lucifer) reassured the woman, "for God knows that when you eat from it your eyes will be opened, and you will be like God, knowing good and evil" (Gen. 3:4-5).[5] The truth of course, was that God gave man the same freedom of choice given to the angels, even after He suffered from their betrayal. The serpent planted the perception that God withheld the means of true exaltation from Adam and Eve, while he was there to illuminate them with an alternative pathway to exaltation—to become gods on their own terms (2 Cor. 11:3-14).

---

heavenly realm. Surely to achieve the same in the earthly realm would seem to him to be trivial in contrast. There are indications of this being the timeline of events, but ultimately this is unknown to man. Remember when God challenged Job by asking him "where were you when I laid the earth's foundation? ... while the morning stars sang together and all the angels shouted for joy? (Job 38:4-7). God revealed that all the angels participated in the celebration of His new creation, suggesting that this was pre-rebellion. But all could still refer solely to all the faithful angels. Another possibility is that the angelic realm rebelled after Lucifer had successfully deceived Adam and Eve because they saw a unique opportunity to challenge the legitimacy of God.

[5] The serpent is directly identified as Lucifer or Satan in Revelation: "the great dragon was cast out, that serpent of old, called the Devil and Satan" (12:9) ... "the dragon, that serpent of old, who is the Devil and Satan" (20:2).

Consider how this promise was given by the most cunning and adept deceiver of all. What could be the ulterior motives? Lucifer had already challenged the supremacy of God and taken a third of the angels into his rebellion (REV. 12:4). Why should we assume that man would be left to their own devices?

> *When the woman saw that the fruit of the tree was good for food and pleasing to the eye, and desirable for gaining wisdom, she took some and ate it. She also gave some to her husband, who was with her, and he ate it. Then the eyes of both were opened, and they realized they were naked; so, they sewed fig leaves together and made coverings for themselves (Gen. 3:6-7 NIV).*

And here the sin nature was inherited. Sin as transgression, lawlessness, and rebellion. Our humanity became embedded with the *body of sin,* and consequently, a *body of death,* which doomed us to an inescapable end (ROM. 6:6; 7:24). The same self-seeking desire that led to rebellion and chaos in the heavenly realm was introduced into the earthly realm. Man discarded the "thou shall not" (GEN. 2:17) ordered by God in favour of the promise by the serpent to "be as gods" (GEN. 3:5).

Adam and Eve had their eyes opened to good and evil, and realised they were naked, not simply physically, but spiritually. It was spiritual nakedness that brought on the feelings of guilt and shame which led them to hide from God's presence (GEN. 3:10-11). Notice that God went looking for them. He never intended on giving up on His beloved creation. Instead, He immediately went and fashioned together "garments of skin" for Adam and Eve to wear as a temporary covering (GEN. 3:7-11, 21). He cloaked them under the skin of an innocent animal substitute to hide their impurity from His sight. Because death was the consequence for eating the fruit, either Adam and Eve had to die, or a substitute had to take their place. Blood had to be continually shed for the forgiveness of our sins (HEB. 9:22) for otherwise, "the soul who sins shall die" (Ezek. 8:4; Rom. 6:23).[6] The blood of animal substitutes served to cover our sins, not to remove our sin nature which doomed us to death, for they were without sin themselves.

God was willing to temporarily cover our sins because a truly redemptive sacrifice had already been slain from before the foundation of the world (Rev. 13:8; Eph. 1:3-7). This could only speak of the human incarnation of the divine God. No other substitute could atone for us. As it was later said: "for this purpose the Son of God was manifested, that He might destroy the works of the devil" (1 John 3:8). The late Chinese evangelist Witness Lee expounded on this truth:

> *Satan was joyful thinking he had taken over man. But God seemed to say, "I also will become incarnated. If Satan wrought himself in to man, then let me enter man and put man upon myself.*[7]

God was not caught by surprise by the cunning deception of the serpent. He promised a day to come when we are covered with an eternal garment of salvation, the same radiant light of purity and innocence which Adam and Eve emanated before their transgression (Isa. 61:10). We deserved death, but God wanted to redeem us.

### The Redemptive Protoevangelium

Immediately after the fall of man into Lucifer's rebellion, the merciful and loving God declared a prophetic plan for man's redemption—the protoevangelium, or first messianic gospel of salvation:

---

[6] B. Talmud Yoma 5a states: *"Isn't atonement accomplished only by the sprinkling of the blood, as it is stated: 'For it is the blood that makes atonement by reason of the life' (Lev. 17:11)?"* See also the Midrashic compilation Yalkut Shimoni Exod. 29 and the tractate Zevahim 6a.

[7] Lee, *The Economy of God*, 111.

> *The woman said, "The serpent deceived me, and I ate."*
> *So, the LORD God said to the serpent: "Because you have*
> *done this, you are cursed more than all cattle ... And I will*
> *put enmity between you and the woman, and between*
> *your seed and her Seed; He shall bruise your head, and*
> *you shall bruise His heel" (Gen. 3:13-15 NKJV).*

We are told from the beginning of mankind that a man is destined to come from the seed or offspring of the woman (Eve) to challenge the seed of the accursed serpent (Lucifer). The seed of the woman is biological (human Eve), but the seed of the serpent is spiritual (spirit Lucifer). The seed of the woman is favoured by God—it is the godly line by birth—but the seed of the serpent is cursed by God—it is the ungodly line by spiritual alignment.[8]

Notice how the battle is oriented around the seed of the woman and the serpent, not his intermediary seed. The serpent is said to bruise the heel of the godly seed, but the godly seed shall ultimately bruise or crush the head of not only the ungodly seed, but the serpent himself. The godly defeats the ungodly, but at a great cost. Equipped with the knowledge of the scriptures, both the Old and New Testaments, the prophetic picture becomes more clear. The language suggests that the war over heaven between God and Lucifer is decided on earth by the seed of the woman. I believe that this is accomplished by the necessary redemptive sacrifice of the seed of the woman, for as the scholar Caroline Stanke said, "the forgiving and covering of sin were always accompanied by a sacrifice":

---

[8] The seed of the serpent is based on spiritual descendancy, not biological. This topic has been poisoned by a racist fringe who posit that Cain was the biological son of Lucifer and use this to denigrate those they claim are the accursed "serpent seed." This is a baseless view, for it is explicitly said that Cain was the son of Adam and Eve (GEN. 4:1). There are certainly peoples who are generally considered to be ungodly, such as the line of Cain, the Canaanites in particular, or even the sons of Esau, the Edomites and Amalekites. However, individuals are not judged based on their blood.

> *God promised in Eden that there will be a redeemer who would, once and for all, crush the head of the serpent. But to really make atonement for sin and to bring man back into close companionship with God, another sacrifice was needed.[9]*

The typology of the substitutionary sacrifice is progressively delineated throughout the Old Testament for a reason. As previously mentioned, God taught the practice of substitutionary sacrifice to Adam and Eve. It was then passed down to their sons Cain and Abel, for we read of the instance when the two boys offered up sacrifices before God, and respect was given unto the sacrifice of sheep by Abel, but not the farm yield by Cain (GEN. 4:3-5). Again, Abraham was ordered to sacrifice a bull in the place of his son Isaac, which is discussed in the following chapter.

It was the blood, the life of the sinless animal, which bought salvation from Egypt. God spared the lives of those who smeared the blood of the innocent and unblemished lamb on their doorposts (EXOD. 12:13). Blood sealed God's covenant with the Hebrew people and brought them under His protection. This covenant was ratified when Moses sprinkled the oxen blood on the altar (EXOD. 24:5-8). God instituted by law the practice of blood atonement when He spoke the law to Moses:

> *For the life of the flesh is in the blood, and I have given it to you upon the altar to make atonement for your souls; for it is the blood that makes an atonement for the soul (Lev. 17:11 NIV).*

The provisions in the law for the cleansing of sins required the blood of animal substitutes. As one example, on the yearly Day of Atonement the high priest sprinkled the blood of a sin offering upon the mercy seat in the temple to cleanse himself and the

---

[9] Stanke, "The Motif of the Messiah in Zechariah 9-14," 72, https://dx.doi.org/10.32597/theses/128.

people of their sins (Exod. 30:10; Lev. 16).

This is all to say that the seed of the woman is prefigured by these substitutionary sacrifices all throughout scripture. The fullness of this revelation was gifted to mankind after the redemptive death and resurrection of Jesus Christ, the son of God (Isa. 53:7; John 1:29, 36; 1 Cor. 5:7; Rev. 5:12; 12:11; 13:8; 22:3):

> *Inasmuch then as the children have partaken of flesh and blood, He Himself likewise shared in the same, that through death He might destroy him who had the power of death, that is, the devil, and release those who through fear of death were all their lifetime subject to bondage (Heb. 2:14-15 NKJV).*

In other words, through his perfect sacrificial death as the seed of the woman he crushed the serpent's head and released man from the curse of everlasting death (Gen. 3:15). The apostle Paul affirmed this to be true of Jesus when he said, "the God of peace will soon crush Satan under your feet" (Rom. 16:20; Isa. 9:6-7; 14:24-26). He did what Adam could not, nor any man, by staying faithful to both man and God as the son of man and God. He vindicated the character of his Father and the unity of the Godhead of which he is joined, and in doing so reconciled man to God.

**The Binary Choice for Man**

C. S. Lewis perfectly encapsulates our binary situation in his classic work *Mere Christianity*:

> *God created things with free will. That means creatures which can go either wrong or right. Some people think they can imagine a creature that was free and had no possibility of going wrong; I cannot. If a thing is free to be good, it is also free to go bad. Why then did God give us free will? Because free will, though it makes evil possible, also is the only thing that makes love or goodness or joy worth having ... If God thinks this state*

> *of war in the universe a price worth paying for free will- that is for making a live world in which creatures can do real, good or harm and something of real importance can happen, instead of a toy world which only moves when he pulls the strings-then we may take it that it is worth paying.*[10]

God gives man every opportunity to be free, even if that freedom separates man from Himself and unites man with His enemy. Repentance—that is the ability to think again and humble oneself towards God—must also be of man's own volition. It cannot be forced or simply a matter of fate—the relationship must be genuine. For God to be just and therefore good, man cannot be excused from the consequences of his actions without being forgiven from a basis of righteousness. If the rebel angels (or the agents of liberty as some suggest) are to be righteously judged for the exact same transgression, it would be contradictory of a just and immutable God to make an arbitrary exception for man. To deny His own nature would void any fair and legitimate judgement He could possibly cast upon Lucifer and his angels (2 TIM. 2:12-13; HEB. 6:13-18). God must therefore balance mercy with justice.

    I personally think God *did* extend the same mercy to Lucifer by offering a final chance of repentance in the tree of the knowledge of good and evil. Lucifer's fate was placed entirely in his own hands and yet he acted upon the inclinations of his rebellious heart by tempting Eve away from God and into his rebellion. The chance for redemption here through humble submission to God was the other more sensible option (LUKE 15:11-32). Nevertheless, he wilfully chose the former and for that there is now no going back for him or the Most High. Enmity will always and forever be the disposition between them (GEN. 3:15).

---

[10] Lewis, *Mere Christianity*, 47-49.

*Godly Line*

Those of the godly line have one way to the God of the tree of life, and that is through faith in His Word for guidance and spiritual revelation. There is either faith or unbelief. No third option is available. True biblical faith directs our efforts away from personal god realisation towards encounter with the living God Himself. All that is asked of us is to understand and accept that it is the promised seed of the woman who makes this restored union possible by crushing the serpent's head through an act of self-denial and sacrifice. Our exaltation is dependent entirely upon the righteous character of God which is imparted to those who believe. By grace (unmerited mercy) He grants the repentant spiritual revelation of this truth so they may be freed from the lie of self-Godhood told by the serpent (ROM. 3:21-31; 4:20-25; 8:14-17; EPH. 2:10).

*Ungodly Line*

The ungodly line glorifies the doctrine of self-Godhood preached by the serpent, directing us to be wise in our own eyes and to claim for ourselves what we accept as right and wrong, or good or evil. The road to salvation for the ungodly is entirely relative—it is purely of our own choosing. The suggested antidote to the suffering and loss of meaning we endure is in the serpent's promise to "be as gods" (GEN. 3:4-5). These sentiments are echoed in the ancient mystery religions, and in the current ecumenical movement which is pushing us towards religious homogeneity. By these means he shall prepare the world for his own seed who endeavours to take the place of the seed of the woman as king.

## Watermarks of Authenticity

To train ourselves to authenticate the word of God we must analyse His many watermarks which will either authenticate or disprove the testimony of Jesus Christ as the seed of the woman. Most of us are aware of how the nations of the world make use of watermarks within currency notes to identify them as legal tender. What is not as commonly known is how God has embedded watermark systems throughout the entire Bible. As it pertains to currency, the banks and governments of the world all take the threat of counterfeiting extremely seriously. Staff are put through rigorous training and ever-evolving identification systems are put in place to outpace the fraudsters. The danger is not simply in people using fake money to enrich themselves at no benefit to others, but the inevitable inflation of the economy that follows. Left unchecked, hyperinflation takes hold and the value of the currency devalues to near worthlessness. We saw this happen in Germany after World War One.

To tie this in with the spiritual economy of the world now, something similar is happening here. The true spiritual currency has always been related to the promised seed of the woman who is to crush the head of the serpent. At the bidding of Satan—the ultimate counterfeiter—plans were devised long ago to dilute, and thus hyperinflate, the spiritual economy. To make many roads to God appear possible and the idea of one exclusive path a sign of foolishness and arrogance. The goal here being to render the legal spiritual tender—the atoning work of the promised offspring of Eve—utterly worthless. Consider how the name Antichrist does not simply mean against Christ, but further—in place of Christ.

This begs the question—if we can detect counterfeits within physical currency, can we do the same for spiritual currency? The answer is a resounding yes. In all His wisdom, God inspired many different conduits of His Word to record His revelation in scripture. Each unknowingly weaved together countless unique threads or watermarks embedded not just within their contributions, but which combined with that of the other writers across time and place. Together they form a complex tapestry that serves as an ultimate seal and as a representation of the totality of His Word. Any disturbances in its original structure can be seen by those who choose to look closely. Just as the bank and government staff are diligent and faithful in their duties to detect counterfeits, we who call ourselves Christian are to be the same, and "contend for the faith which was once delivered unto the saints" (JUDE 3-4).

## Conclusion

Earth has become the battleground for eternal supremacy and dominion. Two heavenly beings profess to be the light and are seeking our allegiance. This conflict demands our deepest consideration to the competing claims made by these two protagonists. Just as God allowed the rebellious serpent into the garden, God affords us the same freedom to disobey and choose our own path. Will it be the godly line, where surrendering of the self brings freedom through reconciliation with God? Or will it be the ungodly line, where self-Godhood becomes the predominant focus—and where "thou shall not" has no application?

# 2

# Living Shadows

In this chapter the watermark to be examined relates to the living shadows of the seed of the woman. These are the great but flawed men whose stories each tell a prophetic story of the promised son and Messiah. The experiences and character traits of these men—both natural and learned through hard trial—combine to become the key that unlocks the reality of this promised seed. As a Christian, I believe this son to be Jesus of Nazareth, so I will be presenting the parallels between Jesus and the living shadows. Each of these men were descended along the godly line from Adam through Seth, then down to Noah, then through his son Shem to a man called Abraham, the spiritual father of the faith. The living shadows to be discussed are all descendants of Abraham whom God called out to lead prophetic lives. I am going to share the ancestral line to these men from the very beginning at Adam and give the associated meanings of their names in the process. I implore you to check the Hebrew translations and pictographs for yourself to see if you agree with my interpretations.[11]

### The First Age of Man

Adam was a direct creation of God, a son of God (ben elohim), but after his transgression with Eve he lost his divine status and

---

[11] To check the Hebrew translations, consider the following sources: Abarim Publications; Köhler and Baumgartner, The Hebrew & Aramaic Lexicon of the Old Testament; Strong, The Exhaustive Concordance of the Bible.

simply became *human* (adam) of the earth (adamah). His descendants, being estranged from God, lived according to their own human desires and corrupted the world with wickedness. During the days of Noah ten generations from Adam, God refreshed life on earth with the great flood. The world was restored, but it was not redeemed. Mankind was still fallen so judgement remained inevitable. The world depended on the birth of a greater Adam, one both man and divine, to defeat this curse of sin and death. The birth of this redeemer, the one and only ontological son of God, Jesus Christ, is the culmination of the following genealogy. Whereas Adam was created from the dust of the earth, Jesus—the second but greater Adam—is begotten of God (1 COR. 15:45-49). He is uniquely capable of reversing our fallen nature which doomed us to judgement by transforming us back into his likeness which is the very image of God (1 JOHN 3:1-3). Let us now investigate the first of these generations to Jesus, starting with the first age of man from Adam to Noah:

*Image 2.1 – Hebrew name meanings from Adam to Noah*

| NAME | HEBREW MEANING |
|---|---|
| Adam | *man* |
| Seth | *appointed* |
| Enos | *mortal* |
| Kenan | *sorrow* |
| Mahalalel | *blessed God* |
| Jared | *shall come down* |
| Enoch | *teaching* |
| Methuselah | *his death shall bring* |
| Lamech | *the despairing* |
| Noah | *rest* |

**INTERPRETATION FROM COMBINED MEANINGS**

Man appointed mortal sorrow, the blessed God shall come down teaching his death shall bring the despairing rest.

As you can see, their names produce a prophecy which mirrors the salvific promise of God from the garden of Eden. God shall come down to earth as a man and His substitutionary death shall overturn the curse of the serpent which doomed us to a body of death and a world of corruption. While it is evident that the despairing rest has yet to materialise, the pathway has been paved by the human incarnation of God that is Jesus Christ. It is by his death and resurrection that we are brought the despairing rest from sin and death. Those who believe in him will enter into this promised rest after he returns and "death is swallowed up in victory" (1 Cor. 15:54). First the dead, then the living, will be caught up (harpazo) to be with the Lord and transformed from mortality to immortality and corruptible to incorruptible (1 Cor. 15:35-56; 1 Thess. 4:13-18).

> And God will wipe away every tear from their eyes; there shall be no more death, nor sorrow, nor crying. There shall be no more pain, for the former things have passed away (Rev. 21:4 NKJV).

We see from the above table that Noah is the tenth generation of man. There is another layer of significance here which comes from the Hebrew meaning of the tenth letter and tenth numeral, *yod*. The letter yod is the smallest or most humble letter of the Hebrew alphabet. The word associated with ten is *eser*, itself comprised of the letters *ayin* (to see or discern), *shin* (separate), and *resh* (authority). By combining these all together, we piece together the following:

*Image 2.2 – Breakdown of the tenth letter and numeral, Yod*

| VALUE | LETTER | PICTOGRAPH | WORD |
|---|---|---|---|
| 10 | Yod (י) | Hand | Eser (עשר) |
| **INTERPRETATION FROM COMBINED MEANINGS** | | | |
| By the hand of God, the humble receive the authority to discern and separate truth from error. | | | |

As a model for all believers, those who humble themselves to God receive His divine truth to steer us away from falsehood and human error. Nowhere is this more clearly shown than by Noah:

> *By faith Noah, being divinely warned of things not yet seen, moved with godly fear, prepared an ark for the saving of his household (Heb. 11:7 NKJV).*

Noah humbly saw by faith what no others could, being "divinely warned" of the impending judgement by the flood (HEB. 11:7). The faithful work of Noah ensured that God's redemptive plan for mankind was not thwarted. The seed of the woman promised to Adam and Eve could be born through the solitary line of Noah.

*The First Covenant with Noah*

Before we continue down the genealogy from Noah it is important to mention the Noahic covenant, the first of five covenants crucial to the story of God's redemptive plan for man (GEN. 8:18-22, 9:1-17).[12] Though the inclinations of man were, and still are, demonstrably evil, God vowed never again to send a flood to destroy all living creatures (GEN. 9:9-12). As a surety of this promise, God designated the rainbow to be a visible sign of the everlasting nature of the covenant (GEN. 9:12-16). This is not to say that the judgement of the flood was redemptive. It was only restorative. All of man, even Noah, the one man found to be blameless before God, were still fallen in the new world (GEN. 6:8-9; 7:1). The works of the old world were washed away in the flood so that life could be regenerated. God's order to propagate mankind in the new world was not because man had become justified or good before Him, it was because the man who *is* justified and good, the seed of the woman, needed to be born for the justification of all mankind. Dr. Michael Youssef expressed this sentiment well:

---

[12] Consider watching the three-part video series by David Pawson entitled "The Five Covenants of God," https://www.davidpawson.org/resources/series/the-five-covenants-of-god-2009.

> *In order for God's previous promise to be fulfilled, God had to sustain and protect mankind. But wickedness and violence had become rampant—so He chose Noah to be like a new Adam on a new earth (9:1, 7)—not a redeemed earth nor a redeemed Adam, but a man who would preserve mankind. In this way, God ensured the Seed of Eve would come to fulfill the covenant of Grace.*[13]

Noah facilitated the coming of the redeemer Jesus Christ by humbling himself before God and believing in His promises by faith.[14] Because of this faith, Noah and his family survived the judgement of the flood—they were saved and not destroyed. Likewise, we today must place our faith in this redeemer to be saved during the final judgement. The works of this world will not be wiped away by water, but utterly destroyed by fire (2 THESS. 1:7-10; 2 PET. 3:3-13).

> *In that day you will say: "I will praise you, Lord. Although you were angry with me, your anger has turned away and you have comforted me. Surely God is my salvation [Hebrew Yeshua (Jesus)]; I will trust and not be afraid. The Lord, the Lord himself, is my strength and my defense; he has become my salvation." With joy you will draw water from the wells of salvation (Isa. 12:1-3 NIV).*

The apostle Peter wrote that baptism itself is an antitype of how Noah and his family were "saved through water" (1 PET. 3:20-21). They survived certain death in the old world and received life in the new world. Likewise, we who place our faith in Christ, as

---

[13] Youssef, "6 Covenants Fulfilled in Christ," *Leading the Way*, https://au.ltw.org/read/articles/2020/04/6-covenants-fulfilled-in-christ.

[14] The substitutionary sacrifice which Noah offered up to God after departing from the ark was a "pleasing aroma" for the same reason as the offering of Abel over Cain (GEN. 8:20-22; 2 COR. 2:14-16). It was an expression of faith in the ultimate substitutionary atonement to come from Jesus Christ.

affirmed through baptism, survive certain death in the old creation under Adam, and receive eternal life in the new creation under the second Adam, Jesus Christ. Jesus walked on water to demonstrate that he is the ark above the waters of judgement which can save us (MATT. 14:22-33; MARK 6:45-52; JOHN 6:15-21). The waters of baptism are for us the outward sign of faithful participation in the new covenant (ACTS 2:38; ROM. 6:3). Those who are in Christ are baptised with the living water of the Holy Spirit, the seal of the new covenant (MATT. 3:11; MARK 1:8; LUKE 3:16). The Holy Spirit has been sent to us by Jesus to be our own personal ark while we navigate through the unrelenting waters of this world. It keeps us above the waters of judgement on the journey to justification, sanctification, and glorification (ROM. 8:29-30).

## The Second Age of Man

God gave Noah and his sons the same mandate given to Adam and Eve. They were to once again "be fruitful and multiply, and fill the earth" (GEN. 1:26-28; 8:15-17; 9:1, 7). By these means the promised seed of the woman could be born. What we find instead is that the sons of Noah specifically journeyed east, a direction associated with rebellion against God, as shared in the companion book "Seed of Satan: Antichrist." In defiance of God's instruction, they coalesced into one place, the plains of Shinar, and established the stronghold at Babel, the base of the ancient mystery religions (GEN. 11:1-4). In the words of Professor of Old Testament Brent A. Strawn:

> *God created humans precisely to fill the earth and steward it (Gen 1:26–30)—a point reiterated after the Flood narrative (Gen 9:1, 7) ... the hunkering down in Gen 11:4 is a refusal to fulfill the creational mandate.*[15]

The rebellious spirit of the people became concentrated in one location, and Babel became the archetype for kingdoms in

---

[15] Strawn, "Focus On Tower of Babel," *Oxford University Press*, https://global.oup.com/obso/focus/focus_on_towerbabel.

opposition to God and His mandate over humanity. It was here where the mighty rebel before the Lord named Nimrod rose to power and fame by building the mighty tower of Babel with the intention of reaching heaven. God acted swiftly to quell or dilute this pervasive Babylonian influence on mankind by undermining their unity as a people. With the confusion of tongues, the people could no longer work together in one mind, so groups formed according to their language and scattered across the world (GEN. 11:9). Scripture tells us that the Babylonian mindset continued to resurface in subsequent evil empires under the influence of the ancient mystery religions founded in Babel (JOHN 2:15-18; 5:19; 18:36; ROM. 12:2). The present-day push for a centralised and fully unified world is symptomatic of this ancient mindset. One of the purposes of the death of Jesus on our behalf was to separate us from this spirit which dominates the present world system:

> May I never boast except in the cross of our Lord Jesus Christ, through which the world has been crucified to me, and I to the world (Gal. 6:14 NIV).

The interpretation of the next set of ten names ties into this story of man hunkering down at Babel and subsequently being dispersed. Starting from the son of Noah, Shem, we end with Abram (Abraham), the father of Israel (GEN. 10:21-31; 11:10-32):

*Image 2.3 – Hebrew name meanings from Shem to Abram (Abraham)*

| NAME | HEBREW MEANING |
| --- | --- |
| Shem | name, fame |
| Arpachshad | stronghold of Chaldea |
| Shelah | branch out |
| Eber | beyond the region |
| Peleg | division (Babel) |
| Reu | friend |
| Serug | branch |
| Nahor | snort, scorched |

| | |
|---|---|
| Terah | *spirit, delay* |
| Abram | *exalted father* |

**INTERPRETATION FROM COMBINED MEANINGS**

The famed stronghold of Chaldea (Babylon) branched out beyond the region of division (Babel means division or confusion). A friend of the branch snorts at the spirit of the exalted father.

Among the peoples dispersed from the Tower of Babel were the Chaldeans. They migrated to the southern regions of Babylonia and established the kingdom or stronghold of Chaldea. Arpachshad, the son of Shem, is said by Josephus and the book of Jubilees to be the father of the Chaldeans (JUB. 9:4).[16] We are not told when the sons of Shem settled in Chaldea, but Jubilees states that the dispersal came in the days of Reu, and that his son Serug and grandson Nahor grew up and lived in Ur of the Chaldeans (JUB. 10:18-27; 11:6-7). Terah, the son of Nahor, is said in Genesis 11 to have lived there with his son Abram (GEN. 11:27-32). According to Jubilees, Abram made an enemy out of Nimrod, the king of Babel, for threatening his self-exaltation (JASH. 7, 9, 11).[17] We see in Genesis that God called Abram out of this idolatrous land of self-exaltation to follow Him by faith. His father Terah journeyed to the land of Canaan with Abram, but because he was comfortable in his idolatrous ways (JOSH. 24:2), Terah chose to delay (Terah also means delay) the journey by settling in Haran. He went on to die there, falling short of the divine destination because he lacked faith. After his death, Abram followed God to the divine destination of Canaan, knowing by faith that he would be exalted (GEN. 12:1-9; ACTS 7:2-4). Contrary to his Babylonian peers, Abram turned away from self-exaltation and looked to God for exaltation. For this he received the land of Canaan as an inheritance and became the exalted father of Israel and the spiritual progenitor of all believers.

---

[16] Josephus, "Antiquities of the Jews," 1.143.

[17] Rabbi Ari Kahn claimed: *"God rescued Avraham when Terah handed him over to Nimrod to be killed for spreading monotheism and rejecting the idolatry and paganism of the society in which he was raised,"* Rabbi Ari Kahn on Parsha," *OU Torah,* https://outorah.org/p/21996/

*Seed of God: Jesus Christ*

## The Second Covenant with Abraham

The first twelve chapters of Genesis covers a period of 2000 years, while the following thirty-eight cover only 430 years. The pace of the narrative slows drastically to focus on the story of Abram (Abraham) from his calling by God at age seventy up until the death of his great-grandson Joseph. As discussed, our first encounter with Abraham came when God called him (then Abram) to venture out from the land of Ur (Mesopotamia) to an unknown land (GEN. 12:1). God intended for Abram to inherit this area and make of him "a great nation" and "a great name" in whom "all the families of the earth shall be blessed" (GEN. 12:2-3). In view of the protoevangelium (GEN. 3:15), the chief one to whom these promises are made is Jesus, the seed of the woman. It is obvious that not Abram, nor any descendant besides Jesus, has become a blessing to all peoples and nations, or even taken full possession of the promised land for that matter. Abram clearly died without ever inheriting the promises made to him, but he was allotted the privilege of fathering the line of the promised seed. The key to salvation was forged by him, but the key itself was his seed—not plural, but seed in the singular (GEN. 22:18).

> *The promises were spoken to Abraham and to his seed. Scripture does not say "and to seeds," meaning many people, but "and to your seed," meaning one person, who is Christ (Gal. 3:16 NIV).*

Abram was under no delusion as to the scope of the promises given to him. Jesus said, "Abraham rejoiced to see My day, and he saw it and was glad" (JOHN 8:56). How did he see it if he was dead? It is because Abraham "died in faith, not having received the promises, but having seen them afar off were assured of them" (HEB. 11:13). Like we do today, Abraham "waited for the city which has foundations, whose builder and maker is God" (HEB. 11:10-16; GAL. 3:7-9; ROM. 4:16). We are sojourners in a temporary land like Abraham. We are called out of our comfortable lives to seek out a better and heavenly country which God has prepared for us (HEB. 11:16).

Let us continue now with the story of Abram and his own sojourning out of Mesopotamia. Throughout his journey with his wife Sarai and nephew Lot, Abram became "very wealthy in livestock and in silver and gold" (GEN. 13:2). In Canaan, Abram and Lot accrued possessions too great for the land to sustain so Abram suggested they part company: "if you go to the left, I'll go to the right; if you go to the right, I'll go to the left" (GEN. 13:5-9). Abram demonstrated true humility in ceding his right as the elder to pick the better portion of land. After this great display of virtue, God appeared to Abram and revealed the area of land to be allotted to him and his descendants forever (GEN. 13:14-17). This was the land of Canaan, later to become Israel—the land always to be contested by the Canaanites, the descendants not of the godly Shem, but his ungodly brother Ham (GEN. 10:15-20). This area of Canaan would come to be known as Phoenicia—ground zero in the battle between the two promised sons.[18]

God appeared to Abram again in a vision to reconfirm the land inheritance with its expanded borders and to reveal he would bear a son to pass on the blessings (GEN. 15:18). Abram wondered to God "how shall I know that I will inherit it?" so God reassured him by formalising the promises within a covenant (GEN. 15:8-20). God cut the covenant with Abram using the Ancient Near East cultural conventions familiar to him. Abram prepared for the ratification ceremony by slaughtering three animals and dividing them in two (GEN. 15:9-11). Normally to seal the covenant the involved parties would walk between the split carcasses to acknowledge in the most visceral sense what the consequences were for reneging on the covenant commitments (death). God instead put Abram into a deep sleep and passed between the animal parts on His own, signalling that the covenant was to be taken as a unilateral and everlasting promise to Abram. For God who cannot die, holding to the covenant curse of death spoke to the surety of His promise (MAL. 3:6; 1 TIM. 1:17; 6:16).

---

[18] The significance of the Canaanites descended from Ham, the brother of Shem, is explored in depth in the companion book "Seed of Satan: Antichrist."

God appeared to Abram again when he was ninety years old to reaffirm the covenant. He said to him, "I am God Almighty; walk before me faithfully and be blameless. Then I will make my covenant between me and you and will greatly increase your numbers" (GEN. 17:1-2). Abram "fell on his face" in obedience so God reassured him that the covenant blessings would be expanded to become everlasting:

> *As for Me, behold, My covenant is with you, and you shall be a father of many nations. No longer shall your name be called Abram, but your name shall be Abraham; for I have made you a father of many nations. I will make you exceedingly fruitful; and I will make nations of you, and kings shall come from you. And I will establish My covenant between Me and you and your descendants after you in their generations, for an everlasting covenant, to be God to you and your descendants after you. Also, I give to you and your descendants after you the land in which you are a stranger, all the land of Canaan, as an everlasting possession; and I will be their God (Gen. 17:4-8 NIV).*

A common interpretation of this passage is that the Abrahamic covenant is conditional, but God was not sneaking in a covenant obligation of moral perfection. Reiterations of the covenant promises were made despite clear instances of disobedience and moral failings. For instance, after God led Abraham into Canaan and famine plagued the land, Abraham doubted God as his provider and protector by departing for Egypt. Depending on the work of his own hands, Abraham engaged in deceit and lies to protect himself (GEN. 12:10-20). Nevertheless, God pressed on with Abram and assured him and his wife Sarai that their heir would be of their own flesh and blood (GEN. 15:1-5). By the time the covenant was formally ratified, the couple were very old and doubted that God would deliver them this son. Their disobedience culminated in the extra-marital relationship with Hagar, their servant, to produce their own heir in Ishmael (GEN. 16). Following the talks of the covenant and the sign of circumcision in this chapter (GEN. 17), God reminded Abraham of this seed promise, yet he remained doubtful (GEN. 17:15-18). Again, Abram suggested that God accept Ishmael as the covenant heir: "Oh, that Ishmael might live before You!" (GEN. 17:18). Notice after how God did not rebuke Abraham, but attended to him with great patience and reassurance (GEN. 17:15-22). If a new condition had been added to the covenant, or a new covenant had been cut, Abraham clearly would have broken it.

God's command to "walk faithfully before me and be blameless" was an appeal to faithfulness. As much as God desired to work through Abraham and his descendants, He was limited by willing participants in His covenant and willing recipients of its promises. After all, a long and unbroken chain of devotees to the ultimate seed was required for him to be born (GEN. 22:18; GAL. 3:16; MATT. 1:1). That is why Abraham and his descendants, both biological and spiritual through Christ (GAL. 3:7-9, 26-29; ROM. 4:11-16; 16:25-27), are called to walk before God and "live by faith, not by sight" (2 COR. 5:7). God pleads with us to remember that He is and will always be behind us, and that His plan for us will not be frustrated (DEUT. 31:6; MATT. 28:20). We only need to trust in His higher purposes and allow Him to work through us like Abraham.

The same was true for Abraham and his children. God instructed Abraham and all males among him to undergo circumcision as an outward physical sign of obedience or participation in the covenant (GEN. 17:10-11, 23-27). Circumcision acted as the sign of the covenant in the same way as the rainbow for the Noahic covenant. All males left uncircumcised were to be cut off from his people for breaking the covenant (GEN. 17:14). Some see this as evidence for the conditionality of the covenant—that it was not unilateral after all, but bilateral. There is however, a subtle but crucial distinction regarding covenant conditions and regulations that needs to be stressed. Covenant obligations indicate what each party obligates themselves to do in the covenant. In contrast, covenant regulations are imposed by the suzerain (controlling power) upon the vassal (subordinate) to regulate the vassal's behaviour after they have entered the covenant. In the case of the Abrahamic covenant, God as suzerain imposed the regulation of circumcision upon the vassal of Abraham and his descendants. For circumcision to be a covenant condition, Jewish defiance of this instruction throughout history would have rendered the covenant null and void (JOSH. 5:2-9). As noted by leading scholar and Messianic Jew Arnold Fruchtenbaum, "God always fulfilled His part, even when the command and the penalty were disobeyed."[19] Israel can never cut herself off from the promises of the Abrahamic covenant. Even at the height of her unfaithfulness, see what God declared through Jeremiah:

> *"Only if the heavens above can be measured and the foundations of the earth below be searched out will I reject all the descendants of Israel because of all they have done" (Jer. 31:37 NIV).*

It is therefore necessary to recognise the sign of circumcision not as a covenantal condition, but as a regulation. Inclusion into the designated promises of the covenant is contingent upon following the regulation of circumcision. This is what it means for the uncircumcised male to be "cut off from his people" (GEN. 17:14). The regulation only serves to limit the beneficiaries of the covenant to those faithful to it. Man cannot break the covenant, nor will God ever forget His forever-binding obligations to His people. As stated by Old Testament Professor Robert Chisholm:

> *"Though future generations were obligated to perform the rite ... their failure in this regard would jeopardize only their personal participation in the promised blessings, not the oath itself."*[20]

---

[19] Fruchtenbaum, *Israelology*, 145-146.
[20] Chisholm, "Evidence from Genesis," chap. 1 in *A Case for Premillennialism*, 45.

## The Final Realisation of the Abrahamic Covenant

As we continue we shall witness the progressive fulfilment of the Abrahamic covenant. It will become clear that the totality of the land that was promised has never been acquired by Israel to this day (GEN. 15:18-21). The promised seed, Jesus, is inextricably linked with this final realisation of the Abrahamic promises. God frequently spoke of a day when His people would be gathered from among the nations and firmly established in all the land of Israel (EZEK. 37:21-28; JER. 31:10-14; 32:36-44). No more judgement, no more exile. Evidently, the outward participatory sign of circumcision did not keep the Jews from transgressing their Lord and warranting their own exile. It served only as a type of the true spiritual circumcision of the heart by the Holy Spirit (DEUT. 10:12-20; 30:6; JER. 4:4; ZECH. 7:8-14; ROM. 4:9-25). For the blessings of the covenant to be uninterrupted by judgement, God required a people transformed from the inside, or circumcised in the heart (ROM. 2:28-29). This is precisely what Jesus enabled when he poured out the Holy Spirit on his faithful and loving believers. All who receive the Holy Spirit through Jesus are circumcised of the heart by the Spirit, not by human hands (COL. 2:11; ROM. 2:28-29). It is through faith in Jesus, the promised seed of Abraham (GAL. 3:16; GEN. 12:7; 13:15; 24:7; MATT. 1:1; ROM. 9:4-5) that all peoples on earth will be blessed (GEN. 12:1-3; GAL. 3:13-16; ROM. 9:30-32). As it is said: "if you are Christ's, then you are Abraham's seed, and heirs according to the promise" (GAL. 3:29).

In another case, God told the prophet Ezekiel in a vision to prophesy to the dry (dead) bones of Israel and tell them to "hear the word of the Lord" (EZEK. 37:4). To proclaim they will be resurrected and brought back into their land one day, and that God will put His Spirit within them (EZEK. 37:11-14). This vision pictured the Church preaching the gospel to the Jews, and ultimately, the end-times when God, having already collected them back into Israel, restores them to life. Paul explained how the gentiles were used to provoke the Jews to jealousy as a means of bringing them to repentance (ROM. 11:11). The imagery of national resurrection in Ezekiel's vision is connected to the following passage from Paul:

> *For if their rejection brought reconciliation to the world, what will their acceptance be but life from the dead? (Rom. 11:15 NIV).*

At that time, God will sprinkle upon them the clean water of the Holy Spirit to transform their hardened hearts into a heart of flesh (EZEK. 11:19-20; 36:25-27; JER. 31:34). The softening of their hearts will awaken their spirits to the goodness of the Lord and His Word so they may love Him with all their heart and soul, and live (DEUT. 30:6). Their inward disposition will be to do only what is good in the eyes of the Lord (JER. 31:33; EZEK. 36:26-27). God will give them a singleness of heart and action (JER. 32:39-41) whereby the divided tribes of Israel will reunite as one nation under one king (EZEK. 37:15-23). They will live in total accordance with Him, and He shall set His sanctuary in their midst forevermore (EZEK. 37:26-28). God identifies this future king not as a mortal appointment, but one who will reign on the throne of David forever (EZEK. 37:24-26). We will soon explain how this points to Jesus, the final king from the line of David, and the source of eternal life. Jesus promised to return as king to establish this worldwide messianic kingdom (MATT. 19:27-29; ISA. 66:18). Upon its inauguration Israel will enter the fullness of their allotted land and into the everlasting new covenant (JER. 31; 32:40-41; HEB. 8:10-13; EZEK. 37:26-28; ISA. 42:1-7).

**1. Living Shadow of Isaac**

Isaac was the son of Abraham whom God chose to inherit His covenant with Abraham (GEN. 17:19-21; 26:3-5, 24-25). As discussed previously, Ishmael may have been the first-born, but God stated emphatically that the son to continue the covenantal lineage was to come by supernatural works (GEN. 15). Ishmael was born out of unfaithfulness to the covenant. God blessed Ishmael greatly, but God did not choose Ishmael for this divine purpose (GEN. 16).

*Living Shadows*

At this stage, "Abraham and Sarah were already very old, and Sarah was past the age of childbearing" (GEN. 18:11). Three angels soon appeared to Abraham and "one of them said, 'I will surely return to you about this time next year, and Sarah your wife will have a son.'" We know from the surrounding context that this angel was the Lord Himself, the preincarnate Jesus Christ (GEN. 17:22; 18:1-2, 9-14, 16, 20-23, 33; 19:1; 19:15).[21] Sarah overheard God's plan to give them another son from inside their tent, and she "laughed to herself as she thought, 'After I am worn out and my lord is old, will I now have this pleasure?'" (GEN. 18:12). Abraham was just as sceptical of their child-bearing prospects, but "God said: 'No, Sarah your wife shall bear you a son, and you shall call his name Isaac; I will establish My covenant with him for an everlasting covenant, and with his descendants after him'" (GEN. 17:17-19). God came through on His promise and Sarah miraculously conceived Isaac (GEN. 21:1-7). God reminded Abraham that it was in "Isaac your seed shall be called," for he was a child not just of the flesh (Ishmael), but of divine promise (GEN. 21:12; GAL. 4:22-23). The apostle Paul expounded on this in Romans, stating how "those who are the children of the flesh [Ishmael], these are not the children of God, but the children of the promise [Isaac] are counted as the seed" (ROM. 9:6-8). Paul emphasised how all belonging to Christ similarly become children of divine promise as Isaac was, not "of the bondwoman [Hagar] but of the free [Sarah]" (GAL. 3:29; 4:28). This is because a similar unbelievable scenario befell Joseph and Mary, the parents of Jesus. An angel alerted Joseph and Mary separately that she would bear a son with the Holy Spirit and that he "shall call his name Jesus" (MATT. 1:18-21; LUKE 1:26-38). Mary reacted as Sarah did to the prospect of a miraculous birth, saying:

---

[21] The attached scriptural references show that God was one of the three angels. The angel of the Lord is the preincarnate Jesus Christ because he is the physical manifestation of the invisible Father, he is the Word of God (ROM. 1:20; HEB. 1:1-3; 1 TIM. 1:17). "No one has ever seen God, but the one and only Son, who is himself God and is in closest relationship with the Father, has made him known" (EXOD. 33:20; JOB 9:11; JOHN 1:18; 5:37; 6:46; 8:38; 14:9; 1 JOHN 4:12, 24). "The Son is the image of the invisible God" (COL. 1:15), who manifested in the flesh (JOHN 1:1-18; 14:9; 1 TIM 3:16; PHIL. 2:5-8).

"How will this be ... since I am a virgin?" (LUKE 1:26-34). Jesus was confirmed to be called from the line of Isaac in the genealogies of Matthew and Luke (MATT. 1:2; LUKE 3:34). Like Isaac, Jesus was a child of promise, the son of God, born through supernatural means for a supernatural purpose.

*Sacrifice of the Son*

Having declared to Abraham, "in Isaac your seed shall be called" (GEN. 21:12), God tested him to determine if he truly believed this would be brought to pass (GEN. 22). God commanded: "take your son, your only son Isaac, whom you love" to the land of Moriah and sacrifice him as a burnt offering (GEN. 22:2). As far as the covenant was concerned, Isaac was the "only son" through which the covenant would come to fruition. God never intended for Isaac to be sacrificed, and I believe Abraham knew this. Abraham concluded through faith "that God was able to raise him up, even from the dead" and ultimately spare his life (HEB. 11:17-19). Consider that Abraham took Isaac to Moriah with two of his young men (GEN. 22:2-3). If he intended on killing Isaac, it would be a peculiar choice to bring witnesses. Notice what he said to them once they reached the mountain God picked for the sacrifice:

> Then Abraham said to his young men, 'Stay here with the donkey, and I and the boy will go over there; and we will worship and return to you' (Gen. 22:5 NASB).

Again, it appears that Abraham expected to return with Isaac, knowing the covenant needed to go through him. Abraham took the wood and placed it on Isaac for him to carry to the mountaintop (GEN. 22:6). Isaac asked his father "where is the lamb for the offering" to which Abraham responded that "God himself will provide the lamb for the burnt offering" (GEN. 22:6-8). Isaac willingly submitted to his father, even in the face of death, prefiguring the unity of God the Father and Jesus the Son in his sacrifice (JOHN 3:14; 10:30; 17:21-23). Abraham proceeded to bind Isaac to the wooden altar and right before he plunged in the knife an angel of God stepped in to spare Isaac (GEN. 22:9-12). Abraham looked up and saw a ram caught by its horns in a thicket (thornbush) so he sacrificed it in the place of Isaac (GEN. 22:13-14). God expanded the covenant blessings for Abraham because of his great display of faith in God's promises (GEN. 22:15-18; 26:1-6).

Jesus, who is called the lamb of God, was the sacrificial lamb alluded to by Abraham (JOHN 1:29, 36). God took Jesus, His only begotten son "whom [He] loves" to Golgotha and sacrificed him as the ultimate burnt offering (MATT. 3:17; MARK 1:11; 9:7; LUKE 3:22; HEB. 5:5). He did this knowing that He could raise him up from the dead (JOHN 3:16; 1 JOHN 4:9). Like Isaac, Jesus carried his own wooden beam up the mountain of sacrifice, Mount Moriah, to the place of the Skull, Golgotha (MATT. 27:33; MARK 15:22; JOHN 19:17). Similar to how the substitutionary ram had its horns caught in the thornbush, a crown of thorns was placed upon Jesus' head (MATT. 27:29; MARK 15:17; JOHN 19:2). Jesus was sacrificed in the place of Barabbas as the ram was for Isaac. He was a substitutionary atonement for all man (MATT. 27:15-26; MARK 15:6-15; LUKE 23:13-24; JOHN 18:39-40). The sacrifice was shrouded from the surrounding witnesses as darkness covered the land (MATT. 27:45; MARK 15:33; LUKE 23:44). The two thieves on the cross next to Jesus were like the two servants of Abraham who stayed behind, they could not see the sacred interaction between the Father and Son. Matching the three-day journey of Abraham and Isaac, Jesus resurrected from the dead after three days. When Jesus humbly sacrificed himself in obedience to fulfil the Abrahamic promises, God expanded the blessings through the new covenant.

## 2. Living Shadow of Jacob

The next living shadow is Jacob (later named Israel), the son of Isaac. Jacob is the third-generation patriarch of the twelve tribes of Israel after his grandfather, Abraham, and his father, Isaac. Again, despite being the second born of Isaac, God prophetically chose the line of Jacob to perpetuate the seed. As with his father Isaac and his descendant Jesus, Jacob was the product of a supernatural birth. His mother Rebekah was barren like Sarah, the wife of Abraham, but after Isaac prayed to God on her behalf, Rebekah became pregnant with twins (Gen. 25:21). She began to feel them struggle against each other in the womb and, in her confusion, inquired God about it:

> The Lord said to her, 'two nations are in your womb, and two peoples from within you will be separated; one people will be stronger than the other, and the older will serve the younger (Gen. 25:23 NIV).

The younger in Jacob grabbed the heel of the elder in Esau as he was being delivered, seemingly trying to claim the first-born birth right (Gen. 25:24-26). Fittingly, the name Jacob means *supplanter*, reflecting his supremacy over Esau. This peculiar story conveys the idea that the divine choice of God is contrary to the natural order—the child of promise was selected for different but higher reasons. The apostle Paul stressed this very point:

> It is not the children of the flesh who are children of God, but the children of the promise are regarded as descendants. For this is the word of promise: "At this time I will come, and Sarah will have a son." And not only that, but there was also Rebekah, when she had conceived twins by one man, our father Isaac; for though the twins were not yet born and had not done anything good or bad, so that God's purpose according to His choice would stand, not because of works but because of Him who calls, it was said to her, "The older will serve the younger." Just as it is written: "Jacob I have loved, but Esau I have hated" (Rom. 9:8-13 NASB).

When the contexts of these two quotations are kept in mind, it becomes evident that the prediction, "the older will serve the younger," concerns two nations, Israel and Edom, and not the twins as persons. The fact that Esau never served Jacob (in fact, it was Jacob who bowed before Esau - Gen. 33:1-4) confirms that it is the nations which descended from the two brothers that are being discussed here. Not until the time of David would descendants of Esau serve descendants of Jacob (2 SAM. 8:14). The subject of the second prophecy, pronounced about 1500 years after the birth of Jacob and Esau, is clearly the nation of Edom and its territory (MAL. 1:2-5). During the intervening centuries, the descendants of Esau—the Edomites and Amalekites—were not only overtly hostile toward Israel, but tried to prevent the realisation of God's plan through Israel (NUM. 20:14-21; EZEK. 25:12-14; DEUT. 25:17-19). Natural descent is clearly not what God looks at, but rather, the spiritual softness of the heart that enables the necessary spiritual circumcision by the Holy Spirit.

God already knew from the time Jacob and Esau were in the womb that it was Jacob who would uphold the godly line. The metaphor of the second born ties in with the statement from Jesus "unless a man is born again, he cannot see the Kingdom of God" (JOHN 3:16). Jesus himself was the second born after Adam, the latter of whom relinquished his birth right to serve the earthly authority of Satan (1 COR. 15:45-48). The responsibility of taking back control was therefore passed into the hands of the second born who serves the spiritual authority of God, and that is Jesus. Just as Adam sold his birth right through disobedience for Jesus to inherit, Esau despised his birth right and sold it to Jacob under oath for a single meal (GEN. 25:27-34; HEB. 12:15-16). The messianic Rabbi Russel Resnik explained the clear difference between the two brothers which dictated how they valued the birth right:

> *Jacob values what God values and Esau does not. Jacob understands what is truly important, although he does not always understand how to obtain it. Esau, who is not altogether evil, does altogether miss the priorities of God. Thus Esau sells his birthright because he has no concept of its worth ... To Esau the promise is meaningless; to Jacob it is invaluable ... Esau falls short of the grace of*

> God because it is unimportant to him. Jacob, in contrast, recognizes the value of the promise.[22]

Only being human, Isaac did not fully grasp the divergent characters of his two sons. He valued Esau for the works of his hands, for he "was a skillful hunter, a man of the field" (GEN. 25:27). On the other hand, Jacob stuck to the tents, prioritising the spiritual over the earthly, which Isaac could not fully appreciate from the outside. "Isaac loved Esau because he ate of his game, but Rebekah [and most importantly, God] loved Jacob" for his inward character (GEN. 25:27-28). Rebekah was faithful and in touch with God. She recognised Jacob was destined to receive the birth right and was prepared to intervene to ensure this happened.

*Passing of the Covenant Blessing*

The story of Isaac passing on the patriarchal blessing of the covenant provides a clear picture of how his physical blindness was symptomatic of a spiritual blindness (GEN. 27:1-40). Isaac favoured Esau over Jacob despite the revelation from the Spirit that the older would serve the younger from birth (GEN. 25:19-28). He was unable to look beyond outward stature and natural attributes. He could not accurately discern which was the son of promise who desired the blessing from the one who despised it.

When Jesus came to Israel, its spiritual fathers—the Sadducees and the Pharisees—could not discern him from a false prophet because of spiritual blindness. On the day that Jesus, the only begotten son of the Father, and Barabbas, whose name means "son of the Father," were presented before them on trial, they incorrectly discerned which was the son of promise (the lot for the Lord) and which son was of the character of Esau (the lot for Azazel) (LEV. 16). They rejected the true son of promise for the false one, and in their blindness conspired to kill the true son.[23]

---

[22] Resnik, *Gateways to Torah*, 32.

[23] This event, along with the significance of Esau and the divergence from the line of Jacob, is discussed in the companion book, "Seed of Satan: Antichrist."

When the day came for Isaac to bless Esau, he asked Esau to hunt his favourite meal. He seemed to prioritise the material pleasures from Esau over his spiritual obligations to Jacob. Rebekah, the wife of Isaac, was not spiritually blind like her husband, and sensed the significance of the moment. She was faithful to the word of God which declared the older would serve the younger of the twins she was to bring forth. Therefore, she instructed Jacob to trick his father into bestowing the blessing upon him by dressing and appearing to him as his brother Esau. As an assurance to Jacob, Rebekah declared she would bear any curse that could come from this deceitful action. But since she was guided by faith, not by sight, she was justified by the order of God which takes precedence. God chose Jacob before Isaac ever chose Esau, and Rebekah recognised this (Gen. 27:13). It is no surprise then that no curse fell on her head for this action. There is no biblical record of her death, only her burial place (Gen. 49:31).

Jacob obeyed his mother, and his father did not discern the exchange of sons, so Jacob was given the firstborn patriarchal blessing. After Isaac unwittingly blessed Jacob with the covenant of his father Abraham, Esau returned from the field and asked for the blessing. Isaac immediately understood the blessing was God appointed so he did not try to reverse it or pass it on to Esau (Gen. 27:30-40). The door had opened for God to personally reveal Himself to Jacob (Gen. 28:3-4).

*The Beginning of Jacob's Transformation*

God soon appeared to Jacob in a dream for the purpose of appointing him as the inheritor of the covenant (Gen. 28:13-15). In this dream, God made His proclamations to Jacob atop a ladder that stretched from earth all the way up to heaven, coupled with angels ascending and descending on it (Gen. 28:12-13). When Jacob woke up (physically and spiritually), he exclaimed:

> "Surely the Lord is in this place, and I did not know it ... this is none other than the house of God, and this is the gate of heaven!" (Gen. 28:16-17 NKJV).

We see that Jacob was transformed by the presence of God. He realised that the Lord dwelled in his place, calling it the house of God and the gate of heaven. In other words the transition point between heaven and earth. This pointed to the future circumcision of the heart undertaken by the Holy Spirit whereby the house of God dwells directly within the faithful—wherever they may be. Jacob had not yet understood the full reality of this revelation that was to come through the promised seed. First he needed to be shown the future of the Messiah like his grandfather Abraham who had seen Jesus' day and was glad (JOHN 8:56). As a living shadow of the true image in Christ, Jacob could only glimpse the significance of the dream, not yet seeing Jesus in it.

> *Then Jacob made a vow, saying, "If God will be with me and will watch over me on this journey I am taking and will give me food to eat and clothes to wear so that I return safely to my father's household,* **then** *the Lord will be my God and this stone that I have set up as a pillar will be God's house, and of all that you give me I will give you a tenth" (Gen. 28:20-22 NIV).*

The self-boldened "then" is the critical word here. It signified that Jacob had not yet been circumcised in the heart. His trust in God was contingent on how things in his immediate future went for him. As we shall soon see, it would take further testing from God before his heart would be truly transformed.

Jesus asserted himself as being the metaphorical reality of Jacob's ladder, stating "you shall see heaven open, and the angels of God ascending and descending upon the Son of Man" (JOHN 1:51). Jacob's ladder is identified as a type of Jesus, the mediator who bridges the gap between God in heaven and man on earth. By portraying himself in the place of Jacob, Jesus was telling the disciples that the Abrahamic covenant given unto Jacob was ultimately given unto him.[24] The messianic significance is further

---

[24] McHugh, *John 1-4*, 168-169.

reinforced by the inclusion of the Son of Man motif (DAN. 7:13-14; REV. 1:13, 14:14) and the opening of heaven motif (EZEK. 1; REV. 4:1; 19:11 MATT. 3:16; MARK 1:10; LUKE 3:21; ACTS 7:56; 10:11). Both are employed in relation to Jesus descending from heaven in the end days. In this light, the angels ascending and descending describes their future duties in enacting the final judgement (REV. 10:1; 11:12; 14:17; 18:1; 20:1). In the case of Jacob, the angels went to and from heaven and earth to protect and instruct Jacob and his descendants, but Jesus announced that it is by his authority and direction that these angels, his messengers, traverse heaven and earth.

*Marriage of Jacob to Rachel and God to Israel*

Isaac, after the careful instruction from Rebekah, commanded Jacob to head to Rebekah's family in Haran to flee the wrath of Esau and find a suitable wife from his own people (GEN. 27:41-45; 28:1-5). Parallel to this, God sent his son Jesus to earth after the wrath and rebellion of Lucifer in heaven to find a suitable wife— the corporate body of the Church (ROM. 11:13-24). Jacob's brother Esau went against his parent's wishes here by courting Hittite women (Canaanite descendants) (GEN. 26:34-35; 28:6-9; 36:1-4). The children of these relationships brought forth the Edomites and the Amalekites, the pre-eminent adversaries of the line of Jacob until the end of the present age (GEN. 36:1-12; DEUT. 25:17-19; 1 CHR. 1:13). The enmity between these peoples parallels that of the seed of the woman and the serpent (GEN. 3:15; 25:19-34). The prophesied Star and Sceptre to come out of Jacob-Israel and take dominion over Edom is Jesus, the seed of the woman (NUM. 24:17-19).

Jacob went to stay with his uncle Laban and offered to work seven years for him as a bride price for his daughter Rachel (GEN. 28:5; 29:13-18). At the end of the seven years Laban prepared a feast for the marriage between Rachel and Jacob but waited for the cover of darkness to replace Rachel with his older daughter Leah (the bride wore a veil until consummating the marriage). Jacob unknowingly consummated the marriage with Leah and not Rachel. In this same manner, Jesus came from heaven and paid the bride price for Israel in accordance with Jewish custom. That price was the blood of the Passover lamb which secured their release from Egypt and allowed for their betrothal at Mount Sinai. As it was for Jacob, Jesus did not receive the bride of his choice, but the two worked with the arrangement nonetheless. Leah was fruitful in childbirth for Jacob, and the gentile nations were fruitful in accepting and spreading the gospel of Jesus.

Laban asked Jacob to work an additional seven years in return for Rachel, and because he loved her more than Leah, he willingly agreed. For the last two-thousand years, Jesus has been working for Israel after paying the ultimate bride price of his own blood unto death. In God's appointed time, Israel, like Rachel, will finally come to their husband and bear the fruit of obedience and blessing, but it will take the greatest period of tribulation in their history, "the time of Jacob's trouble" (JER. 30:7). During this coming time of travail of the soul, the veil of unbelief over the nation will be pulled off. At last, not only a remnant, but all of Israel shall cry out "blessed is he who comes in the name of the Lord" and "we will not let you go unless you bless us" (JER. 30:3-17; GEN. 32:26). They will finally recognise Jesus as their heavenly bridegroom and accept the only condition of their betrothal which is simply obedient faith and love (2 COR. 3-14; MATT. 23:39).

Those within the gentile church (Leah) who have been fruitful in their relationship with the Lord will ultimately acknowledge Israel as the first love of God and extend mercy and understanding to help restore this union. This is akin to Ruth (a Moabite gentile) clinging to Naomi (an Israelite) in love and faithfulness whereby Boaz (a type of the Messiah) could redeem the inheritance of Naomi (RUTH 1-4). Leah (gentile church) wanted to be loved by Jacob (Jesus) as Rachel (Israel) was, but being His chosen bride, the firstfruits, "his love for Rachel was greater than his love for Leah" (GEN. 29:30). However, because of His love and grace, we read that "when the Lord saw that Leah was not loved, he enabled her to conceive, but Rachel remained childless" (GEN. 29:31). This is symbolic of how it was predominately the gentile church that spread the gospel of Christ throughout the world while the Jews

*Living Shadows*

generally remained unbelievers and were therefore unfruitful in bringing the unsaved into the kingdom. Leah was fruitful, but with every child she longed for her husband Jacob to finally love her as he loved Rachel. The emotional anguish she suffered was reflected in the names she gave to her children:

> *So, Leah conceived and bore a son, and she called his name Reuben; for she said, "The Lord has surely looked on my affliction. Now therefore, my husband will love me." Then she conceived again and bore a son, and said, "Because the Lord has heard that I am unloved, He has therefore given me this son also." And she called his name Simeon. She conceived again and bore a son, and said, "Now this time my husband will become attached to me, because I have borne him three sons." Therefore his name was called Levi. And she conceived again and bore a son, and said, "Now I will praise the Lord." Therefore, she called his name Judah. Then she stopped bearing (Gen. 29:32-35 NKJV).*

Leah refused to let her placement behind Rachel deter her from loving God and was rewarded by Him for her faithfulness. Despite not being Jacob's first love, she was the one who was fruitful in childbearing, which for the time, was a most honourable position for a woman. Rachel on the other hand bore the stigma of infertility and childlessness:

> *When Rachel saw that she was not bearing Jacob any children, she became jealous of her sister. So she said to Jacob, "Give me children, or I'll die!" Jacob became angry with her and said, "Am I in the place of God, who has kept you from having children?" (Gen. 30:1-2 NIV).*

The jealousy of Rachel (Israel) towards her sister Leah (gentiles church) was intended to stir her to faithfulness. After Jesus brought salvation to the world, Paul stated that it was primarily the gentiles who would receive it as to make Israel envious—for them it was to be a stumbling block (ROM. 11:11-15). But God fully intended on placing them back on their feet. We see this play out by God eventually allowing Rachel to conceive. To this she said, "God has taken away my disgrace" and she gave birth to Joseph (GEN. 30:22-24). Jacob then said to Laban in the following verse, "Send me on my way so I can go back to my own homeland" (GEN. 30:25). This appears to be a picture of the unification between Israel, the Church, and God in Christ within the millennial kingdom, the homeland situated in the land of Canaan, followed by the new heaven and earth.

> *Through the gospel the Gentiles are heirs together with Israel, members together of one body, and sharers together in the promise in Christ Jesus (Eph. 3:6 NIV).*

Rachel and Leah—the spiritual embodiment of Israel and the faithful in the gentile Church—will become united around one greater than Jacob. They will all return to the house of the living God, their Father (GEN. 31:11-18). This is the consummation of God's plan to restore all things in Jesus, the seed of the woman (ACTS 3:21).

## Birth of Israel

To affect this consummation of the age, Jacob had to face one final challenge, a direct confrontation with the Most High. In Genesis 32 we read the story of Jacob wrestling through the night with a man (the Lord) until the break of day. After being bested, the man put Jacob's thigh out of joint and said, "let me go," to which Jacob responded, "I will not let you go unless you bless me" (GEN. 32:25-26). Being humble in defeat, the man (the Lord) agreed and blessed him with the name Israel, which means a "man who has struggled with God and prevailed." Jacob had a direct encounter with the member of the Godhead who, according to Meno Kalisher, "men can see and not die."[25] That being the human incarnation of God,

---

[25] Kalisher, *Jesus in the Hebrew Scriptures.*

Jesus Christ. This was the crossover point for Jacob to receive the circumcision of the heart and the name of Israel to reflect his fatherhood over the twelve tribes of Israel. It foreshadowed Jesus wrestling with God in the darkness on the cross over our sin. As with Jacob, he too prevailed after bearing the wounds of that divine encounter and was rewarded with a name above all names (PHIL. 2:5-11). Jesus chose twelve disciples to mirror the twelve tribes of Israel and granted them apostolic oversight of the Church (MATT. 5:16). These twelve tribes and twelve disciples were called by God to be a light to the nations. The New Testament scholar David R. Kirk illustrated this typology:

> *Just as Jacob represents his descendants before the LORD and gives his name Israel to them, Jesus portrays himself as the representative of a new Israel, a new people of God. The significance of Jesus's self-identification with Jacob is that it portrays Jesus as the originator of a New Israel ... the title the Son of Man carries the New Israel motif to its telos—a New Humanity.*[26]

The apostle Paul used the metaphor of the olive tree of Israel to describe this new humanity (ROM. 11). The olive tree is bound up in the covenantal relationship God maintains with Abraham, Isaac, and Jacob (EXOD. 3:6, 14-15; MATT. 22:29-32). The believing remnant of Israel who are circumcised in the heart by covenantal faith are joined to this tree like Abraham, their biological and spiritual father (JOHN 8:56). For accepting the gospel, believing gentiles are grafted into the tree as a part of the household of God (ROM. 11:24; EPH. 2:11-22). Unbelieving Israel who are blinded to the reality of Jesus will remain outside of the tree until the fullness of the gentiles have joined their Jewish counterparts in the tree of faith (ROM. 11:25). Following this, the God of Abraham in the person of

---

[26] Kirk, "Heaven Opened," *Tyndale Bulletin* 63 no. 2 (2012): 237-256, https://legacy.tyndalehouse.com/Bulletin/63=2012/05_Kirk-20.pdf.

Jesus will transform the remaining hardened hearts of the children of Israel in a national supernatural encounter akin to the one experienced by Jacob (ROM. 9-10-11; JER. 31:27-37).[27]

## The Three Patriarchs of the Hebrews

Now we share the link between Abraham, Isaac, and Jacob, as the three patriarchs of the Hebrew people. To breakdown three in Hebrew, three denotes permanence, unity, and wholeness. The letter with the numeric value of three is *gimel*, which means pride or to lift up. The pictograph for gimel is a foot and this is thought to symbolise a rich man running after a poor man to give him charity. The word for three is *shalosh*, comprised of the letters *shin* (to separate or destroy) and *lamed* (to shepherd, teach or go toward). By combining these together I interpret the following:

*Image 2.4 – Breakdown of the third letter and numeral, Gimel*

| VALUE | LETTER | PICTOGRAPH | WORD |
|---|---|---|---|
| 3 | Gimel (ג) | Foot | Shalosh (שלש) |

| INTERPRETATION FROM COMBINED MEANINGS |
|---|
| The path to being lifted up is to destroy pride and follow the shepherd, the rich man from whom we receive charity and obtain permanent wholeness. |

*Image 2.5 – Hebrew name meanings for the three patriarchs*

| NAME | HEBREW MEANING |
|---|---|
| Abraham | *father of multitudes, protection* |
| Isaac | *laughter* |
| Jacob (Israel) | *he who follows, supplanter* |
| Israel (Jacob) | *one who prevails, retains God* |

| INTERPRETATION FROM COMBINED MEANINGS |
|---|
| A father of multitudes laughs, knowing he who follows is the one who prevails. |

---

[27] For more insight on this I would recommend the video by Jacob Prasch titled "The Mandrakes - The Jewish Valentine."

### 3. Living Shadow of Joseph

Joseph was the most beloved son of Jacob and the first-born of his most beloved wife, Rachel. Jesus is the most beloved son of God, His first and only begotten son (JOHN 3:16).

At seventeen, Joseph had two unique dreams (God given) in which he was exalted above his brothers, and even his parents (GEN. 37:4-11). While his father pondered the significance of these dreams, the brothers were greatly angered by them—to the point of despising Joseph:

> *His brothers said to him, 'Do you intend to reign over us? Will you actually rule us?' And they hated him all the more because of his dream and what he had said (Gen. 37:8 NIV).*

The religious authorities hated Jesus, who was meant to be a brother, because to them he claimed to be exalted over them and threatened their rule (MATT. 12:14; LUKE 23:2-4; JOHN 11:45-53).

When the older brothers were grazing the flocks near Shechem, Jacob ordered Joseph to go there to check on them and report back to him (GEN. 37:14). God sent Jesus down from heaven to earth to check up on his brothers and tend to His flock before reporting back to Him (MATT. 3:15-17).

When the brothers saw Joseph, they quickly conspired to kill him, but his brother Reuben dissented and persuaded the others to throw him into a cistern instead (GEN. 37:18-20-22). "So, when Joseph came to his brothers, they stripped him of his robe—the ornate robe he was wearing—and they took him and threw him into the cistern" (GEN. 37:23-24). Nicodemus dissented at the unfair judgement against Jesus and championed his right to defend himself (JOHN 7:45-52). At his execution, Jesus was stripped of his garments by the guards and thrown into the tomb (MATT. 27:35).

Luckily a caravan of Ishmaelites arrived from Egypt, so Judah insisted they sell Joseph instead. He was sold for twenty shekels of silver and left in their bondage (GEN. 37:26-28). Judas Iscariot sold

Jesus out to the religious authorities for thirty pieces of silver (MATT. 26:14-16, 47-56; MARK 14:43-50; LUKE 22:1-6, 47-54; JOHN 18:1-13).

Joseph's coat of many colours was shown to Jacob to confirm his apparent death (GEN. 37:31-34). Jesus left his linen clothes in the tomb for his disciples to confirm he had resurrected from apparent death (JOHN 20:1-9).

Over in Egypt, Joseph was sold again into the hands of Potiphar, a captain to the Pharaoh (GEN. 37:36). Joseph became successful serving in Potiphar's household initially, but soon found himself in prison over false accusations. The empty charge came from the wife of Potiphar, who grew spiteful after repeated unsuccessful efforts at tempting Joseph (GEN. 39:11-23). Jesus was sold out again to the Roman authorities and imprisoned because of the false testimony of the Sanhedrin (MATT. 26:3-4, 59-68).

Joseph was judged as guilty along with two other men—a butler and a baker—both there for offending the king. During conversation, the men shared their dreams with Joseph for him to interpret. Joseph envisioned the butler restored to his position of favour before the Pharaoh within three days but saw the baker being hanged (GEN. 40:12-19). Joseph asked the butler to speak well of him before the Pharaoh when the interpretation proved to be true, so that he may be released (GEN. 40:14). "Two other men, both criminals, were also led out with Jesus to be executed" and insulted Jesus, the king (MATT. 27:41-44; LUKE 23:32). Initially both criminals next to Jesus hurled insults at him, but eventually one rebuked the other and asked Jesus to remember him after he re-entered his kingdom (LUKE 23:39-42). Jesus promised to restore his position of favour before the Lord and join him in paradise after three days (LUKE 23:43). In both cases, one criminal died while the other was saved.

After two years, Pharaoh suffered from troubling dreams, and at the butler's suggestion, requested an interpretation from Joseph. Pharaoh was pleased greatly by Joseph, who advised him to store extra grain for the next seven years of abundance before seven years of famine (GEN. 41:29-30). This advice saved Egypt from a severe food shortage. For this remarkable assistance, Pharaoh gave Joseph the keys to the kingdom of Egypt as his second-in-command at only thirty-years old (GEN. 41:39-46). Pharaoh gave Joseph a new name and a gentile woman to be his wife (GEN. 41:45). After Jesus was baptised at thirty-years old, God anointed him as His second-in-command, for He was "well pleased" in him (LUKE 3:23; MATT. 3:13-17; ACTS 2:32-33). God gave Jesus a name above all names and a wife of his Church which became predominately gentile (PHIL. 2:9-11; EPH. 3:6).

The famine devastated Canaan, the land of Jacob (Israel) and his eleven sons. The conditions were such that Jacob sent his ten oldest sons down to Egypt to buy grain supplies from the Pharaoh. When they arrived it was Joseph they stood before, but they did not recognise him. The same was true for Jesus at his first coming. "Though the world was made through him [Jesus], the world did not recognize him. He came to his own, and his own did not receive him" (JOHN 1:10-12).

Joseph refused to acknowledge their reasoning for being there and acted roughly towards them. They began talking among themselves in Hebrew, lamenting the fact that this situation was their own doing for selling their brother into slavery. Secretly listening in, Joseph realised how guilty they began to feel over their mistreatment of him and he removed himself to weep. When he returned, he demanded they go back to Canaan to fetch their younger brother Benjamin to prove their story. Benjamin, the only other son of Rachel, was now his father's favourite and received preferential treatment in Egypt. Joseph was setting up a test to determine if his brothers had truly repented, or if they would abandon Benjamin as they did him. After returning to Joseph, they were told to depart under this test. In the period before the second coming of Jesus, the Jewish people are similarly tested and appear to be deserted by God until they finally acknowledge how they rejected their exalted brother (JER. 30:4-10; MATT. 23:39).

Joseph commanded his servant to fill their sacks with food and money and to place a silver cup in Benjamin's sack, a tool often used for divination (GEN. 44:5, 15). Would the brothers think that Benjamin was trying to be a "dreamer" like Joseph? In the morning he sent the eleven brothers on their way back to Canaan but quickly ordered his servants to catch them and search their sacks for a supposedly stolen cup. After finding the cup in Benjamin's sack, the brothers were again brought before Joseph. Judah stepped forward and asked how they could clear themselves, to which Joseph declared Benjamin had to stay behind so the others could return to their father. Once again Judah (note it is Judah) spoke up to argue that since their father had already lost one favoured son, if he were to lose another, he would be utterly heartbroken (GEN. 44:17, 20-22). Judah pleaded to take the place of Benjamin as a slave for the sake of his father, and so the others could all return to Canaan. Upon hearing of Judah's readiness to sacrifice himself for his brother and the good of his father, Joseph asked his gentile servants to remove themselves before making his identity known to his brothers (GEN. 45:1). To their utter astonishment, Joseph declared:

> "I am your brother Joseph, the one you sold into Egypt! And now, do not be distressed and do not be angry with yourselves for selling me here, because ... God sent me ahead of you to preserve for you a remnant on earth and to save your lives by a great deliverance" (Gen. 45:4-7 NIV).

Joseph embraced his brothers who once betrayed him and wept bitterly (GEN. 45:14). He organised for the relocation of his family to Egypt to be provided for throughout the famine. Jesus was sent into the world by God to preserve and save a remnant unto eternal life by a great deliverance (MIC. 2:12; ISA. 10:20; 11:16; 28:5). Just as Joseph was considered a gentile Lord by his brothers until he revealed himself, the Jews who did not recognise Jesus as their Lord at his first coming, will at his second coming after a time of great tribulation. Israel (Judah) will be similarly tested by God and come to recognise Jesus as their exalted brother they had once betrayed. Jesus will transfigure the Church (that is, he will remove them) during the harpazo before presenting himself to his Jewish brothers, unbelieving Israel, as the source of their deliverance from the wrath of Satan and his seed, the Antichrist (MATT. 24:30-31; ISA. 63:1-9). The Jews shall weep bitterly over their mistreatment of him (ZECH. 12:10-14) and Jesus will be so moved by their repentance that he will accept them into his heavenly household to be provided for forever (EZEK. 37:24-28).

Through this crisis, Joseph had brought about a change of heart in Judah and shifted the trajectory of the family—and thus the godly line. Joseph (Jesus) had to suffer so Judah (Israel) could have this change of heart and recognise their father's grief (God). Joseph prefigured the remarkable faithfulness and loyalty of the Messiah in an unparalleled way. The ability to suffer and not become bitter and disheartened requires exceptional fortitude, and Joseph possessed this trait in abundance.

### 4. Living Shadow of Judah

Even though Judah acted wickedly on many occasions, even selling his own brother (GEN. 37:27; 38:2-10, 24), the Messiah still chose to descend through his bloodline:

> *He rejected the tent of Joseph, and did not choose the tribe of Ephraim, but chose the tribe of Judah, Mount Zion which He loved (Psa. 78:67-68 NKJV).*

In contrast to Judah and his brothers, Joseph seemed to be the obvious choice. He always displayed the goodness of his character and faithfulness to God, even while enduring the deepest levels of betrayal and rejection. What could the Lord have seen in Judah?[28]

Perhaps Judah was predestined by God to inherit the messianic bloodline contrary to the natural choice. This would fit in line with the divine call of his predecessors (GEN. 17:18-21; 25:23). Abraham chose Ishmael, but God chose Isaac; Isaac chose Esau,

---

[28] Another possibility or factor for why God chose Jesus to descend through Judah is the strange incident between Judah and Tamar which is interpolated into the story of Joseph (GEN. 37). I will explore the significance of this event on the website beholdmessiah.com.

but God chose Jacob. Jacob favoured Joseph, but God chose Judah. Justification for this perspective can be gleaned from the already discussed Rachel and Leah connection. Due to the difficult situation of being the less desired of the two wives, Leah experienced much pain and grief. This reflected in each of the names she gave her children, each calling to mind the predicament she was in. When it came to birthing Judah, her fourth child, her focus suddenly shifted from herself to the Lord, despite her circumstances being unchanged:

> *And she conceived again and bore a son, and said, "Now I will praise the Lord." Therefore she called his name Judah. Then she stopped bearing (Gen. 29:35 NKJV).*

Notice how the passage mentioned she thereafter stopped bearing children and the attention moved to Rachel. It is as if this so pleased God that He blessed Leah and her son Judah right then and there. Could Leah's change of heart in the midst of great suffering have influenced God's decision to give the sceptre to Judah? The impact which powerful acts of faithfulness can have upon God is also shown in the New Testament when Paul and Silas were being imprisoned (ACTS 16:16-36). Having been severely beaten and put in shackles, the men had reason to doubt divine providence and descend into self-pity, but they prayed and sang praises to God (v. 25). God was moved by their faith as He was by Leah's and responded with a great earthquake that opened all the prison doors and broke apart their chains (v. 26). The prisoners and the guard came together to put their faith in Christ because of the love and faithfulness they saw on display by Paul and Silas. They were all set free in the spiritual and physical sense (vv. 27-36).

Another possibility is that the pledge of safety which Judah made to his father factored into God's decision-making. Remember that Judah vowed to protect the life of Benjamin with his own life as a surety (GEN. 43:8-9). Judah lived up to his word when tested by Joseph and begged to suffer in the place of Benjamin (GEN. 44:18-34). What we saw was a repentant man, a loyal son, and a loving brother willing to die in the place of another. All attributes God loves and desires from His kings and shepherds (John 10:11). Remember how Jesus told his disciples that "greater love has no one than this, than to lay down one's life for his friends" (John 15:13; 1 John 3:16). Judah substituted himself for his brother Benjamin, whose name means "son of the right hand" as a type of Jesus who offered up his own life to save mankind. We take the place of Benjamin, being sons and daughters of God's right hand, Jesus Christ (Matt. 22:44; Acts 2:33; 7:55-56; Rom. 8:34; Eph. 1:20; Col. 3:1; Heb. 1:3; 8:1; 10:12; 12:2; 1 Peter 3:22; Rev. 3:21).

### Sceptre from Judah to Jesus

When it came time, "Jacob called unto his sons, and said, gather yourselves together, that I may tell you that which shall befall you in the last days" (Gen. 49:1). To be clear on the eschatological implications here, the Hebrew words for last days or days to come in the first verse is *acharit hayamim*, which is often used in the context of end days or the latter end (Isa. 2:2; Mic. 4:1). The blessings and curses which Jacob prophesied to his sons reflected the last days of their posterity—their tribes.

The blessing portion given to Judah was that the sceptre, the tribal staff of authority to enforce the Mosaic laws, would not depart "until Shiloh comes," to whom the obedience of the people would ultimately be (Gen. 49:8-12). As evidenced by many early rabbinical writings, the term *Shiloh* was always understood to be a personal designation of the Messiah.[29] Fittingly, the phrase "until Shiloh comes" has a Hebrew gematria (numerical value) of 358—the same as Messiah and Thy Redeemer. The Hebrew word for serpent, *nahash*, also has a gematria of 358. His seed, the Antichrist, seeks to counterfeit the Messiah and thy redeemer and claim the sceptre of authority for himself.

---

[29] B. Talmud Sanhedrin 98b:14; Targum Onkelos, Jerusalem, Jonathan, and Pseudo-Jonathan on Genesis 49:10-11; Midrash Genesis Rabbah 98.8, 99.9. For more Jewish sources read the following: https://www.kolhator.com/shilo-jewish-sources-interpretation-shiloh.

## Seed of God: Jesus Christ

With this understanding, we can deduce who Shiloh is from the point in time that the sceptre departed from Judah. One might assume the Babylonian conquest marks the spot since the national sovereignty of Judah was lost as a consequence. However, we learn from Ezra 1 that the tribal sceptre, or political structure, remained intact even during the captivity (EZRA 1). The Jews retained their own lawgivers and judges over the people. This political arrangement persisted when the Jews became a vassal state of Medo-Persia, and later, the Greek and Roman empires.

The first sign for the removal of the sceptre from Judah, according to Josh McDowell in *The New Evidence that Demands a Verdict*, was the transfer of royal power from the Jews (as in Judeans or Judahites) to the gentiles with the succession of King Herod the Great.[30] Only a generation later in 6-7 AD, the Roman-backed Herodian dynasty was ousted and Judea became a Roman province. Emperor Augustus appointed a Roman procurator named Caponius to wield "the power of life and death" in the region.[31] In line with all the nations that were assimilated into the Roman empire, it seems Judah lost the sovereign power to adjudicate capital cases, dubbed the *ius gladii* ("right of the sword"). No longer could they fully self-govern themselves according to the Mosaic laws. If this were the point in which the sceptre departed from Judah, it would coincide with the time a boy from Nazareth called Jesus was growing up.

According to the Talmudic tractate *Sanhedrin* however, "the Sanhedrin ceased judging cases of capital law forty years before the destruction of the temple":[32]

> *Forty years before the destruction of the Second Temple, the Sanhedrin was exiled from the Chamber of Hewn*

---

[30] McDowell, *The New Evidence That Demands a Verdict*, 195; B. Talmud Sanhedrin, folio 24, 97; Maccabees 2.

[31] Josephus, "The Wars of the Jews," 2.117; Ibid., "Antiquities of the Jews," 18.1, 18.2.2.

[32] B. Talmud Sanhedrin 41a:26; Shabbat 15a:9-10.

> *Stone and sat in the store near the Temple Mount ... the Sanhedrin no longer judged cases of capital law. Once the Sanhedrin left the Chamber of Hewn Stone, the court's power to judge capital cases was nullified.*[33]

The Chamber of Hewn Stone was a council chamber inside the Second Temple.[34] It was the equivalent of a Supreme Court for the Sanhedrin where they would congregate to exercise their legal powers, including capital punishment.[35] The fact that there is no explanation for why the Sanhedrin left the Chamber of Hewn Stone is peculiar. Due to this omission, if one were to research what could have transpired at the temple in 30 AD, one would be faced with the gospel accounts. This is what we are told happened at the temple when Jesus yielded up his spirit on the cross:

> *And Jesus cried out again with a loud voice, and yielded up His spirit. Then, behold, the veil of the temple was torn in two from top to bottom; and the earth quaked, and the rocks were split (Matt. 27:50-51 NKJV).*

We make the case in the chapter *New Covenant for a New Creation* that Jesus was crucified at this very time, forty years before the destruction of the temple. This would mean that the trial of Jesus was most likely the last capital case the Sanhedrin carried out. Biblically speaking, forty is commonly used to represent a time of testing, or a probation period, such as the forty-years the Jews wandered the wilderness. It is my contention in that chapter that Jesus similarly allotted forty years to the religious authorities to accept that the sceptre had departed from them into his hands as Shiloh. I present as evidence the Talmudic reports of many unusual events, or portents of destruction, that occurred for these forty years before the temple was destroyed.

---

[33] B. Talmud Sanhedrin 41a:25.

[34] Ibid. Yoma 25a.6-9.

[35] Ibid. Sanhedrin 88b.

The first-century Roman-Jewish historian Flavius Josephus recorded an instance of the Sanhedrin overstepping their legal boundaries in 62 AD when high priest Ananus sentenced none other than "James the brother of Jesus, who was called Christ" to be stoned to death:

> *All the wise men and strict observers of the law who were at Jerusalem expressed their disapprobation of this act ... some even went to Albinus himself ... to bring this breach of the law under his observation, and to inform him that Ananius had acted illegally in assembling the Sanhedrin without the Roman authority.*[36]

Notice how the Sanhedrin were not even permitted to assemble without Roman permission. This would explain the earlier remark from the Jewish authorities to Pontius Pilate: "It is not lawful for us to put anyone to death" (JOHN 18:31).

In summary, if the first example of 6-7 AD was not the correct date for the sceptre departing from Judah, but 30 AD, the Shiloh figure in view would still be the same. The former date concerns the time Jesus the Messiah was coming into his own as a young man, and the latter fits firmly with the time of Jesus' crucifixion. Since the temple was destroyed in 70 AD and the Jews were dispersed from the land in 132 AD, the most reasonable candidate for Shiloh we are left with is Jesus Christ. Significantly, the tribe of Judah was the last surviving tribe of Israel by the time of Jesus (the tribe of Benjamin was assimilated). God depended on Judah to hand over the sceptre to Jesus, or Shiloh, upon his arrival.

### Shiloh in the Last Days

Given the messianic context of the blessings and prophecies Jacob specifically gave to Judah, the last days in his case pertain to the very last days, the final judgement and restoration after Shiloh comes. With this in mind, the prophecy that Jacob relates to the

---

[36] Josephus, "Antiquities of the Jews," 20.197.

Messiah fits under a familiar Christian eschatological framework.

First, Jacob says of the Messiah: "He will tether his donkey to a vine, his colt to the choicest branch" (GEN. 49:11). The prophet Zechariah made the same allusion: "Behold, your King is coming to you; He is just and having salvation, lowly and riding on a donkey, a colt, the foal of a donkey" (ZECH. 9:9). Jesus, whom we claim to be this Shiloh figure bringing salvation, rode into Jerusalem in this manner, and Matthew and John explicitly state that it was so the prophecy be fulfilled (MATT. 21:1-5; JOHN 12:14-16). The people expected him to be the conquering king, or *Mashiach ben David*, but he came for peace as the suffering servant, or *Mashiach ben Joseph* (MATT. 21:1-11; MARK 11:1-11; LUKE 19:28-40; JOHN 12:12-19). This reversal of expectations was explained by the scholar Caroline Stanke:

> *Because the king is riding on a donkey and not on a horse, it also implies that he will take away all weapons and build a kingdom of peace. Instead of riding a horse, he rides a beast of burden and shows his peaceful mission.*[37]

But it could also be the case that this prophecy is recapitulated after Jesus returns as the messianic king, the Mashiach ben David, to inaugurate the millennial kingdom. Some commentators see the vine strong enough to tether a donkey as a metaphor for the magnificence and strength of this kingdom.

The remainder of the prophecy Jacob revealed to Judah states how this Shiloh figure "will wash his garments in wine, his robes in the blood of grapes [and] his eyes will be darker than wine, his teeth whiter than milk" (GEN. 49:11-12). Rabbinic sources tend to view this as a hyperbolic depiction of abundance that will come upon the entire house of Judah. The donkey tethered to the vine is likewise interpreted as a signal of strength. My contention is that

---

[37] Stanke, "The Motif of the Messiah in Zechariah 9-14," 28, https://dx.doi.org/10.32597/theses/128.

the subject of the prophecy is in the *singular*, not the plural, and the Messiah figure Shiloh is clearly in view here. To interpret this otherwise requires us to dispense with the obvious reading of the prophecy. For this reason, I am comfortable continuing with the exegetical approach of Jesus, or Shiloh, as being the subject. The passage points to a time beyond ourselves to the second coming of Jesus. The imagery herein is pictured in many OT prophecies of the Messiah, and of Jesus directly in the NT. We will discuss these in detail, but first, it is wise to find precedent for the approach I am about to take. Put simply, the idea of Jesus partially fulfilling aspects of a single prophecy in both of his incarnations on earth.

The precedent I will focus on is found in Luke 4, which both illustrates this idea and connects perfectly with the prophecies on his second coming for judgement. We heard about Jesus reading from the book of Isaiah in the synagogue, and how he turned to the beginning of Isaiah 61 to relate it to himself as Messiah (ISA. 61:1-3; LUKE 4:17-19). The passage was the following:

> *The Spirit of the Lord is upon Me, because He has anointed Me to preach the gospel to the poor; He has sent Me to heal the brokenhearted, to proclaim liberty to the captives and recovery of sight to the blind, to set at liberty those who are oppressed; to proclaim the acceptable year of the Lord (Luke 4:18-19 NKJV).*

In Isaiah, you will notice the second verse continues with "and the day of vengeance of our God" but Jesus closed the book and sat down instead of finishing it (LUKE 4:20; ISA. 61:2). Sensing the bemusement of the people, he told them, "today this Scripture is fulfilled in your hearing" (LUKE 4:21). This emphasises how Jesus only addressed the first fragment; the remainder was yet to come. I believe the first portion of Jacob's prophecy to Judah relates to Jesus coming as the suffering servant and peacemaker. The first coming was the acceptable year of the Lord, but it was not yet time for the day of vengeance. Parallel to this example, the remainder of Jacob's prophecy relates to the day of vengeance, a double prophecy. First judgement came upon the Jews when the gentile Romans destroyed Jerusalem in 70 AD and in 135 AD with their forced exile following the Bar Kokhba revolt. The second judgement is yet future, the day of the Lord, when God extends His mercy to the Jews and defeats the gentile forces that are under the authority of the Antichrist (ISA. 34-35; 61-63; JOEL 2-3; OBAD. 1; ZEPH. 1:14-18; ZECH. 14; MATT. 24:29-31; LUKE 21:22; 1 THESS. 5:1-11; REV. 6; 14; 18).

In an apocalyptic vision of John, Jesus is seen in heaven sitting not upon a donkey of peace, but a white horse, symbolic of impending war (REV. 19:11). On the day of vengeance, Jesus, the Lion of the Tribe of Judah (REV. 5:5), returns to earth as the conquering Davidic king to strike down his enemies (REV. 14:14; 19:15-16; DAN. 7:13; PSA. 110; MIC. 5:2; MATT. 2:6). As Jeremiah prophesied, Jesus executes judgement and righteousness in the earth and restores Judah and Israel to an eternal peace (JER. 23:5-6; 33:14-17). With sickle in hand, he treads the winepress of the fierce wrath of God, filled to overflowing with his enemies (REV. 14:15-20; 19:15; JOEL 3:13-14). His garments are sprinkled with their blood, the same grape and blood metaphor employed in Jacob's prophecy (ISA. 63:1-4). His eyes are described by Daniel and John as being like a flame of fire (REV. 1:14; 2:18; 19:12; DAN. 10:6). This could be an allusion to the eyes darker than wine (red like fire) from Jacob's prophecy.

*Image 2.6 – Hebrew name meanings from Judah to David*

| NAME | HEBREW MEANING |
| --- | --- |
| Judah | *praises God* |
| Perez | *breach, breaks open a way* |
| Hezron | *area surrounded by a wall* |
| Ram | *of great height* |
| Amminadab | *my kinsman is noble and generous* |
| Nahshon | *a prophet, oracle* |
| Salmon | *garment* |
| Boaz | *strength* |
| Obed | *who serves* |

| | |
|---|---|
| Jesse | my husband, Lord exists |
| David | beloved |
| **INTERPRETATION FROM COMBINED MEANINGS** | |
| The one who praises God breaches an area surrounded by a wall of great height. My kinsman is noble and generous, he is a prophet wearing a garment of strength who serves my husband (God), my beloved. | |

## 5. Living Shadow of Moses

Before moving on to David we shall look at a living shadow that is outside of the lineal line of the seed of the woman, but is still an important son of Abraham, Isaac, and Jacob, through Levi. I am speaking of Moses, the great mediator and lawgiver. The list starts with Levi, going through Moses and his two sons Gershom and Eliezer and their descendants:

*Image 2.7 – Hebrew name meanings from Levi to Shelomoth*

| NAME | HEBREW MEANING |
|---|---|
| Levi | joined, to join |
| Kohath | obedience, congregation |
| Amram | exalted people, bound |
| Moses | drawn out of water |
| Gershom | strange land, exile |
| Eliezer | God helps |
| Shebuel | restored (or captive) of God |
| Rehabiah | God is wide, enlarging |
| Jeshaiah (Isaiah) | salvation of God |
| Joram | God exalted (or exalts) |
| Zichri | remembered |
| Shelomoth | peace, peacemaker |
| **INTERPRETATION FROM COMBINED MEANINGS** | |
| One joined to an obedient congregation of exalted people is drawn out of water in a strange land. God helps restore His captive people through His wide salvation and the God exalted is remembered as a peacemaker. | |

Moses was Hebrew by birth, the exalted people of God, born during their time of bondage under Egypt (Exod. 1:8-14). As a Hebrew baby boy, Moses had to be killed according to the Pharaoh's decree (Exod. 1:15-22). His parents desperately sent him down the Nile river to find refuge among the Egyptians (Exod. 2:1-10). He was drawn from water in a strange land by the Pharaoh's daughter, a gentile, and she raised him as one of her own (Exod. 2:5-10). Jesus was born a Jew during their time of bondage under Rome. King Herod ordered a similar decree within Bethlehem that all males under two years old were to be killed. God told Jesus' father Joseph to take the baby Jesus to Egypt for refuge. He was raised among the Egyptians until the death of Herod (Matt. 2:13-18).

God exalted Moses to become His mediator to the Hebrews so they could be delivered from slavery. Moses had to humble himself by relinquishing his power and life of luxury and seek the confidence of his captive people (Exod. 3:1-22; 4:28-30; 32:1-14). God sent Jesus from heaven to earth to seek our confidence as a mediator. He had to voluntarily relinquish his comfort in heaven as the second-in-command to God in order to "proclaim deliverance to the captives" under the slavery of Satan and sin, a much greater Pharaoh (Luke 4:18; Rom. 5:1).

Moses fled from Pharaoh and stopped at a well in the land of Midian. There he met seven gentile women and graciously watered their flocks. The women all rushed home to their father and were told to return to Moses and welcome him into their home. This led to Moses marrying Zipporah, one of the gentile daughters (Exod. 2:15-22). Jesus fled from the temptations of Satan in the wilderness and not long after stopped at Jacob's well on his journey through Samaria (John 4:1-6). There he met a Samaritan woman (considered worse than gentiles) and revealed himself to her as the Messiah who gives living water unto eternal life (John 4:6-26). She rushed to the town to spread the good news and from her account many believed (John 4:27-42). While they did not get married as individuals (the well pattern of marriage applies also to Isaac and Jacob), their marriage is as part of a larger, corporate body of believers of Jews and gentiles—the Church.

Moses' promises of deliverance fell on deaf ears initially, but he persisted through rejection (EXOD. 5:14-21; LUKE 4:14-30). Out of desperation from their persecution under Pharaoh, the people accepted him the second time (EXOD. 4:28-31). With Moses as their leader, the Hebrews challenged the authority of Pharaoh and the gods of the age (EXOD. 7-10). Jesus was rejected by his people and sent outside the camp (LUKE 4:14-30). At his second coming, his people will finally accept him after suffering great persecution under the Antichrist (REV. 7:9-17).

Moses, as the mediator between the Lord and the Hebrews, was singularly responsible for their deliverance (GAL 3:19-20). Outside of him, none could escape slavery in Egypt. They were delivered out of the land because they faithfully obeyed the God-given instructions from Moses to avert the judgement of death upon their firstborn sons (EXOD. 11-13). Because all mankind is under the curse of sin, all households, whether Hebrew or Egyptian, were able to escape death by smearing the blood of an unblemished lamb on their doorframes. God thereafter commanded the Hebrews to observe the Passover festival every year in remembrance of His deliverance through the blood of the lamb (EXOD. 12:14). Jesus, as the mediator between God and mankind, became the singular path to our deliverance from the slavery of sin under the ultimate Pharaoh—Satan (JOHN 1:29; 1 COR. 5:7; 1 TIM. 2:5; HEB. 8:6; 9:14-15; GAL. 1:3-5). In the hours before the Passover sacrifice, Jesus told his disciples to observe a new Passover, the Eucharist, in remembrance of the act of salvation he was to perform before them as the Lamb of God, the ultimate fulfilment of the Passover sacrifice (MATT. 26:17-30; MARK 14:12-26; LUKE 22:7-20; 1 COR. 11:23-26):

> ... the Lord Jesus on the same night in which He was betrayed took bread; and when He had given thanks, He broke it and said, "Take, eat; this is My body which is broken for you; do this in remembrance of Me." In the same manner He also took the cup after supper, saying, "This cup is the new covenant in My blood. This do, as often as you drink it, in remembrance of Me." For as

*often as you eat this bread and drink this cup, you proclaim the Lord's death till He comes (1 Cor. 11:23-26 NKJV).*

Following the judgement upon the firstborn sons of Egypt, the Hebrews quickly departed with unleavened bread for the journey ahead (Exod. 12:31-39), "and Moses took the bones of Joseph with him, for he had placed the children of Israel under solemn oath, saying, 'God will surely visit you, and you shall carry up my bones from here with you'" (Exod. 13:19). Jesus was taken down from the cross in haste and placed in the tomb of Joseph of Arimathea before the feast of Unleavened Bread (Matt. 27:59-60; Mark 15:42:45; Luke 23:50-54). Matthew told us that many dead saints, perhaps even Joseph himself, were raised up from their graves in Jerusalem after Jesus became the first fruits of the resurrection (Matt. 27:50-54).

Upon reaching the Red Sea, the Israelites found themselves closed in by the Egyptian army and began to question the authority of Moses and of God (Exod. 14:1-12):

> *And Moses said to the people, "Do not be afraid. Stand still, and see the salvation [yeshuat] of the Lord, which He will accomplish for you today. For the Egyptians whom you see today, you shall see again no more forever. The Lord will fight for you, and you shall hold your peace" (Exod. 14:13-14 NKJV).*

From a pillar of cloud above, God gave light to His people, but darkness for His adversaries (Exod. 13:21-22; 14:19-25; Psa. 105:39). To one He promised salvation, to the other judgement. He told Moses, "lift up your rod, and stretch out your hand over the sea and divide it" (Exod. 14:16). Moses did as he was commanded and guided the Israelites through the parted waters away from the wrath of Pharaoh and his army (Exod. 14:21-23). After reaching the land, God instructed Moses to stretch his hand over the sea a second time to release the waters over the Egyptian army (Exod.

14:26-29). For one the waters brought sanctification and rebirth, to the other destruction and death. David Smith made the observation that "the enemies of God are judged and vanquished in the same water through which God's people are cleansed and rescued."[38] The late preacher Witness Lee likened this to the resurrection of Christ:

> *Israel went into the Red Sea with Pharaoh and his army following, but Israel was resurrected from the death water without Pharaoh and his army. Pharaoh and his army were buried in the death water. Christ brought man with Satan into death and the grave and brought man without Satan out of death and the grave. He left Satan buried in the grave. Now the resurrected man is one with Christ.*[39]

With his hands outstretched upon the wooden cross, akin to the staff of Moses, Jesus (Yeshua) accomplished "the salvation [yeshuat] of the Lord" to which the first Exodus pointed (EXOD. 14:13-14). God saves (meaning of Jesus) all mankind through the blood and water of Jesus (Yeshua) (1 JOHN 5:6). This metaphor of salvation was reinforced quite literally when blood and water flowed out from his pierced side on the cross (JOHN 19:34). Those who pass through the second Red Sea crossing of judgment by being baptised into Christ are "rescued from the dominion of darkness" under Satan, paid for by Jesus' own blood (COL. 1:13-14). They are freed from the shackles of sin and death and begin their journey through the wilderness of life towards the promised rest of heaven (ACTS 3:19-26; JOHN 8:34-36; ROM. 8:2; REV 21:1-7).

Paul the Apostle compared this baptism into Christ with the Red Sea crossing, stating that the Hebrews "were all baptized into Moses in the cloud and in the sea" (1 COR. 10:1-2), whereas Christians

---

[38] Smith, "The Exodus and Christian Baptism," *The Village Church Resources*, https://www.tvcresources.net/resource-library/articles/the-exodus-and-christian-baptism.

[39] Lee, *The Economy of God*, 113.

are "baptised into Christ Jesus," in body and in death. We too must immerse ourselves (literal meaning for baptise) in the deep waters of his afflictions and suffer his death (2 TIM. 2:11-13; EPH. 4:8-13) to be raised up in him in bodily resurrection (ROM. 6:3-5; MATT. 28:19; MARK 10:38; LUKE 12:50; JOHN 5:28-2; 1 COR. 15:50-55; 1 THESS. 4:13-17).

Paul emphasised the point that, although the Hebrews in the wilderness were baptised and partook of the sacraments which were the "spiritual food" (bread or manna) and "spiritual drink," it was of no benefit to them, for they neglected the faith of which baptism was but a symbol, and therefore God kept that generation in the wilderness (1 COR. 10:1-10; EXOD. 15:22-17:7; NUM. 14; DEUT. 1-2:23; HEB. 3:7-19; JUDE 5). The journey through the wilderness was determined for the children of Israel to demonstrate their faithfulness to God, and therefore warrant entrance into the land promised to their forefathers. The supremacy of faith is evidenced by the fact that although the next generation were uncircumcised in the flesh, God nevertheless allowed them to cross the Jordan river under Joshua (Hebrew *Yehoshua*—Jesus or *Yeshua* is the contraction of Yehoshua) and enter the promised land because of their faithful obedience—or circumcision of the heart (JOSH. 5:2-8).[40]

---

[40] The law under Moses can lead us only so far, it cannot bring us into the promised land. That must be done by the one after Moses, a figure like Joshua. Before the Israelites entered the promised land through Joshua (a type of Messiah), who inherited the role of Moses, he waited three days for the two spies in Jericho to report back with the assurance of victory over the Canaanites (JOSH. 2). A gentile woman named Rahab who believed and feared the God of Israel protected these spies and ensured their safe passage back to the camp of Israel (JOSH. 2). Jesus' disciples waited three days for the report from Mary Magdalene that Jesus had resurrected and assured our victory over death. The gentile Church who believe and fear the God of Israel are protectors or custodians of the faith and the faithful until Israel comes into the promised rest and are united as one with the Church in Christ (ISA. 14:3-7; ROM. 11:25-32; EPH. 2:14). Israel encircled the mighty city of Jericho and marched around the city walls in silence six times for six days, but on the seventh a great trumpet was blasted and a great shout came from the people, and with it the ungodly Canaanite stronghold of Jericho fell (JOSH. 6). In John of Patmos' vision of the apocalypse, there is shown to be silence in heaven at the opening of the seventh seal, and then a blast of seven trumpets and a shout of great voices in heaven saying: "the kingdoms of this world have become the kingdoms of our Lord and

Only once they became settled in the promised land did Joshua have them circumcised.

The symbolism is clear—we are as the children of Israel in the wilderness, delivered from slavery, but still yet to come into our promised rest (HEB. 4). We too must endure in the wilderness of life by clinging to God in faith and subsisting on His Word, the body and blood of Christ, symbolised by the bread and wine of the Eucharist, the analogue of the spiritual bread and water God showered upon the Hebrews from heaven (MATT 4:4; JOHN 6:51).

> *For if we died with Him, we shall also live with Him. If we endure, we shall also reign with Him. If we deny Him, He also will deny us. If we are faithless, He remains faithful; He cannot deny Himself (2 Tim. 2:11-13 NKJV).*

We must take heed of the lessons from the first Exodus to ensure we are counted among those who cross over the river of life (Jordan river) and enter into eternal rest within the kingdom of God (HEB. 4; 2 PET. 3:13; REV. 22:12-14). Paul stated that the first Exodus under Moses "happened to them as examples and were written down as warnings for us, on whom the culmination of the ages has come" (1 COR. 10:11). Even Moses, before the Israelites had entered into the promised land, looked ahead to the day of this second Exodus under a prophet and mediator greater even than himself:[41]

---

of His Christ, and He shall reign forever and ever!" (REV. 11:15). When the soles of the feet of the priests bearing the ark of the covenant dipped in the river Jordan, under the command of Joshua, the waters banked up so Israel could proceed across into the promised land on dry ground (JOSH. 3). At this time Israel experienced a great circumcision and the manna from heaven stopped (JOSH. 5). Jesus leads us in triumphal procession through the flood of death to the eternal promised land, the new heaven and earth through resurrection (2 COR. 2:14; HEB. 6:20). This enabled a great national circumcision of the heart for God's people where he becomes their bread of life (manna), as the living Word.

[41] The rabbinic assessment of this prophet greater than Moses only considered the royal accomplishments of the Messiah. The medieval Rabbi Maimonides summarised the historical perspective of the Jews: *"The King Messiah will arise and re-establish the monarchy of David as it was in former times. He will build the Sanctuary and gather in the dispersed of Israel. All the earlier*

> *The Lord your God will raise up for you a prophet like me from among you, from your fellow Israelites. You must listen to him ... The Lord said to me: "What they say is good. I will raise up for them a prophet like you from among their fellow Israelites, and I will put my words in his mouth. He will tell them everything I command him. I myself will call to account anyone who does not listen to my words that the prophet speaks in my name (Deut. 18:15-19 NIV).*

The apostle Peter reaffirmed what was told to Moses in relation to Jesus but went even further by boldly declaring that "every soul who will not hear that Prophet shall be utterly destroyed from among the people" (ACTS 3:22-23).

> *Therefore, as the Holy Spirit says: "Today, if you will hear His voice, do not harden your hearts as in the rebellion, in the day of trial in the wilderness, where your fathers tested Me, tried Me, and saw My works forty years. Therefore I was angry with that generation, and said, 'They always go astray in their heart, and they have not known My ways.' So I swore in My wrath, 'they shall not enter My rest'" (Heb. 3:7-11 NKJV).*

The typology of the covenant and the law, specifically the feasts, which were given to Moses at Mount Sinai, will be discussed in greater depth throughout this book. As mentioned in the introduction, in addition to the living shadows explored here, the biblical covenants and the law are completed and fulfilled in Christ. For this reason I will refrain from including all of the remaining parallels between Moses and Christ and move on to discuss the Mosaic covenant.

---

statutes will be restored as they once were ... Anyone who does not believe in him or one who does not anticipate his coming not only denies the Prophets, but also the Torah and Moses our Teacher" (Maimonides, *Mishneh Torah: Kings and Wars*, 11:1).

*Seed of God: Jesus Christ*

## The Third Covenant with Moses

Forty-seven days from the crossing of the Red Sea (three days before receiving the Law) God told Moses to inform the Hebrews that having seen how He delivered them from the Egyptians and brought them unto Himself, He would promise them three things if they were willing to obey His voice and keep His commands (Exod. 19:1-5):

> *[1] Out of all nations you will be my treasured possession ... [2] you will be for me a kingdom of priests and [3] a holy nation (Exod. 19:5-6 NIV).*

They were then instructed to sanctify themselves for three days before personally meeting with God at Mount Sinai. It was on this day, the fiftieth day (Pentecost), that God descended upon the mountain with thunder and fire to meet them (Exod. 19:10-24). Moses acted as mediator for the people to receive the covenant, thus the name, the Mosaic covenant (Exod. 20-24). To all of the stipulations of the covenant, the people "responded with one voice, 'everything the Lord has said we will do'" (Exod. 24:3). Forty days after his deliverance by resurrection (First Fruits), Jesus instructed his disciples to wait in Jerusalem for the full power of the Holy Spirit to be poured out on them. On the fiftieth day, the second great Pentecost, the Spirit came upon the disciples like a mighty rushing wind and baptised them with fire (Acts 2). Because they accepted the new covenant, Jesus called them out to become part of his Church, a holy nation and kingdom of priests (1 Pet. 2:9).

With the Mosaic covenant, the descendants of Abraham were defined more narrowly as the Israelite people or nation to whom the promised land inheritance belonged. Israel agreed as a collective to become a holy nation of priests set apart from the gentiles to serve God (Exod. 19:5-6; Deut. 7:6; 14:2; Psa. 147:19–20). As the first fruits of the holy nations, God intended for Israel to exhibit the qualities He desired from all the nations (Jer. 2:3). The Mosaic law instructed them on the responsibilities of this divinely appointed role, which, if followed, demonstrated to themselves and to the gentiles the perfect ways of God (DEUT. 32:44-47; PSA. 119:9, 104). In line with the Abrahamic promise for all the peoples of the world to blessed, Israel was not chosen instead of the world, but *for* the world. To live in total accordance with the goodness of God would naturally increase the quality of life for all people, and thus participation would bring joy, not misery.[42] The promised blessings of the Abrahamic covenant could easily flow on through Israel as the vehicle for the salvific plan to be realised.

The sign of participation was corporate or collective. Of concern were not only the individuals, but the people and their land. As a nation, Israel was required to observe the sign of the Lord's sabbaths for as long as they occupied the land (EXOD. 31:13-17; LEV. 25; 26:2, 32-35). The Abrahamic sign of circumcision was formalised under the Mosaic covenant for individuals to enter into the holy nation. Crucially though, the Abrahamic covenant was not superseded or abrogated by the Mosaic, nor would this be the case for any future covenant. The two covenants were complimentary, and so were the signs. The land was for the people, and the people for the land. The Mosaic covenant promulgated faithful participation for the sake of the nation and its people, and thus, the Abrahamic promises. Paul made this point in the epistle to the Galatians, stating that, "if the inheritance [Abrahamic] depends on the Law [Mosaic], then it no longer depends on the promise; but God in his grace gave it to Abraham through a promise" (GAL 3:15-19).

Even with the new covenant which Jesus ratified, he stressed how the Mosaic covenant was not abolished, but fulfilled (MATT. 5:17-20; LUKE 16:16-17). Again, in Hebrews 8:13, a common passage used to support supersessionism or replacement theology, the Mosaic covenant is not described as being abrogated, but merely

---

[42] Kaiser, "God's Promise Plan and His Gracious Law," *Journal of the Evangelical Theological Society* 33, no. 3 (September 1990): 294.
https://www.etsjets.org/files/JETS-PDFs/33/33-3/33-3-pp289-302_JETS.pdf.

made "obsolete" or "old" by the new covenant (HEB. 8:13). In the words of Old Testament Professor William Barrick:

> *Each covenant advanced the previous without overturning it through the process of progressive revelation. In fact, the very focus of the covenant was the formation of a nation through whom the promises of the Abrahamic Covenant could be mediated. Both covenants were particularistic—the former identified an individual and his descendants, the latter identified a national entity composed of those descendants.*[43]

The Mosaic covenant was a conditional and bilateral covenant or marriage. As with any marriage, both parties entered into the agreement freely and willingly on Pentecost at Mount Sinai (EXOD. 24:3-8; 34:27-28; DEUT. 4:13; 26:16-17). For all their days, Israel was marked as the bride of God, and God the bridegroom (ISA. 54:5; JER. 3:14; 31:32; HOS. 2:19-20). Israel vowed to keep their marital obligations of perfect obedience to God and His law, and God vowed to act in return with abundant blessings and protection (EXOD. 19:5-8; DEUT. 7:12-26; 11:8-25; 28:1-13). Failure to honour the marital vows called for disciplinary curses for the purpose of reconciliation (LEV. 26; DEUT. 4:40; 11:26-28; 27:11-26; 28:15-68; 29-30).

As evidenced by their history, Israel repeatedly violated the terms of their sacred marriage with God and were duly corrected through the curses (LEV. 26:1-46; DEUT. 28–30), but God was quick to forgive and forget their adulterous ways. The Old Testament Professors William Barrick and Walter Kaiser pointed out how: "disobedience annulled the blessings of God for that individual or generation in their own time, but disobedience did not invalidate the unconditional terms of the covenant,"[44] and how: "the 'breaking' or conditionality can only refer to personal and

---

[43] Barrick, "The Mosaic Covenant," *Journal of The Master's Seminary* 10, no. 2 (Fall 1999).

[44] Ibid.

individual invalidation of the benefits of the covenant, but it cannot affect the transmission of the promise to the lineal descendants."[45]

It is clear that for as often as Israel was reprimanded for her marital unfaithfulness, God refused to abandon Israel entirely. The kingdom of Israel was issued a certificate of divorce, and without the protection of God, was subsequently destroyed by the Assyrians, but the kingdom of Judah, to which many of the Israelites fled, was spared from divorce. The consequence of unfaithfulness was harsh, but mercy and grace always outweighed righteous judgement. For every judgement there is a restoration to even greater heights. The final restoration will be the reconciliation of Israel and Judah under God.

God's commitment to those whom He calls is not predicated on what He stands to receive in return, for He lacks nothing, and everything belongs to Him (JOB 2:2-4; 41:11; PSA. 24:1; 50; ROM. 11:35-36; ACTS 17:24-25; JAMES 1:17). All divine intervention is solely out of sovereign grace and concern for our wellbeing (EPH. 2:4-5). Remember how God called Abraham out of Ur to be the father of the promise. He established an everlasting covenant with him not on the basis of faithfulness or works, but grace. In this same way, God called Moses and the Israelites out from Egypt to be the nation of the promise. It was not the law that established their relationship, for He first rescued them out of Egypt. Note how God declared Israel His chosen people and treasured possession before the covenant was ratified (EXOD. 20:1; 24:7; DEUT. 26:18-19). This was a divine choice based out of God's love for Abraham and his descendants (DEUT. 4:37; 7:6-9; 10:15). Again, the decision was not contingent upon obedience, but grace and love (DEUT. 7:6–11). In fact, the golden calf incident occurred immediately after the Israelites agreed to the terms, and even then, God forgave them (EXOD. 32-34). As put by theologian Hoyt Woodring:

---

[45] Kaiser, *Toward an Old Testament Theology*, 157.

> *It is true that gross disobedience of the Mosaic covenant as well as blatant unbelief did in effect suspend temporal and local enjoyment of covenant blessings ... [but] whatever discipline fell upon His people came from the hands of Jehovah as a discipline of grace. When concrete manifestations of grace were thus suspended, it was possible to reverse the situation by repentance, confession, and supplication on the ground of immutable divine grace alone apart from any merit of the law.*[46]

What then was the purpose of the Mosaic covenant if the Israelites were incapable of remaining faithful? As it is said: "cursed is anyone who does not uphold the words of this law by carrying them out" (DEUT. 27:26) and "whoever keeps the whole law and yet stumbles at just one point is guilty of breaking all of it" (JAMES 2:10; GAL. 5:3). Were the Israelites set up to fail? By the righteous standard of God, for man to attain righteousness outside of His grace, all of the law had to be followed all of the time (LEV. 18:5; DEUT. 6:24-25; 12:32; GAL. 3:10). Such a prospect was difficult enough for a motivated individual, let alone an entire nation.

Consider the stubbornness of the Israelites throughout the forty-years of testing in the wilderness. Even after direct, physical encounters with the God who delivered them from bondage and provided them daily with manna from heaven, still they were quick to abandon Him. This trial period perfectly encapsulated the weak moral and spiritual fortitude of fallen man. The destiny of man apart from God always ends with self-ruin.

> *Remember that the Lord your God led you all the way these forty years in the wilderness, to humble you and test you, to know what was in your heart, whether you would keep His commandments or not. So He humbled you, allowed you to hunger, and fed you with manna which you did not know nor did your fathers know, that*

---

[46] Woodring, "Grace Under the Mosaic Covenant," 197.

> *He might make you know that man shall not live by bread alone; but man lives by every word that proceeds from the mouth of the Lord. Your garments did not wear out on you, nor did your foot swell these forty years. You should know in your heart that as a man chastens his son, so the Lord your God chastens you (Deut. 8:2-5 NKJV).*

God needed to bring man to an understanding of the trappings of the serpent curse for true repentance to be desired. Here the adage "failure is the greatest teacher" comes to mind. If man so desired righteousness by works rather than faith like Abraham, God would facilitate this futile endeavour (GEN. 15:6). Not for the twisted pleasure of condemnation or judgement, but to humble the proud and reveal sin to the sinner (DEUT. 8). The power and penalty of sin shown to be unavoidable, and judgement a given, man would look to God for redemption. The apostle Paul, himself once a Pharisee, emphasised the futility of seeking righteousness by the law as opposed to living by the faith of Abraham:

> *It was not through the law that Abraham and his offspring received the promise that he would be heir of the world, but through the righteousness that comes by faith. For if those who depend on the law are heirs, faith means nothing and the promise is worthless (Rom. 4:13-14 NIV).*

God purposed Israel to become a nation of priests but before the Israelites had even reached the promised land they repeatedly failed in their priestly duties (NUM. 14:11; DEUT. 1:32; 9:23; 31:14-29; 2 KGS. 17:14; PSA. 78:22, 32; 106:24; HEB. 4:2). As a concession, God chose the tribe of Levi who had remained faithful after the golden calf incident to serve as holy priests on behalf of all Israel (EXOD. 32:25-29; LEV. 21:6-8; NUM. 1:47-53; 3-7). The Levitical priesthood acted as an intermediary between God and Israel until the greater priesthood was ushered in under Jesus Christ. The Levites were redeemed unto God as a substitute for the firstborn of Israel and stood in the gap as mediators on her behalf. Paul testified that the remnant according to election, the chosen apostles and those who believed their testimony, were called, sanctified, and redeemed as the firstfruits of the harvest to act as mediators through a priest greater than Levi (ROM 8:28-31; 11:5-7).

Within the ceremonial section of the law, termed as such for convenience, God included provisions for forgiveness and sin covering to reconcile the people to Himself. The temporary means of atonement mediated by the Levitical priesthood foreshadowed the ultimate substitutionary atonement by Jesus, and his ensuing role as high priest of a greater priesthood. In the words of Paul, this was the express purpose of the law—to guard from sin and tutor the people in Christ until the time of his coming (GAL. 3:19-25). At that moment, the object of their faith would be revealed as Jesus, and in him they would be justified by faith (ROM. 3:23-24). Edward Fisher explained this concept wonderfully in his influential book *The Marrow of Modern Divinity:*

> *The moral law being delivered unto them with great terror, and under most dreadful penalties, they did find in themselves an impossibility of keeping it; and so were driven to seek help of a Mediator, even Jesus Christ, of whom Moses was to them a typical mediator; so that the moral law did drive them to the ceremonial law, which was their gospel, and their Christ in a figure; for that the ceremonies did prefigure Christ, direct unto him, and require faith in him, is a thing acknowledged and confessed by all men.*[47]

God harnessed the power of legal obedience to testify to the salvation that was to come by faith, not by works under the law. Salvation was never the objective of the Mosaic covenant (ROM. 3:20). In a sense, through the ceremonial law, they rehearsed the

---

[47] Fisher, *The Marrow of Modern Divinity*, 73.

expression of faith that was to one day be directed at Jesus, the bringer of salvation, the subject of these very ceremonies and sacrifices. This topic is explored in great depth in the chapter *Righteous Atonement*.

*Precedent for a New Priesthood*

God fully intended to supersede the Levitical order by one day establishing an everlasting priesthood in the order of Melchisedech—the king of righteousness and peace (HEB. 5:5-6; 7:11-15; PSA. 110:1-7). This priest, called Melchisedech, preceded the call of Levi as the head of a priesthood by four hundred years (GEN. 14:18-20; PSA. 110:4; HEB. 5:5-17). He was prophetically appointed by God (HEB. 7:12-22). In this same way, God planned on directly appointing Jesus, who was a Judahite and therefore ineligible for the Levitical priesthood, as the eternal high priest in the order of Melchisedech (HEB. 5:5-10; 7:11-21; PSA. 110). By following the order of Melchisedech— that is to be divinely appointed independent of the law—Jesus could circumvent the Levitical priesthood entirely and become a high priest uniquely capable of accomplishing the atonement:

> *And what we have said is even more clear if another priest like Melchizedek appears, one who has become a priest not on the basis of a regulation as to his ancestry but on the basis of the power of an indestructible life (Heb. 7:15-16 NIV).*

Even from an honest reading of the Old Testament it is clear that the Levitical priesthood was to be superseded from one to come who bore the messianic title of the Branch:

> *"'Listen, High Priest Joshua, you and your associates seated before you, who are men symbolic of things to come: I am going to bring my servant, the Branch. See, the stone I have set in front of Joshua! There are seven eyes on that one stone, and I will engrave an inscription on it,' says the Lord Almighty, 'and I will remove the sin*

> of this land in a single day. "'In that day each of you will invite your neighbor to sit under your vine and fig tree,' declares the Lord Almighty" (Zech. 3:8-10 NIV).

God told Joshua that the priesthood is "symbolic of things to come" from the "servant, the Branch." The terms *my servant* and *Branch* are frequently used as titles for the coming Messiah (Isa. 11:1; 42:1; 49:3; 50:10; 52:13; 53:11; Jer. 23:5; 33:14-15; Ezek. 34:23, 24) and the same goes for the term *stone* (Psa. 118:22-23; Isa. 8:13-15; 28:16; Dan. 2:35, 45; Matt. 21:42; Acts 4:11; 1 Cor. 10:4; Eph. 2:19-22; 1 Pet. 2:6-8). The Lord revealed to Zechariah that these seven eyes upon the stone were symbolic of His spirit which roams the earth (Zech. 4:8-10). [48] This is affirmed in the book of Revelation in relation to Christ with the imagery of the slain Lamb with "seven eyes, which are the seven Spirits of God sent out into all the earth" (Rev. 1:4; 3:1; 4:5; 5:6). These seven spirits were prophesied of the Messiah by Isaiah, and Jesus became the cornerstone of the spiritual temple of God after he removed the sin of the land in a single day on the cross (Isa. 1:12; Psa. 118:22; Isa. 28:16; 1 Pet. 2:4-7):

> "Tell him this is what the Lord Almighty says: 'Here is the man whose name is the Branch, and he will branch out from his place and build the temple of the Lord. It is he who will build the temple of the Lord, and he will be clothed with majesty and will sit and rule on his throne. And he will be a priest on his throne. And there will be harmony between the two'" (Zech. 6:12-13 NIV).

Coming not "to destroy but to fulfill" the law, Jesus stepped in the place of Israel to obey the law which they could not (Matt. 5:17-18). Not one jot or tittle of the law went unfollowed. Jesus as high priest accomplished what was beyond even the Levitical priesthood. We read of this in Hebrews 7 which is devoted to the

---

[48] For more information on the biblical significance of the number seven, refer to the appendix.

typological role of the priesthood in light of Christ as high priest:

> *If perfection could have been attained through the Levitical priesthood—and indeed the law given to the people established that priesthood—why was there still need for another priest to come, one in the order of Melchizedek, not in the order of Aaron? (Heb. 7:11 NIV).*

Even before the high priest of Israel could begin the ceremonial atonement for the people during the yearly Day of Atonement, it was necessary for him to cover his own sins with a pure and unblemished substitute (HEB. 5:1-4). After his own covering, he would perform a sacrifice on behalf of the nation to temporarily cleanse them before God. For as long as fallen man was appointed to this role, these sacrifices had to be performed in perpetuity. This was the dilemma of the Levitical order under the law, and that which cried out for one greater. As Paul said, neither perfection nor salvation could be attained through, or by, the Levitical priesthood, but only through Christ (HEB. 7; 10:1-4, 11:22):

> *Now there have been many of those priests, since death prevented them from continuing in office; but because Jesus lives forever, he has a permanent priesthood. Therefore he is able to save completely those who come to God through him, because he always lives to intercede for them (Heb. 7:23-25 NIV).*

Jesus bore the covenantal curses due to us and freed us from its grip. In its wake, the greater new covenant which God promised through Jeremiah was established by him (JER. 31:31-34; HEB. 8):

> *Behold, the days are coming, says the LORD, when I will make a new covenant with the house of Israel and with the house of Judah—not according to the covenant that I made with their fathers in the day that I took them by the hand to lead them out of the land of Egypt, My covenant*

> which they broke, though I was a husband to them, says the Lord (Jer. 31:31-32 NKJV).

The day is coming when Israel will collectively accept Jesus Christ as king and high priest and enter into the new covenant. The hearts of all Jews will be circumcised by the Holy Spirit to know and love their high priest in Jesus Christ, and in him they will finally be fit for holy service as a nation of priests:

> But this is the covenant that I will make with the house of Israel after those days, says the LORD: I will put My law in their minds, and write it on their hearts; and I will be their God, and they shall be My people. No more shall every man teach his neighbor, and every man his brother, saying, 'Know the Lord,' for they all shall know Me, from the least of them to the greatest of them, says the Lord. For I will forgive their iniquity, and their sin I will remember no more (Jer. 31:33-34 NKJV).

Under the Mosaic covenant of works, the impetus was on the Israelites to circumcise their own hearts to follow in the ways of God (DEUT. 10:16). Under the new covenant entered through faith, the Israelites will finally allow God to circumcise their hearts for them (JER. 31:33-34; ZECH. 12:10; ROM. 11:26-27).

> For the Law came by Moses, but grace and truth through Jesus Christ (John 1:17 KJV).

With His law in their minds and on their hearts, their hardened hearts dead in spirit will become soft and malleable to finally accept the Word of God in order that they may be ministers of the new covenant, "not of the letter but of the Spirit; for the letter kills, but the Spirit gives life" (2 COR. 3:6). They will look not to the mediator of the law of the letter, Moses, but the mediator of the law of faith, Jesus Christ (ROM. 3:27-28).

## 6. Living Shadow of David

Now we shall resume the journey down the messianic line of Judah. The next important stop is the great warrior-king David, the youngest son of Jesse (1 CHR. 2:13-14; 1 SAM. 16:1-13; 17:12-14). The biblical narrative surrounding David begins with the royal drama between David and King Saul. This battle for supremacy over the kingdom of Israel typifies the ongoing battle between Jesus and Satan for authority over both heaven and earth. Adam and Eve chose earthly self-determination over the protection of God and became subjects of Satan, the first king of humanity after God. Israel was similarly set apart as holy to tabernacle with God and receive His protection. They too rejected God as their king and demanded a king "like all the nations" so they could be "like all the nations." This all came after being forewarned of the tyrannical conduct of the prospective king (1 SAM. 8:5-20; 12:12). At their behest, God reluctantly installed Saul as the first earthly king over Israel (1 SAM. 8:22; 10:17-24). Because the people did not follow the commandments of God, His hand went against them and their king (1 SAM. 12:13-15, 25). Saul began to disobey God and His commandments (1 SAM. 13; 15). He became unfit to rule over God's people, and so the prophet Samuel, under the anointing of the Holy Spirit, told him: "you have rejected the word of the Lord, and the Lord has rejected you from being king over Israel" (1 SAM. 15:26). Predictably, as it was with Satan, Saul rejected God's verdict and when Samuel turned to leave he tore the tassel of his tallit, an Israelite symbol of authority (NUM. 15:37-41; DEUT. 22:12):

> *And as Samuel turned around to go away, Saul seized the edge of his robe, and it tore. So Samuel said to him, "The Lord has torn the kingdom of Israel from you today, and has given it to a neighbour of yours, who is better than you (1 Sam. 15:27-28 NKJV).*

This was not only a symbolic picture of Saul's kingdom being ripped from him by a second man, David, but of Satan's kingdom by the second man, Jesus (ROM. 5:12-15; 1 COR. 15:45-47).

> "The Lord has sought for Himself a man after His own heart [David], and the Lord has commanded him to be commander over His people, because you [Saul] have not kept what the Lord commanded you" (1 Sam. 13:13-14 NKJV).

To these ends, God sent the prophet Samuel to Jesse in the town of Bethlehem where He had chosen His replacement for King Saul (1 SAM. 16:1-3). Though Bethlehem was small among the clans of Judah, God later announced through the prophet Micah that it was to be the birthplace of the Messiah, the greater King David:

> "But you, Bethlehem Ephrathah, though you are little among the thousands of Judah, yet out of you shall come forth to Me the One to be Ruler in Israel, whose goings forth are from of old, from everlasting" (Mic. 5:2 NKJV).

The prophet Isaiah reinforced the Davidic heritage of this coming ruler when he prophesied, "there shall come forth a Rod from the stem of Jesse, and a Branch shall grow out of his roots" (ISA. 11:1). Isaiah employed "rod" or sceptre as a metaphor for authority, he was speaking of the king promised under the Davidic covenant from the "stem" or lineage of Jesse, the father of David. He would not only be a king like David, but he would be a son of David. All of these criteria were met by the one whose origins are truly from everlasting, Jesus Christ, "the Root and the Offspring of David" (REV. 22:16; MATT. 2:1-8; LUKE 2:4-11; JOHN 7:42). At the time of his birth, the magi from the East saw "his star" and recognised it as the birthplace of the prophesied "King of the Jews" (MATT. 2:1-8). They may have been aware of the scripture: "a star will come out of Jacob; a sceptre will rise out of Israel" (NUM. 24:17). King Herod was informed by the chief priests and scribes that Bethlehem was indeed the prophesied birthplace of the Messiah:

> "But you, Bethlehem, in the land of Judah, are by no means least among the rulers of Judah; for out of you

*will come a ruler who will shepherd my people Israel"* (Matt. 2:6 NIV).

God told Samuel his choice of king from the house of Jesse was based not upon outward appearance, but the heart (1 SAM. 16:7). Each of the eldest sons were passed over by God until it came to David, the youngest. Unlike his brothers, David was not even put up for consideration by his father, he was out tending to the sheep during the selection process (1 SAM. 16:8-11). Nevertheless, God testified of David: "I have found David the son of Jesse, a man after My own heart, who will do all My will" (ACTS 13:22). God saw in David a great shepherd capable of leading and protecting His people Israel (2 SAM. 5:2; 1 CHR. 11:1-3; PSA. 78:70–71). David was selected by God to be anointed, and from that time forward, "the Spirit of the Lord came upon David" (1 SAM. 16:13). He was anointed by God to one day usurp Saul as king and reign over Israel (1 SAM. 18:6-7; 2 SAM. 7:16-17).

> *He chose David his servant and took him from the sheep pens; from tending the sheep he brought him to be the shepherd of his people Jacob, of Israel his inheritance (Psa. 78:70-71 NKJV).*

This same Spirit of God came upon Jesus to anoint him as Messiah and the "beloved son" of God at his baptism (MATT. 3:17; 12:18; 17:5; MARK 1:11; 9:7; LUKE 3:22; 9:35; COL. 1:13; 2 PET. 1:17; ISA. 42:1). Unlike David, Jesus was the beloved son of God in a truly unique way. He was the only begotten son of God the Father—he was in the Father, and the Father was in him (JOHN 14:11). We will look into these divine claims of Jesus in the chapter *God Manifested in the Flesh*.

With God as his protection, David spent the next fourteen years evading the wrath of King Saul as he gathered to himself the dispossessed and disheartened, the lost sheep (1 SAM. 22:2). Even though Saul knew God had anointed David to become king of Israel, he continued to relentlessly pursue him (1 SAM. 27). Saul refused to come to true repentance after each failed attempt to take David's life, always seeking to retain his kingship despite God's rejection. Likewise, Jesus gathered the dispossessed during his ministry while withstanding attacks from Satan (MATT. 9:36; LUKE 4:1-13). Satan recognised the virtue of Jesus after each failed attempt to kill him but he remains firmly fixed in his rebellion against the true Davidic king that is Jesus.

Looking back to when Saul tore the tassel from Samuel's tallit and was warned that his authority had been taken away, the day came when Saul's own tallit was cut off by David. The unsuspecting Saul was delivered into David's hands, but instead of killing Saul, he removed the equivalent of the king's crown:

> *Then the men of David said to him, "This is the day of which the Lord said to you, 'Behold, I will deliver your enemy into your hand, that you may do to him as it seems good to you.'" And David arose and secretly cut off a corner of Saul's robe (1 Sam. 24:4 NIV).*

This marked the moment when Saul finally acknowledged the transfer of power prophesied by Samuel. He admitted that his days as king were numbered when he remarked to David: "Now, behold, I know that you will certainly be king, and that the kingdom of Israel will be established in your hand" (1 SAM. 24:20).

It was not long after that David succeeded Saul as king while only being thirty years old. Before long, David had unified the tribes of Israel, defeated her enemies, and conquered Jerusalem (2 SAM. 5:4; 6; 1 CHR. 13-16; 22). **But even as the prototype and the model for a perfect king of Israel, David was not infallible, nor could he save his people from their sins. When David trusted in his own judgement over that of God, he brought a plague of pestilence upon Israel, and required atonement for his own sins** (2 SAM. 24). We are reminded that all of mankind, even the earthly kings chosen by God, are slaves to sin and cannot even save themselves, let alone anyone else. As we shall see in the following section, it took only one generation for the Davidic kingdom to face judgement from God, and another for it to become fractured into two kingdoms. Israel would not settle into the rest God to promised to Abraham under David.

Clearly then, the often-used phrase for God's shepherd, "my servant David," does not speak of the literal King David, but of the Davidic covenant, in which it is promised a descendant of David will reign as king on his throne forever (EZEK. 34:23-24; 37:24-28):

> *My servant David will be king over them, and they will all have one shepherd. They will follow my laws and be careful to keep my decrees. They will live in the land I gave to my servant Jacob, the land where your ancestors lived. They and their children and their children's children will live there forever, and David my servant will be their prince forever. I will make a covenant of peace with them; it will be an everlasting covenant. I will establish them and increase their numbers, and I will put my sanctuary among them forever. My dwelling place will be with them; I will be their God, and they will be my people. Then the nations will know that I the Lord make Israel holy, when my sanctuary is among them forever (Ezek. 37:24-28 NIV).*

David merely portrayed the role of the good shepherd, an ancient metaphor for a just and loving king. Jesus, who referred to himself as the good shepherd, was the true reality behind this picture:

> *"I am the good shepherd. The good shepherd lays down his life for the sheep. The hired hand is not the shepherd and does not own the sheep ... I am the good shepherd; I know my sheep and my sheep know me—just as the Father knows me and I know the Father—and I lay down my life for the sheep. I have other sheep that are not of this sheep pen. I must bring them also. They too will listen to my voice, and there shall be one flock and one shepherd" (John 10:11-16 NIV).*

Jesus was anointed by God to become the Messiah on the throne of David and confirmed this to the world at his baptism (REV. 1:12-18; 19:11-16). Following his baptism he began his ministry to proclaim His kingdom at *about* thirty years old, the same age when David became king (LUKE 3:21-23). The full blessings of the Abrahamic covenant are manifested during his reign over all creation. Besides the following section, we shall focus on the typology of the Davidic king in the following chapter *Messiah on the Throne of David*.

## The Fourth Covenant with David

Once King David was firmly settled in the land promised to Abraham, he expressed his desire to build a permanent dwelling place for the Lord (2 SAM. 7:1-2). God took this opportunity to establish a new covenant with David and his seed. Although He laboured to turn David into a great name among the likes of Abraham (2 SAM. 7:9-11; 1 CHR. 17:8; GEN. 12:2), the building of His temple was to be the responsibility of David's son, Solomon (1 CHR. 22:6-13; 28:1-10).

Moving along the trajectory of the Abrahamic covenant, God swore to David, "your seed I will establish forever and build up your throne to all generations" (PSA. 89:3-4). Remember that God assured Abraham: "I will make you very fruitful; I will make nations of you, and kings will come from you" (GEN. 17:6) and reaffirmed it to Isaac and Jacob (GEN. 26:3-4; 35:11-12). The kings in question were at last specified as those of the royal progeny of David. To the seed of David, the throne of his kingdom would endure forever, or "as the days of heaven" (2 SAM. 7:12-16; 22:51; 1 CHR. 17:11-14; PSA. 89:29). The Davidic covenant thus established the royal lineage of the promised king, the seed of the woman.

As with the Abrahamic covenant, no conditions were placed upon the participants in the Davidic covenant, but there was the regulation of faithfulness. The king was expected to rule in accordance with the stipulations of the Mosaic covenant to reflect the values required of the nation.⁴⁹ All the days of his life he was required to read the law so that his heart would not be lifted above his fellow Israelites, and he could lead them in keeping Torah (DEUT. 17:18-20). The fate of the nation was thus dependent on conformity to the conditional Mosaic covenant. The Professor of Old Testament Michael Grisanti wrote about this "convergence between the Mosaic and Davidic covenants":

> *The stipulations of the Mosaic Covenant provide the "measuring stick" for the reign of each of these kings (2 Kgs 18:6; 21:7-9; 23:24-25). The function of the God-fearing king was to lead Israel in keeping covenant and in relying on God for deliverance ... The proper role of the Davidic king was to lead his people in keeping Torah. Herein lies an important convergence between the Mosaic and Davidic covenants. The Davidic ruler should epitomize the standards of the Mosaic Covenant, even though his conformity or lack of conformity to those standards does not determine whether or not Yahweh will one day bring to realization the provisions of the Davidic Covenant.*⁵⁰

Obedience prolonged the days of the kingdom, but rebellion doomed it (DEUT. 17:20). Nevertheless, the perpetuation of the Davidic covenant was fully assured. It was unilateral and unconditional. Discipline and punishment may be necessary, but no king, nor the nation as a whole, could undermine it (2 SAM. 7:14-15; 11-12; 1 KGS. 2:1-4; 6:11-13; 8:25; 9:4-9; 1 CHR. 17:13; 2 CHR. 7:17-22; PSA. 89:29-37; 132:12). The distinguished Professor of Old Testament Eugene H. Merrill emphasised this point in his book *Kingdom of Priests*:

---

⁴⁹ Grisanti, "The Davidic Covenant," *Journal of The Master's Seminary* 10, no. 2 (Fall 1999): 233-250. https://www.tms.edu/m/tmsj10p.pdf.
⁵⁰ Ibid., 245.

> *Israel as the servant people of Yahweh might rise and fall, be blessed or cursed, but the Davidic dynasty would remain intact forever because God had pledged to produce through Abraham a line of kings that would find its historical locus in Israel, but would have ramifications extending far beyond Israel.*[51]

As we will learn in the next chapter, the treachery of Solomon, the very first king after David, caused the kingdom of Israel to split in two (1 Kgs. 11:1-13). Even after this divine judgement, the kingdom of Judah continued to degenerate until their iniquities had again overflowed. The prophet Amos was forewarned by God of the inevitable destruction of this "sinful kingdom" and the exile of the people (Amos 9:1:10). Even still, God planned for their restoration in the land before their judgement was meted out (Amos 9:11-15). Once judgement was rendered, the Babylonians sacked Jerusalem, destroyed the temple Solomon built, and hauled the Jews off into exile (2 Kgs. 24:13-14). History attests to their partial restoration after returning from exile, but it is clear that we await a final recapitulation when Israel is never again uprooted from the promised land (Amos 9:15).

By the time of Jesus, the land had passed through the hands of the Babylonians, Medo-Persians, Greeks, and Romans (Dan. 2; 7). Israelite autonomy had become a relic of the past, and sentiment surrounding the Davidic covenant had turned fatalistic (Psa. 89:30-51; 132). But looking back to Amos and the other prophets, a great rebirth of the Davidic kingdom was assured. A king greater than David was said to one day emerge and live fully in accordance with Mosaic law. Isaiah saw a future in which this great king "from the stump of Jesse" branches out and restores life to the lifeless Davidic dynasty (Isa. 11:1). Isaiah elaborated on the nature of this anointed one (Messiah) in chapter 53, again describing him as "a root out of dry ground" (Isa. 53:2). This indicates that the king will reinstate the defunct kingdom to its former glory. I implore you to

---

[51] Merrill, *Kingdom of Priests: A History of Old Testament Israel*, 185.

read this chapter and take note of how closely it resembles the life of Jesus. The NT writers quote Isaiah 53 in many passages to reinforce this connection of Jesus as the sin-bearing Messiah (ACTS 8:26-35; MATT. 8:14-17; LUKE 22:37; JOHN 12:37-41; ROM. 10:16; 1 PET. 2:23-25). Isaiah said again of this Messiah that the Lord will establish him upon the throne of David and "of the increase of his government and peace there shall be no end" (ISA. 9:6-7). This is to say he will be the Davidic son whose reign is everlasting and encompasses the entire world. Isaiah supported this elsewhere by stating the king will not only reunify Israel but extend "a light to the Gentiles" so the entire world may be saved in him (ISA. 42:6-7; 49:6). Amos similarly predicted the messianic kingdom will be rebuilt from the fallen tabernacle of David and the believing gentiles will be full participants (AMOS 9:11-12). The apostle James quoted directly from this prophecy in the context of the gentile inclusion in the Church grafted into the olive tree of Israel (ACTS 15:14-18; ROM. 11:11-25).

Under the anointing of the Holy Spirit, King David himself acknowledged the pre-eminence and pre-existence of this coming king in a manner that made clear his own subservience to his authority (PSA. 110). Even David realised he was but a shadow or type of the ultimate king. Jesus related this extraordinary chapter of the Psalms to himself:

> *While the Pharisees were gathered together, Jesus asked them, "What do you think about the Messiah? Whose son, is he?" "The son of David," they replied. He said to them, "How is it then that David, speaking by the Spirit, calls him 'Lord'? For he says, "'The Lord said to my Lord: "Sit at my right hand until I put your enemies under your feet."' If then David calls him 'Lord,' how can he be his son?" No one could say a word in reply, and from that day on no one dared to ask him any more questions (Matt. 22:41-46 NIV).*

Following on from that verse in Psalm 110, David announced that God swore to the Lord of David (Jesus), "you are a priest forever according to the order of Melchisedech" (Psa. 110:4; Heb. 5:10; 6:20; 7:17-22). Melchisedech was the king of Salem, the king of righteousness and peace, and the eternal priest of God (Gen. 14:18-20; Heb. 7:1-3). Furthermore, Melchisedech is said to have resembled the son of God, being "without father or mother, without genealogy, without beginning of days or end of life" (Heb. 7:3). This attests to the divine and immortal character of Jesus the Messiah revealed by David in the first verse. Jesus is the unique ben Elohim—the son of God, who existed before him in heaven (Root) and after him on earth (Branch). In the model of Melchisedech, Jesus currently sits at the right hand of God waiting until the day of the Lord to execute final judgement on the nations (Psa.2 Psa. 110:5-7). On that day, God will raise up Jesus, the righteous branch of David, to judge the rebellious nations of the earth who set themselves against Israel (Jer. 23:5-6; 33:14-17). After Jesus triumphs over the kingdoms of the earth and inaugurates the kingdom of God, the faithful who remain from all nations, tribes, peoples, and tongues will stand next to his throne (Psa. 2; 72; Luke 11:30-32; Rev. 3:21; 7:9; 11:15). Like David, Jesus will unite the tribes of Judah and Israel, capture Jerusalem, the designated city of God, and tabernacle with them there forever, restoring them to the tree of life (Ezek. 37:15-28. Zech. 14:1-11 Rev 22:14). At last it will truly be said that the seed of Abraham has blessed all the nations of the earth (Gen. 22:18). They will all dwell peacefully forevermore (Psa. 72:17). After all of his enemies are put under his feet, death itself is destroyed, and he himself is made subject to God, "so that God may be all in all" (Psa. 110:1; 1 Cor. 15:24-28).

## 7. Living Shadow of Daniel

Our final living shadow is Daniel, the prophet and writer of the book of Daniel (Dan. 1:6). Like Moses, he is outside of the direct lineage of Jesus Christ, but he remains an important figure. Daniel was among the first wave (605, 597, and 586 BC) of prominent citizens who were deported to Babylon by Nebuchadnezzar during his successful siege of Jerusalem (Dan. 1:1-7; 5:13). This time of captivity had been prophesied more than one hundred years earlier by the prophet Isaiah (ISA. 39:6-7). The Babylonians sent the house of Judah into exile and selected only the brightest minds to become eunuchs and serve in the palace of King Nebuchadnezzar of Babylon (2 KGS. 20:16-18; DAN. 1:3). Daniel was one of these young boys because he was found to be "gifted in all wisdom, possessing knowledge and quick to understand" (DAN. 1:3-4). Even in this foreign land where polytheism was strictly enforced, Daniel always walked before the Lord blamelessly. Living in an environment where defiance equalled death, Daniel nevertheless stood firm in his obedience to the Torah. One obvious example was his refusal to abandon the dietary regulations and worship practices of the Law inside the royal palace (DAN. 1:8-16; 6:6-12). Not once did Daniel doubt the power of the Spirit, instead he utilised it in total accordance with the will of God (DAN 2:16-23). For this great sensitivity and faithfulness to the Spirit, God loved Daniel greatly and accelerated his knowledge, wisdom, and understanding ten times further than all the other men in the palace (DAN 1:17-20). He excelled in all of his duties and quickly proved himself to be indispensable to the kingdom. According to the Babylonians, he carried "the spirit of the holy gods in him," and "insight and intelligence and wisdom like that of the gods" (DAN. 5:11-14). The depth of his wisdom is corroborated in the Talmud tractate *Yoma*:

> *If all the wise men of other nations were placed on one side of the scale, and Daniel the beloved man were on the other side, would he not outweigh them?*[52]

In the same way, after Jesus reached the age of thirty, God anointed him with the Holy Spirit at his baptism for a life of perfect obedience, fulfilling the messianic prophecy of Isaiah 11 (ISA. 11; MATT. 3:16-17; MARK 1:9-11; LUKE 3:21-22; JOHN 1:32-34; ACTS 10:38). Even as a young boy of twelve, Jesus was filled with wisdom which

---

[52] B. Talmud Yoma 77a:7.

outmatched even the learned Rabbis in Jerusalem, and they were astonished by his insight and understanding (LUKE 2:40, 52).

Owing to these attributes, and for his unique "ability to interpret dreams, explain riddles and solve difficult problems," King Nebuchadnezzar made Daniel ruler over the province of Babylon and chief of its wise men—the magicians, enchanters, astrologers and diviners (DAN. 2:48; 5:12). Even after the kingdom was taken over by the Medes under Darius and then the Persians under Cyrus the Great, Daniel remained in an esteemed position and prospered (DAN. 6:3; 28). It is said that after Darius the Mede conquered the Babylonian kingdom (DAN. 5:30-31), "Daniel distinguished himself above the governors and satraps, because an excellent spirit was in him; and the king gave thought to setting him over the whole realm" (DAN. 6:3). Naturally, there was much resistance from the governors. They sought to find a charge against Daniel, but due to his faithfulness to God, they all agreed that they "shall not find any charge against this Daniel unless [they] find it against him concerning the law of his God" (DAN. 6:4-5). Together they convinced King Darius to sign a written decree stating that for thirty days, whoever petitioned any god or man other than the king shall be cast into the den of lions (DAN. 6:6-9). Once Daniel heard of the decree, he went home and prayed to God three times with his window open toward Jerusalem (DAN. 6:10). There he was caught by his adversaries and they went off to alert King Darius of Daniel's disobedience. They impressed upon the king the burden of executing the innocent Daniel, and while Darius set his heart on delivering Daniel and laboured to these ends, the authorities pressured him to uphold the law (DAN. 6:14-15). Darius reluctantly followed the decree and commanded that Daniel be cast into the den of lions and the entrance to be covered with a stone seal (DAN. 6:16-23).

Now for the trial of Jesus. Anticipating his own imminent arrest, Jesus prayed to God three times in the garden of Gethsemane overlooking Jerusalem (MATT. 26:36-56; MARK 14:32-50; LUKE 22:39-53; JOHN 18:1-13). He was found and seized by the religious authorities and became the subject of their mock trial (MATT. 26:57; LUKE 22:54, 66; JOHN 18:12-13):

> The chief priests and the whole Sanhedrin were looking for false evidence against Jesus so that they could put him to death. But they did not find any, though many false witnesses came forward (Matt. 26:59-60 NIV).

Recognising how faithful Jesus was to God, they looked for a charge against him under the law of God and the Romans. They accused him of blasphemy for identifying himself as the Messiah and condemned him worthy of death (MATT. 26:63-66; MARK 14:61-64; LUKE 22:66-71). Since capital punishment was reserved for the Romans (JOHN 18:29-32), the religious authorities appealed to the Roman law which could secure a death sentence. They insisted that Jesus was guilty of sedition: "we have found this man subverting our nation. He opposes payment of taxes to Caesar and claims to be Messiah, a king" (LUKE 23:2). Pilate recognised that Jesus posed no threat to Roman authority and found "no fault in him at all" throughout the trial (LUKE 23:3-5, 13-15; JOHN 18:38; 19:4-6). "From then on Pilate sought to release him, but the Jews cried out, saying, 'If you let this Man go, you are not Caesar's friend. Whoever makes himself a king speaks against Caesar'" and again, "they insisted, 'He stirs up the people all over Judea by his teaching. He started in Galilee and has come all the way here'" (LUKE 23:5; JOHN 19:12). The religious authorities burdened Pilate with the responsibility of killing the innocent Jesus. Pilate reluctantly condemned Jesus to death and later ordered for him to be placed in a tomb behind a large stone with a Roman seal (MATT. 27:57-60; MARK 15:42-46).

Darius, like Pilate, lamented the punishment of Daniel. Early the next morning, Darius "went in haste to the den of lions" to check on Daniel (DAN. 6:19-23). There he found that God had indeed delivered Daniel from death as he hoped (DAN. 6:20). Daniel told him that God had sent his angel to shut the mouths of the lions because he was found innocent in His sight (DAN. 6:22). Darius overruled the judgement of death against Daniel and "gave orders to lift Daniel out of the den" (Dan. 6:23). His accusers were judged in his place and thrown into the lion's den (Dan. 6:24-28). In their sorrows, Mary Magdalene and Mary the mother of Jesus went to Jesus' tomb early in the morning and found it empty (Matt. 28:1; Mark 16:1-4; Luke 24:1-3; John 20:1). Seeing an angel there, they were told that Jesus had risen, and they realised God had delivered Jesus from death (Matt. 17:23; Mark 9:23; Luke 9:22). God overruled the judgement of death against Jesus because he too was found innocent in his sight, and God lifted him out of the grave (Dan 6:22-3; Luke 24:1-7). To be judged in his place are the accusers of Satan, the Beast, and the False Prophet, who will be hurled down into hell (Rev. 12:10; 19:20-21; 20:10).

Darius henceforth signed a decree "to all peoples, nations, and languages that dwell in all the earth" which declared they must fear the God of Daniel for delivering him from death (Dan. 6:25-26):

> *For He is the living God, and steadfast forever; His kingdom is the one which shall not be destroyed, and His dominion shall endure to the end. He delivers and rescues, and He works signs and wonders in heaven and on earth, who has delivered Daniel from the power of the lions (Dan. 6:26-27 NKJV).*

God issued a decree after the obedient death, burial, and resurrection of His son that all must fear the God of Jesus and accept that Jesus was delivered from death:

> *For this reason also God highly exalted Him, and bestowed on Him the name which is above every name, so that at the name of Jesus every knee will bow, of those who are in heaven and on earth and under the earth, and that every tongue will confess that Jesus Christ is Lord, to the glory of God the Father (Phil. 2:9-11 NASB).*

## Advent of the Messiah in Prophecy

Knowing God better than anyone at that time, it is easy to understand why Daniel was granted access to prophetic revelation to an unparalleled degree (DAN. 1:17; 2:46-48). The many prophecies revealed to Daniel became crucial for our understanding of salvation history and the role of Messiah. In the companion book "Seed of Satan: Antichrist," we delved into a few of the great prophetic visions of Daniel, most notably the statue from Nebuchadnezzar's dream and the four beasts (DAN. 2; 7). These visions looked at the power of gentile domination over the people of Israel and Jerusalem, the city God has chosen for Himself forever, and the final Antichrist kingdom that will fight in opposition to Jesus on his return (2 CHR. 6:6; PSA. 48:1-2).

Another crucial prophecy recorded by Daniel is the seventy sevens of years (490 years) allotted for the fulfilment of all prophecy regarding the Jews, Jerusalem, and their everlasting restoration (DAN. 9:24-27). It is outside the scope of this book to adequately unpack this prophecy due to its complexity, but because of its relevance, the portion of the timeline which predicts the coming of the Messiah and his atoning death is important to discuss. This is the second of the three sets within the 490-year span which ends after 483 years with the arrival of "Messiah the Prince." Without going into detail here, the beginning of this timetable, the time of the decree to rebuild Jerusalem, until the advent and death of Jesus the Messiah, fits within its historical deadline. In fact, the only messianic figure that can be reliably connected to these dates, and live up to all biblical prophecy, *is* Jesus Christ. This we know because the conclusion of the second set, and Messiah's arrival and death before the final set of one seven must have taken place before the Second Temple in Jerusalem was destroyed in 70 AD (DAN. 9:26).

The angel Gabriel told Daniel that the Messiah shall be cut off after this time and, depending on the translation, that he shall "be left with nothing" or be cut off "but not for himself" (DAN. 9:26). God sent the angel Gabriel to earth during this time to proclaim to the virgin Mary that she was to bear this Messiah to be called Jesus (meaning salvation) and that he was to be the son of God and king over the messianic kingdom (DAN. 9:20-27; LUKE 1:26-38). In alignment with the prophecy, Jesus the Messiah was cut off after the sixty-two sevens, the second set, but not for himself, but all mankind (DAN. 9:26). It is clear that Jesus had nothing after his execution. Not reputation, nor acceptance among his people, not even clothes—they were gambled away while he hung on the cross (JOHN 19:23-24).

*Prophecy Diminished*

As we have briefly discussed, much of Jesus' eschatological teachings was based upon the foundational groundwork laid by Daniel, the purpose for which he was called. When we deeply study the prophetic words of Daniel and Jesus, we are shown the history and future of humanity to the end of this age, and the coming of two divine Messiahs, the "son of Man," revealed to be Jesus Christ, the seed of the woman, and the Antichrist from the fourth beast kingdom, the seed of the serpent. It is unfortunately the case that many Jews, and even Christians, neglect their prophetic force. Instead, they undermine their authority as prophets by neutering the prophetic intent of their words. An example of this is how, sometime in the early rabbinic period, the book of Daniel was moved from the Prophets section of the Hebrew Bible (Tanakh) into the Writings section. As you may know, at some point in time the books in the Hebrew Bible (Tanakh) became divided by three sections: the Pentateuch or Law (Torah); Prophets (Nevi'im); and Writings (Ketuvim). Jesus referred to this threefold division in Luke 24:44, and on many other occasions spoke of a two-fold division between the law and the prophets (MATT. 7:12; LUKE 24:27; ACTS 13:15; 24:14; ROM. 3:21; JOHN 1:45).

In his journal article *Is Daniel also Among the Prophets?* Old Testament Professor Klaus Koch pointed out how there had always been "a rather unanimous consensus among the copyists and readers that Daniel was to be placed in the prophetic corpus":

> "There is not a single witness for the exclusion of Daniel from the prophetic corpus in the first half of the first millennium A.D. In all the sources of the first century A.D. - Matthew, Josephus, Qumran - Daniel is reckoned among the prophets. In fact the earliest literary evidence of Daniel's inclusion among the Ketubim is to be placed somewhere between the fifth and eighth centuries A.D. This leads to the conclusion that at some point the rabbis transferred the book from the prophetic corpus to the last third of their collection of Holy Scripture."[53]

As a consequence of Daniel being moved out from the prophetic corpus, Koch rightfully contends that the readers focus is shifted away from its true eschatological significance. Without a doubt, the moral character and faithfulness of Daniel is well worth our study and practice, but a purely moralistic approach fails to honour the clear eschatological purpose of the historical-yet-future narrative structure. We have much to learn from Daniel the man, but even more to learn from Daniel the prophet. The eschatological significance of the book of Daniel has been downplayed by Jews and Christians alike over the centuries. This is the same phenomena which plagues interpretation of the prophetic words of Jesus. Both Daniel and Jesus tend to be examined as moral teachers or archetypal purveyors of good, with little room for their prophecies of the end of the age. If one does not believe in Daniel's prophecy which Jesus reaffirms as being sound end-times prophecy, how will they believe Jesus? One is left to assume that the prophetic statements of Jesus have no future application beyond the happenings of the first-century AD, namely the destruction of the Second Temple. One must also extinguish the life from the book of Revelation, which testifies to the prophecies of Jesus and Daniel. The eschatological harmony that exists between the books of Daniel and Revelation in content

---

[53] Koch, "Is Daniel also Among the Prophets?" *Interpretation* 39, no. 2, (April 1985): 123. https://doi.org/10.1177%2F002096438503900202.

and in style must be diminished to reflect a purely literary genius. Just as first-century Jewry were unable to discern the signs of the times with the Messiah's first advent in history, so it is, and will be, for the people before his second advent. Man and woman, Christian and non-believer, they will all reject Daniel and Jesus as prophets of the impending apocalyptic judgement.

## Conclusion

This great witness of the seven living shadows unlocks part of the mystery that is Jesus of Nazareth:

*Image 2.8 – Jesus as a composite image of the Living Shadows*

| NAME | HEBREW MEANING |
|---|---|
| A willing sacrifice like Isaac | laughter |
| An overcomer like Jacob | one who prevails |
| A suffering servant like Joseph | he shall increase |
| A humbled son like Judah | God's praise |
| A deliverer and lawgiver like Moses | he rescues |
| A warrior king like David | much loved (or beloved) |
| A prophet and statesman like Daniel | God shall judge |
| All culminating in Jesus | salvation |
| **INTERPRETATION FROM COMBINED MEANINGS** ||
| Jesus is the one who in laughter prevails. He shall increase God's praise to those he rescues, and those much loved God shall judge with salvation. ||

The genealogy from Adam down to David bears witness to one person and one person only, Jesus of Nazareth. The living shadows we have learned about were by no means perfect, in some cases they committed grave sins. What must be stressed here is that they humbly accepted their flawed nature and had faith that a seed was to come through them who *could* and *would* be perfect. They held close the love of God and His truth both in prosperous times, and in times of great tribulation. Their example is given to us to model our own lives upon. From the perspective of God, every man has to undergo a deep spiritual change through repentance or self-abasement to be set straight from their wayward path. The living shadows were no different, nor were the apostles closest to Christ. Nevertheless, this is the clear distinguishing factor between those aligned to the godly line from those aligned to the ungodly line. For us today, many similar obstacles can lead us astray from the word of God and lead us towards excessive earthly indulgences and selfish aspirations. The apostle James reminded us that "Blessed is the man who endures temptation; for when he has been approved, he will receive the crown of life which the Lord has promised to those who love Him" (JAMES 1:12). We must be like the living shadows of Christ who held true to the word of God in times of both blessing and suffering.

# 3

# Messiah on the Throne of David

The living shadows have cast an extraordinary image for us to contemplate the nature of the promised seed of the woman. We have left off at King David in the genealogy, the necessary ancestor and forerunner of the promised Messiah of Israel. From David came two sons responsible for propagating the godly line—Solomon and Nathan. The line of Solomon is given by Matthew and leads down to Joseph, the father of Jesus, and the line of Nathan is given by Luke and it leads down to Mary, the mother of Jesus (MATT 1:1-17; LUKE 3:23-38). The importance is thus, Jesus must be a son of David to be the promised son of Judah, son of Abraham, son of the covenant (Law), son of Adam, and most importantly, the son of God. The son of God promised to all of these men must become the Messiah on the throne of David in order for his people to be brought into God's everlasting kingdom.

Indeed, if Jesus is to be the Messiah, he must meet these messianic conditions ordained by God. It follows therefore that the two genealogies must be deeply examined. Some of those who are familiar with the two genealogies struggle to reconcile the differences between them, and might even wonder how Jesus could possibly be the rightful Davidic king, the Messiah, when he was fathered by the Holy Spirit. These are serious concerns, but I believe the solution is simpler than we make it out to be, and that the two genealogies are used to support the kingship of Christ from differing perspectives. Allow me now to outline my thinking and defend the messianic legitimacy of Jesus Christ.

## Jesus' Royal Lineage via Solomon, son of David

In the genealogy of Jesus according to Matthew, we are shown his patrilineage to David via his son Solomon, the ancestor of Jesus' father, Joseph (MATT. 1; LUKE 2:4). As mentioned, the significance of this is clear—to sit on the throne of David, the expectation is that Jesus can trace his descent from David through his father. On these grounds, some critics argue Jesus could not be the prophesied Messiah since God is his father—not Joseph. While it is true that Joseph is not the biological father of Jesus, he *is* the legal father, which by most accounts was sufficient in his time (MARK 10:47-48; 12:35-37; ROM. 1:3-5; 2 TIM. 2:8; REV. 3:7; 5:5; 22:16).[54] To quote the biblical scholar Jack Dean Kingsbury:

> *Since in Jewish circles it was the acknowledgment of a male child by a man that made that child his son and not the physical act of procreation as such, the fact that Matthew depicts Jesus as being adopted into the line of David does not mean that his Davidic lineage is in any sense questionable.*[55]

These statements are affirmed by the ancient Jewish law and tradition preserved in the Mishnah and the Talmud.[56] In the Talmudic tractate *Sanhedrin*, it is said "anyone who raises an orphan in his house, the verse ascribes him credit as if he gave birth to him" and "anyone who teaches another person's son Torah, the verse ascribes him credit as if he sired him."[57] Again, in the Mishnah tractate *Bava Batra*, the understanding expressed is

---

[54] Meier, *A Marginal Jew: Rethinking the Historical Jesus*, 217.

[55] Kingsbury, "The Title 'Son of David' in Matthew's Gospel," *Journal of Biblical Literature* 95, no. 4 (December 1976): 591-602.

[56] The Mishnah was an early third-century collection and codification of ancient Jewish oral laws and traditions supplementary to the law of Moses. The Mishnah was later compiled into the Talmud with a collection of commentaries and elaborations called the Gemara. The Talmud has become the counterpart of the Old Testament (Tanakh) in Judaism.

[57] B. Talmud Sanhedrin 19b:13-17.

that: "if a man said, 'This is my son,' he is believed."[58]

Furthermore, there is no record of the Pharisees or the Sadducees questioning the Davidic pedigree of Jesus, nor does this attack show up in the apologia of the early church. This is noteworthy because the priesthood took the utmost care to preserve the genealogical records.[59] Jesus' genealogy would have been heavily scrutinised by his adversaries, and if news circulated that those written by Matthew or Luke were inauthentic, the world would have known. There may even be a rabbinic acknowledgement of Jesus' Davidic heritage in the Talmudic tractate *Sanhedrin* 43a, where in some translations Jesus is said to have been "near the kingdom" or "near to the kingship."[60]

These genealogical records have long since been lost because of the destruction of the Second Temple and later of Jerusalem when the Jews were forced out. Most of the written genealogical records that have managed to survive are fragmented, and Jews are largely uninterested in preserving the purity of their tribe. Because of the diaspora, they have long since intermixed with the gentiles and assimilated into their cultures. No longer is there an authoritative record of the Davidic lineage that stretches beyond Jesus. According to the Jewish scholar David Einsiedler in the Jewish genealogy journal, *Avotaynu: The International Review of Jewish Genealogy*:

> *Careful examination of all available sources leads to the inescapable conclusion that there is no complete, reliable and positive proof of claims of descent from King David, whether via Rashi, Judah Loew the Elder, or any of the other families claimed. There are at present no known sources that could fill the gaps or set the record straight.*

---

[58] Mishnah Bava Batra 8:6.

[59] Josephus, "Against Apion," 1.28-38; Ibid., "The Life of Flavius Josephus," 1; Einsiedler, "Can We Prove Descent from King David?" *Avotaynu: The International Review of Jewish Genealogy* 9, no. 2, (1993): 34.

[60] McDowell and Wilson, *Evidence for the Historical Jesus*, 65; B. Talmud Sanhedrin 43a.

> It is possible that there may be actual descendants somewhere, but at present, no one can produce sufficient and unquestionable proof of this claim. Conservative genealogists would say that since there is no solid proof, and what is available is incomplete or subject to differing interpretations, such claims cannot be accepted as valid.[61]

For this to be the case we must be able to reconcile God's promise that "David will never fail to have a man to sit on the throne of Israel" as long as the days and nights come at their appointed time (JER. 33:17-25). Could there be any legitimate heirs to the throne of David after Jesus?

Besides the issue of the legal inheritance, detractors question the legitimacy of the genealogy because of several missing kings, and most of all—whether the line which Jesus descends from according to Matthew is cursed from ever producing a king. To address these issues, we shall trace their origins at Solomon, the very first king after David.

Solomon was said to be "wiser than anyone else" in his time (1 KGS. 4:31), and valued these facilities of his over those of the Most High—the direct source of these endowments in the first place (1 KGS. 3:7-14). While the wisdom of the true son of David is of the spiritual, which is eternal, the wisdom of Solomon was of the natural, which is ephemeral, and by it he descended into apostasy. Solomon became consumed by his own lustful desires and welcomed in those whom God had explicitly warned against:

> But King Solomon loved many foreign women, as well as the daughter of Pharaoh: women of the Moabites, Ammonites, Edomites, Sidonians, and Hittites—from the nations of whom the Lord had said to the children of Israel, "You shall not intermarry with them, nor they

---

[61] Einsiedler, "Can We Prove Descent from King David?" *Avotaynu: The International Review of Jewish Genealogy* 9, no. 2, (1993): 34.

> *with you. Surely they will turn away your hearts after their gods." ... For it was so, when Solomon was old, that his wives turned his heart after other gods; and his heart was not loyal to the Lord his God, as was the heart of his father David. For Solomon went after Ashtoreth the goddess of the Sidonians, and after Milcom the abomination of the Ammonites. Solomon did evil in the sight of the Lord, and did not fully follow the Lord, as did his father David. Then Solomon built a high place for Chemosh the abomination of Moab, on the hill that is east of Jerusalem, and for Molech the abomination of the people of Ammon. And he did likewise for all his foreign wives, who burned incense and sacrificed to their god (1 Kgs. 11:1-8 NIV).*

He developed a close relationship with the Phoenician king Hiram of Tyre, who introduced him to their false gods and ungodly women (1 KGS. 11:1-33; 2 KGS. 23:13). Solomon continued to ignore the Word of God as the kingdom progressively devolved into the idolatrous ways of the Phoenicians. God recognised that Solomon would continue to dishonour the law of Moses and the covenant of his father David, so He righteously ordered the division of the kingdom, as warned in various scriptures (DEUT. 17:15-20; 1 KGS. 2:1-4; 6:11-13; 8:25; 9:1-9; 11; 1 CHR. 22:9-13; 28:6-9):

> *"Since this is your attitude and you have not kept my covenant and my decrees, which I commanded you, I will most certainly tear the kingdom away from you and give it to one of your subordinates. Nevertheless, for the sake of David your father, I will not do it during your lifetime. I will tear it out of the hand of your son. Yet I will not tear the whole kingdom from him, but will give him one tribe for the sake of David my servant and for the sake of Jerusalem, which I have chosen" (1 Kgs. 11:11-13 NIV).*

In accordance with His Word, after the death of Solomon, the kingdom was split into Judah and Israel, and the Phoenician bloodline soon infiltrated both of them (1 KGS. 9:13; 12). King Ahab of Israel married Jezebel, the daughter of the Phoenician king Ithobaal I, and their daughter Athaliah married Jehoram, the king of Judah (1 KGS. 21:20-29; 2 KGS. 3:1-2; 8:16-19). Jehoram followed in the footsteps of Solomon by ignoring God's warnings (MIC. 6:16; 2 CHR. 21) and "caused the people of Jerusalem to prostitute themselves and [lead] Judah astray" (2 CHR. 21:11). He corrupted the Davidic kingdom by siring children with Athaliah—thereby integrating her condemned strain into the line of Davidic kings (2 KGS. 8:25-26; 11:1; 2 CHR. 24:7). In keeping with the first commandment, God punished the next three generations of kings from Jehoram's line for persisting with, and building upon, his kingdom of idolatry (EXOD. 20:5). These kings—Ahaziah, Joash, and Amaziah—are listed as kings of Judah in Chronicles and Kings but are excluded by Matthew (2 KGS. 8:16-27; 12:1-3; 14:1-4; 1 CHR. 3:10-16; MATT. 1). Being only a few generations removed from Jehoram at most, these kings could not feign ignorance of their moral wrongdoings and God deemed them fully culpable for their actions. This may have been the impetus for Matthew to omit their names. It was after all a common practice of Hebrew genealogies to include only the names of most significance for future generations.

Jehoiakim, the father of Jeconiah, is the fourth and final king omitted, and for the same reasons (2 KGS. 23:36; 24:6; MATT. 1). During the beginning of his reign, God called for national repentance from the people to avoid the disaster due them because of their continuous transgressions (JER. 26:4-6). King Jehoiakim responded to the warning by killing Uriah, a man who prophesied these things in the name of the Lord (JER. 26:20-23). A few years later, God told the prophet Jeremiah to write this same warning upon a scroll to try turn the people from their wicked ways and warrant forgiveness (JER. 36:1-4). Jehoiakim once again responded with disdain for the Lord by burning the scroll three lines at a time (JER. 36:22-26). Reading that the king of Babylon would destroy the land, Jehoiakim was enraged and called for the arrest of Jeremiah and the scribe, Baruch (JER. 36:26-29). Jeremiah was instructed to copy this scroll again and tell Jehoiakim, among other things, that "he will have no one to sit on the throne of David," he and his children will be punished for their wickedness, and every disaster he pronounced will fall upon Judah for their rebellion (JER. 36:30-31).

The judgement came upon the throne and the people in this same manner. The son of Jehoiakim, Jeconiah (or Jehoiachin) reigned only three short months before he was dethroned by the king of Babylon and thrown into exile. The final king of Judah after him, Zedekiah, was appointed by Nebuchadnezzar the king of Babylon to reign in his place (JER. 37:1). God then pronounced a curse upon Jeconiah which appeared to extend to his posterity, including his descendant, Jesus. This is the verse which some believe undermines the claim of Jesus to become the Davidic king:

> *This is what the Lord says: "Record this man as if childless, a man who will not prosper in his lifetime, for none of his offspring will prosper, none will sit on the throne of David or rule anymore in Judah" (Jer. 22:30 NIV).*

On the surface it could be argued that this curse is forever binding, thereby disqualifying all his posterity from sitting on the Davidic throne, including Jesus. This being the case, the messianic claim of Jesus would be null and void. Luckily, there are strong arguments against the perpetuity of the curse. The simplest of all is that "his offspring" referred simply to his own children, not all of his lineal descendants. Next is the conditional clause "in his lifetime," which indicates his offspring would not prosper or rule for as long as he was alive (JER. 22:30). What happened after he died was out of the picture. This would make sense because Jeconiah was the subject of the punishment. For a former king to be deprived the privilege of seeing his children take up his mantle, or be adequately cared for by them in his old age would be a fitting curse. Not having the social programs we enjoy today, the elders depended on their family for their survival. Furthermore, the conditional nature of God's judgement and quickness to forgive is shown within the surrounding context. First, we read:

> "'As surely as I live,' declares the Lord, 'even if you, Jehoiachin son of Jehoiakim king of Judah, were a signet ring on my right hand, I would still pull you off. I will deliver you into the hands of those who want to kill you, those you fear—Nebuchadnezzar king of Babylon and the Babylonians ... You will never come back to the land you long to return to'" (Jer. 22:24-27 NIV).

We see here that God condemns Jeconiah (Jehoiachin) and the people to exile but in the verses which immediately follows He promises deliverance to greater heights (JER. 23:1-8). God reminds us how He is more willing to forgive and restore than He is to condemn (NUM. 14:17-18). This is perfectly in line with the following events which further illustrate the direct influence that repentance or disobedience have on His decisions:

> In the thirty-seventh year of the exile of Jehoiachin king of Judah, in the year Awel-Marduk became king of Babylon, ... he released Jehoiachin king of Judah and freed him from prison. He spoke kindly to him and gave him a seat of honour higher than those of the other kings who were with him in Babylon. So Jehoiachin put aside his prison clothes and for the rest of his life ate regularly at the king's table. Day by day the king of Babylon gave Jehoiachin a regular allowance as long as he lived, till the day of his death (Jer. 52:31-34 NIV).

As expressed by Michael L. Brown, "in light of the divine fury directed against Jehoiachin, this reversal of circumstances is quite striking, suggesting a change of heart in the king."[62] It seems as if Jehoiachin had repented, and the Lord had forgiven the curse in turn, because only two generations later the Lord declared to

---

[62] Brown, *Answering Jewish Objections to Jesus*, 115.

Jehoiachin's grandson, Zerubbabel, "I will take you ... and I will make you like my signet ring, for I have chosen you" (Hag. 2:23). The signet ring the Lord once pulled off from Jeconiah was restored. Zerubbabel was allowed to "come back to the land he longed to return to" (Jer. 22:27) and furthermore, was heaped with such favour from the Lord that he was tasked with rebuilding the temple (Ezra 3:8; 5:2; Hag. 1:14; 2:1-23; Zech. 4:6-10). Ra McLaughlin noted that "if the curse had been unconditional and permanent, Zerubbabel would not have been able to return ... proving that the curse did not permanently ban all Jeconiah's posterity."[63] God made this point abundantly clear throughout the scriptures. For example, through the prophet Jeremiah, God relayed the message that impending judgement can be averted by repentance:

> *Then the word of the Lord came to me. He said, "Can I not do with you, Israel, as this potter does?" declares the Lord. "Like clay in the hand of the potter, so are you in my hand, Israel. If at any time I announce that a nation or kingdom is to be uprooted, torn down and destroyed, and if that nation I warned repents of its evil, then I will relent and not inflict on it the disaster I had planned. And if at another time I announce that a nation or kingdom is to be built up and planted, and if it does evil in my sight and does not obey me, then I will reconsider the good I had intended to do for it" (Jer. 18:5-8 NIV).*

We read here that God is the potter and Israel is the clay (Jer. 18:3-6). As the potter, God can beautifully shape the clay if Israel chooses to conform to His hands. Otherwise, what could have been a beautiful piece of pottery becomes unusable. Even in their continual failure and disobedience, God still intends on outpouring His Spirit, the living water, to bring the clay of Israel to repentance so they may run perfectly in His hands. We see an

---

[63] McLaughlin, "Jesus and Jeconiah," *Biblical Perspectives Magazine* 1, no. 1 (March 1999).

example of this interplay between repentance and judgement in the story of the prophet Jonah. After Jonah preached to the wicked Ninevites that judgement from God was upon them, they all repented of their sins, and out of compassion God spared them from destruction. Sadly, just a generation later, in fulfilment of the word of the prophet Nahum, Nineveh was destroyed by the Medes in 612 BC for returning to their evil ways (JON. 3; NAH. 1:2-3).

### Genealogy According to Matthew

"There were fourteen generations in all from Abraham to David, fourteen from David to the exile to Babylon, and fourteen from the exile to the Messiah" (MATT. 1:17). The first set of fourteen generations from Abraham to David brings to mind the covenantal promise made to them of a son who will forever rule and bless all the nations. We have already covered these names in the previous chapter so we shall move onto the second set. The second set could be considered the "Times of the Jews"—when kings from the line of Judah reigned on the throne of David. Logically, and according to Matthew's own rendering, David appears again as he is the first of the Davidic kings. Because of Solomon's idolatry, God took from his sons the United Kingdom of Israel so that the Kingdom of Judah became their only dominion. The first three omissions lie between Jehoram and Uzziah, and the last after Josiah.

*Image 3.1 – Hebrew name meanings from David to Josiah*

| NAME | HEBREW MEANING |
| --- | --- |
| David | *beloved* |
| Solomon | *one peaceful* |
| Rehoboam | *people of width* |
| Abijah | *my father the Lord* |
| Asa | *man of sorrows, healer* |
| Jehoshaphat | *Lord has judged* |
| Jehoram | *Lord exalts* |
| Uzziah | *my strength is in the Lord* |

*Seed of God: Jesus Christ*

| | |
|---|---|
| Jotham | who is perfect |
| Ahaz | he has grasped |
| Hezekiah | strength of the Lord |
| Manasseh | made me forget my misery |
| Amon | mother, nourisher, master builder |
| Josiah | despair of the Lord, Lord heals |
| **INTERPRETATION FROM COMBINED MEANINGS** ||
| One beloved and peaceful from a people of width is my Father the Lord. A man of sorrows, whom the Lord judged and exalted, is my strength in the Lord, who is perfect. He has grasped the strength of the Lord and made me forget my misery. He is like a mother who nourishes those who despair of the Lord and heals them. ||

The third and final set of fourteen starts from Jeconiah, marking the beginning of the exile to Babylon. Contrary to the second set, it is now the "Time of the Gentiles," to trample upon the Jews until the second coming of the Messiah (LUKE 21:24):

*Image 3.2 – Hebrew name meanings from Jeconiah to Jesus*

| NAME | HEBREW MEANING |
|---|---|
| Jeconiah | God has established |
| Shealtiel | I asked God |
| Zerubbabel | seed of Babel (Babylon) |
| Abiud | father of praise |
| Eliakim | God sets up |
| Azor | a helper |
| Zadok | righteous or just |
| Achim | established or raised up |
| Eliud | my God is praise |
| Eleazar | God has helped |
| Matthan | gift |
| Jacob | supplanter, one who follows |
| Joseph | increaser, he will add |
| Jesus | salvation |

**INTERPRETATION FROM COMBINED MEANINGS**

The Lord establishes he who asks Him about the seed of Babylon. The father of praise sets up a helper to the righteous to be raised up by Him. As a gift, the supplanter who follows will bring increase and he will add salvation.

The genealogy of Matthew highlighted the futility of earthly rule and the need for something greater. Ever since man rejected God as their king and demanded earthly kings in His place, what they received were power-hungry megalomaniacs and vicious tyrants (1 SAM. 8:6-20). The third set from Matthew indicates how the Davidic kingdom was defunct, but that by the oath of God, Jesus was to be the descendant God would establish on the Davidic throne—never to be succeeded—for in him God will never again be transgressed (ACTS 2:30-36; REV. 22:16; MATT. 22:41-46). He was raised up to give freedom to the exiles and supplant the present Babylonian age with a kingdom and age of his own. In the meantime, because Israel submitted to the Babylonian mindset, they are to be trampled down by the gentiles until the return of their Davidic king (LUKE 21:24). In these final days, the surviving members of the nation shall look to Jesus as their Judahite-Davidic king to save them from the gentiles who seek to destroy them (PSA. 2; ZECH. 12:8-14; 14). The same people God had uprooted and tore down He shall build up as something greater under a new covenant (JER. 31:28-34; 32:30-42). They will be established as a kingdom in the land promised to their patriarchal father Abraham for a millennium, and Christ shall be their Davidic king. Those gentiles who extend mercy to his people, both Jewish and Christian, will be allowed to enter this millennial kingdom (MATT. 24:21-22), for as Jesus said, "whenever you did this to the least of my brethren, you did it to me" (MATT. 25:31-40).

## Jesus' Natural Lineage via Nathan, son of David

I believe the genealogy given by Luke works to reinforce that given by Matthew by emphasising the divine and universal nature of Christ and his kingship over *all* creation, not particularly of the Jews. Let us first investigate the differences between these two genealogies and work through the supposed contradictions.

The genealogy given by Luke starts all the way back at God, the father of Adam, and reaches Joseph not by the way of Solomon, but by Nathan, his brother (LUKE 3:23-38). We are presented with a reality in which Joseph, the father of Jesus, doubles as a son of both lines. Many solutions to this seeming contradiction have been proposed across time. One plausible explanation was proposed back in the fourth century by Augustine of Hippo. He posited that Joseph was adopted, and that Matthew held by the biological lineage of Joseph, while Luke held by the legal lineage.[64] This could explain why Matthew used the explicitly biological pattern of "X begat Y" while Luke opted for the more legal rendering of "X son of Y."

To me, the simplest and most fitting scenario is that Luke outlined the lineage of "Mary, the daughter of Heli," the mother of Jesus.[65] Joseph was begotten by Jacob as listed in the genealogy of Matthew but is counted as the legal son of Heli through his marriage with Mary, and is substituted in her place in accordance with the familiar Jewish (and biblical) custom (MATT. 1:16-20).[66]

Furthermore, since Jewishness is passed on matrilineally—from the mother, not the father[67]—it is therefore the case that Jesus became a Jew from Mary, and most of all—the promised seed of the woman (GEN. 3:14-15; GAL. 4:4-5). Jesus was, as Paul declared, born of the seed of David according to the flesh (ROM. 1:3). However, he was not of the flesh of Joseph, only of Mary, for she conceived Jesus with the supernatural intervention of God's Spirit which Isaiah had prophesied:

---

[64] Augustine of Hippo, "The Harmony of the Gospels, Book II," chap. 3 in *Nicene and Post-Nicene Fathers, First Series, Vol. 6*.

[65] B. Talmud Shabbat 104b.

[66] Torrey, "Luke 3:23," in *The Treasury of Scripture Knowledge*, https://www.sacred-texts.com/bib/cmt/tsk/luk003.htm.

[67] Shurpin and Freeman. "Why Is Jewishness Matrilineal?" *Chabad*. https://www.chabad.org/library/article_cdo/aid/601092/jewish/Why-Is-Jewishness-Matrilineal.htm.

> *Therefore the Lord himself will give you a sign: the virgin will conceive and give birth to a son, and will call him Immanuel [God with us] (Isa. 7:14 NIV).*

God declared to Mary that Jesus will be their "beloved Son," the only begotten son of God, and that he will reign on the Davidic throne forever (LUKE 1:31-35; 3:21-22; HEB. 1:5). This was in fulfilment of His decree from the book of Psalms:

> *I will declare the decree: the Lord has said to Me, 'You are My Son, today I have begotten You. Ask of Me, and I will give You the nations for Your inheritance, and the ends of the earth for Your possession' (Psa. 2:7-8 NKJV).*

God expressed this fact to Jesus directly at his baptism, proclaiming with His voice from heaven: "You are My beloved Son; in You I am well pleased" and the Holy Spirit went upon him as testimony (MATT. 3:16-17; LUKE 3:21-22). Luke positioned this statement immediately before the genealogy of Christ to make it clear that while Joseph was the *legal* father of Jesus, God was his father in *essence*.

Whereas Matthew traced the tribal identity of Christ to legitimise his Davidic kingship, Luke asserted that his divine nature proves he is, as David prophesied, the Lord who is to forever reign on his throne (PSA. 110). The two genealogies work together to prove that Jesus is not merely a son of David, but the son of God. As the son of God, Jesus is uniquely capable as king upon the throne of David to defeat all of God's enemies (LUKE 1:32, 35; 4:3, 9; EZEK. 36), to restore Israel spiritually, and to reunite the divided kingdom into a cohesive whole (EZEK. 37:1-28).

*Genealogy According to Luke*

In the genealogy given by Luke, there are seventy-seven generations in total, symbolic of the seventy sevens prophecies of Daniel before blessing, and of Lamech before judgement (GEN 4:23-24; DAN 9:24-27). The number of generations from Nathan down to

*Seed of God: Jesus Christ*

Joseph consist again of forty-two names. Since there are so many names, many of which are duplicates, I will refrain from tabulating these names and giving my interpretation. I would however implore you to investigate them for yourself.

Luke formatted his genealogy such that Jesus was rendered implicitly as the son of Mary (the final woman in the chain), and then the son of each of the men ascending up to Adam, and then of God Himself:

> *He [Jesus] was the son, so it was thought, of Joseph, [Jesus] the son of Heli, ... [Jesus] the son of David ... [Jesus] the son of Abraham, ... [Jesus] the son of Adam, [Jesus] the son of God (Luke 3:23-38 NIV).*

The pattern of sonship extending up to the first man of Adam and beyond to God makes it clear that Jesus was the son of man prophesied by Daniel, the divine and everlasting king of all creation (DAN. 7:13-14). The chain of men begins with the first son of God in Adam and terminates with Jesus, the second Adam, and the one begotten son of God. Jesus is shown to be the son who God promised to Eve to crush the head of the serpent and redeem her and all mankind. The same son who God promised to Abraham as a blessing to *all* the nations. Indeed, he is not only the awaited Messiah for the Jews, but also for the gentiles—he shares a common humanity with every man and woman.

Perhaps the boldest indication of this universality of salvation comes from the genealogy of Matthew (not Luke). Matthew goes out of his way to mention five women who were instrumental in preserving and continuing the godly line down to Christ. What makes this significant is that not only were they women, who were seldomly mentioned in Jewish genealogies and were generally second-class citizens, but included were gentiles and blatant sinners. The implication is obvious, Jesus came into the world to save more than just the law-abiding Jews. Jesus came to save all people without concerning himself with race, gender, status, or background. These women were Tamar, Rahab, Ruth, Bathsheba, and Mary. Together they embodied the obedience, resilience, faithfulness, and determination of each woman who had worked to secure the next generation down to Christ, the seed of the woman. Just as man and woman caused their own downfall, so it was for their redemption. Women had as much a part to play as the men in bringing the promised seed to fruition. It should be remembered that the first two witnesses to the resurrected Christ were women (MATT. 28:1–10; JOHN 20:10–18), the first to be alerted of the time of the Messiah was a woman (LUKE 1:31), and the first to evangelise was a woman (JOHN 4:28). This was especially striking considering that Jewish society totally disregarded the testimony of women. If the gospels were written without God's direct inspiration, these honours would undoubtedly have been given to men. But the Father did not create another man to be a suitable helper for Adam, He created woman.

## Conclusion

The genealogy of Christ given by Matthew emphasises his royal lineage as the Messiah for the Jews, but at the same time stresses the importance of women and non-Jews in the promises of Christ. Luke in his genealogy generally looks more broadly at how Jesus is the Messiah for all humanity as the divine son of God and the seed of the woman. It is my view that the two genealogies do not contradict each other but are complementary, both communicating different things about the Messiah on the Throne of David.

# 4

# God Manifested in the Flesh

> *And without controversy great is the mystery of godliness: God was manifested in the flesh, justified in the Spirit, seen by angels, preached among the Gentiles, believed on in the world, received up in glory (1 Tim. 3:16 NKJV).*

Up to this point, we have investigated the most important biblical figures in the godly lineage of man (Adam) down to Jesus. Before we can confidently point to Jesus as the promised seed of the woman, further illumination is necessary to move in one direction or the other. Jesus declared that he alone was one with God the Father—the implication being that he was God manifested in the flesh (MATT. 26:63-65; MARK 14:60-62; LUKE 22:67-70; JOHN 5:18; 8:24, 48-59; 10:30-33; 14:6-14; 17:11-26; REV. 1:8, 17-18; 22:13; ISA. 44:6). Taken at face value, it could be assumed that Jesus openly denied the undeniable oneness of God. This was certainly how his critics responded to him. To them he was a blasphemer worthy of judgement. It follows therefore that there must be a strong scriptural basis for his assertion which does not contradict the nature of God. If they were correct in their assessment of Jesus, we would have to simply discard him as a false prophet and abandon our faith altogether (DEUT. 18:20-22; PROV. 30:5-6).

*God Manifested in the Flesh*

**Jesus and the Triune God**

To begin our investigation into the divine nature of Christ, let us unpack the Hebrew meaning of the *Shema*, the great declaration of monotheistic Judaism starting from Deuteronomy 6:4:

> *Hear, Israel, the Lord is our God, the Lord is one.*
> *Shema Yisrael Adonai Eloheinu, Adonai echad.*

Here in the Shema, the most emphatic statement on the oneness of God, Moses opted for the plural first person possessive of *Elohim* (God), *Eloheinu* ("our God"), and chose *echad* (one) over *yachid* (one and only) to describe His oneness. In Hebrew, echad is the word for one, but it often signifies a compound unity of oneness (one in essence), whereas yachid always refers to a solitary oneness (one and only, or unique). It is noteworthy that yachid is never used in reference to God in the Bible.[68] Another example of echad being used to denote unity comes from Genesis 2, where God declared Adam and Eve, while being two, "became one [echad] flesh" through marital union (GEN. 2:22).[69] Marriage creates a compound oneness where two distinct beings unite as one to produce a transcendental trinity of love and truth between them. This earthly institution of marriage is an earthly projection of the heavenly reality of the Godhead, similar to how the tabernacle and temple are projections of the heavenly sanctuary; the ten commandments of God's character; and the ark of the covenant of God's heavenly throne.[70]

Because Moses referred to God in the plural, both in name and essence, when the singular forms were available, the Shema seems to present a greater dimensionality to the oneness of God than it first appears. It is significant that when Jesus quoted both the Shema and the above declaration of marriage from Genesis, he

---

[68] Strong, "3173. יָחִיד (yachid)," in *The Exhaustive Concordance of the Bible*. https://biblehub.com/hebrew/strongs_3173.htm.

[69] See also: Exod. 24:3; Zeph. 3:9; 2 Chr. 30:12; Ezek. 37:19-22.

[70] Payne, "The Trinity and Marriage," *WISEN*, https://www.wisensda.org/blog/2018/3/12/the-trinity-and-marriage.

chose the Greek equivalent of echad, the masculine *heis*, when yachid could have been rendered as *mono* or *monogenes* (Matt. 19:5; Mark 10:7-8; 12:29).

On its own this may seem speculative, but there are many different types of evidence in the Old Testament for the plurality of God. As one example, consider when God said, "let us make man in our image," and ask yourself, who was he speaking to? (Gen. 1:26). Some contend that God was referring to the angels, the ben elohim, but nowhere in scripture are they associated with the act of creation, only in its celebration, by shouting for joy at the majestic display of God's power (Job 38:4-7). Furthermore, we see God employ this same language on other occasions. For example, after the temptation and subsequent fall of man, He said, "the man has become like one of us" (Gen. 3:22).[71]

Another type of evidence are the masculine plural nouns used in the Hebrew for "Maker" (makers) and "Creator" (creators) (Job 35:10; Psa. 149:2; Isa. 54:5; Eccl. 12:1). The creation account indicates these makers or creators were three agents of creation—God, the Spirit of God, and the Word of God (Gen. 1). Interestingly, the third word of the Bible is the plural yet singular form of God, *Elohim* (Gen. 1:1). While not explicitly mentioned, the idea that the Word of God was responsible for creation is not only implicit through God speaking creation into being, but in Psalm 33, we read:

> *For the word of the Lord is right and true; he is faithful in all he does ... [b]y the word of the Lord the heavens were made, their starry host by the breath of his mouth ... [f]or he spoke, and it came to be; he commanded, and it stood firm (Psa. 33:4, 6, 9 NIV).*

In the New Testament, John referenced the opening of Genesis to express the full reality of the Word as the agent of creation:

---

[71] See also: Gen. 11:7; Isa. 6:8.

*In the beginning was the Word, and the Word was with God, and the Word was God. He was with God in the beginning. Through him all things were made; without him nothing was made that has been made (John 1:1-3 NIV).*

John continued that "the Word became flesh" in the person of Jesus Christ, "the one and only Son, who came from the Father" (JOHN 1:1-14). He became the bodily embodiment and personification of God expressed through creation, His Word (COL. 1:15-18; 2:9; HEB. 1:3; 1 TIM. 3:16; REV. 1:8). We see this claim confirmed by the apostle Paul:

*The Son is the image of the invisible God, the firstborn over all creation. For in him all things were created: things in heaven and on earth, visible and invisible, whether thrones or powers or rulers or authorities; all things have been created through him and for him. He is before all things, and in him all things hold together (Col. 1:15-17 NIV).*

For more scriptural attestation for Jesus being the architect of the old and new creation read on to the final chapter and also consult the appendix. The point that is to be stressed here is how despite this astounding revelation of Christ as the divine Word, never is the oneness of God rejected by Jesus, or by the New Testament writers (EPH. 4:4–6; 1 TIM. 2:5; JAMES 2:19; MARK 12:29-31; 1 COR. 8:4-6). Where the Jews had until this time thought of God the Father in purely a corporate sense (ISA. 63:16; 64:8; JER. 3:19; 31:9; MAL. 2:10; HOS. 1:10; DEUT. 14:1; PSA. 82:6), the personal sonship of the Messiah was not a new development (PSA. 2; 45:6-7; 110; PROV. 30:4; ISA. 7:14; 9:5-7; HOS. 11:1; MIC. 5:2-3; DAN. 3:25). In some Old Testament passages, God and the Son are even used interchangeably, or in relationship to each other (PSA. 45:6-7; GEN. 19:24; ZECH. 2:8-9). The third dimension of the Godhead, the Holy Spirit (ACTS 5:3-4; JOHN 4:24; LUKE 12:10; 2 COR. 3:17), is similarly attested to in the Old Testament in many places (PSA.

*Seed of God: Jesus Christ*

51:11–13; 139:7; Isa. 11:2; 48:16; 63:10-14; Zech. 4:6; Exod. 31:3; Job 33:4; Gen. 1:2; 6:3; 2 Sam. 23:2-3).

According to this trinitarian view put forth, the *creators* we see in the Old Testament are revealed as one essence but three distinct entities, God the Father, Jesus the Son, and the Holy Spirit. It was not until the son of God had manifested himself in the world and the Holy Spirit was imparted to all of his followers that a more explicit scriptural basis for this triune view of God was developed:

*Image 4.1 – Testification to God the Father, Son, and Holy Spirit*

| SCRIPTURE | REFERENCE |
|---|---|
| From the beginning I have not spoken in secret, from the time it took place, I was there. And now the Lord God has sent Me, and His Spirit. | Isa. 48:16 NASB |
| Be filled with the Spirit ... giving thanks always for all things to God the Father in the name of our Lord Jesus Christ. | Eph. 5:18-20 NKJV |
| There are diversities of gifts, but the same Spirit. There are differences of ministries, but the same Lord [Jesus]. And there are diversities of activities, but it is the same God who works all in all. | 1 Cor. 12:4-6 NKJV |
| God from the beginning chose you for salvation through sanctification by the Spirit and belief in the truth, to which He called you by our gospel, for the obtaining of the glory of our Lord Jesus Christ. | 2 Thess. 2:13-14 NKJV |
| [W]ho have been chosen according to the foreknowledge of God the Father, through the sanctifying work of the Spirit, to be obedient to Jesus Christ and sprinkled with his blood. | 1 Pet. 1:2 NIV |
| And the Holy Spirit descended in bodily form like a dove upon Him [Jesus], and a voice came from heaven which said, "You are My beloved Son; in You I am well pleased." | Matt. 3:13-17; Mark 1:9-11; Luke 3:21-22 NKJV |
| Jesus came to them and said, "All authority in heaven and on earth has been given to me. Therefore go and make disciples of all nations, baptizing them in the name of the Father and of the Son and of the Holy Spirit." | Matt. 28:18-19 NIV |
| May the grace of the Lord Jesus Christ, and the love of God, and the fellowship of the Holy Spirit be with you all. | 2 Cor. 13:14 NIV |
| I [Jesus] will pray the Father, and He will give you another Helper, that He may abide with you forever—the Spirit of truth. | John 14:16-17 NKJV |
| But when the Helper comes, whom I shall send to you from the | John 15:26 |

| | |
|---|---|
| Father, the Spirit of truth who proceeds from the Father, He will testify of Me [Jesus]. | NKJV |
| For the one whom God has sent [Jesus] speaks the words of God, for God gives the Spirit without limit. The Father loves the Son and has placed everything in his hands. | John 3:34-35 NIV |

It must be stressed that the oneness of Jesus and the Father is not only a unity of purpose and will but one of essence. The Jews would not have tried to kill him for blasphemy on many occasions for simply living in accordance, or unity, with the will of God. It was obvious to his Jewish audience that by "calling God his own Father" he was "making himself equal with God" in nature, not simply in purpose (JOHN 5:18). Jesus distinguished his relationship with God in this uniquely personal sense by calling God, "my Father" or "my God," but when speaking of others, referring only to a corporate sense of sonship, "your Father" or "your God" (JOHN 8:54; 20:17).[72]

This distinction was not lost on the New Testament writers either. They clearly understood the implications of Jesus' words because they testified to the Godhood of Jesus Christ extensively (TITUS 1:3-4; 2:13; 1 JOHN 1:2; 5:20; 1 TIM. 3:16; HEB. 1:8-9; ROM. 9:5; PHIL. 2:5-11):

*Image 4.2 – Testification to the oneness of the Son and the Father*

| SCRIPTURE | REFERENCE |
|---|---|
| "'I and the Father are one.' Again, his Jewish opponents picked up stones to stone him ... 'for blasphemy, because you, a mere man, claim to be God.'" | John 10:30-33 NIV |
| Jesus said to him, "... He who has seen Me has seen the Father; so how can you say, 'Show us the Father'? Do you not believe that I am in the Father, and the Father in Me? | John 14:9-14 NKJV |
| "Holy Father, protect them by the power of your name, the | John 17:11, 21- |

---

[72] Carson, *The Gospel According to John*, 395: *"If instead Jesus' will is exhaustively one with his Father's will, some kind of metaphysical unity is presupposed, even if not articulated. Though the focus is on the common commitment of Father and Son to display protective power toward what they commonly own (17:10), John's development of Christology to this point demands that some more essential unity be presupposed."*

| | |
|---|---|
| name you gave me, so that they may be one as we are one … that all of them may be one, Father, just as you are in me and I am in you. May they also be in us so that the world may believe that you have sent me. I have given them the glory that you gave me, that they may be one as we are one—I in them and you in me—so that they may be brought to complete unity." | 23 NIV |
| For this reason they tried all the more to kill him; not only was he breaking the Sabbath, but he was even calling God his own Father, making himself equal with God. | John 5:18 NIV |
| 'I am ascending to my Father and your Father, to my God and your God.' | John 20:17 NIV |
| "All things have been committed to me by my Father. No one knows the Son except the Father, and no one knows the Father except the Son and those to whom the Son chooses to reveal him." | Matt. 11:27; Luke 10:22 NIV |
| The Father loves the Son and has placed everything in his hands … the Father loves the Son and shows him all he does. | John 3:35; 5:20 NIV |
| Christ Jesus, who, being in very nature God, did not consider equality with God something to be used to his own advantage. | Phil. 2:5-6 NIV |

The sacred name of God in Hebrew is יהוה, comprised of the letters *yod hey vav hey*, which, when transliterated into English, comes to YHWH (Yahweh). Since Hebrew reads from right to left, we write it as HWHY. God ensured His work on the cross would be reflected in His sacred name of the tetragrammaton: [73]

*Image 4.3 – Hebrew pictographic meaning of Yahweh (God)*

| LETTER | PICTOGRAPH | MEANING |
|---|---|---|
| **H** - Hey | man with arms raised | behold, look, reveal |
| **W** - Vav (waw) | peg or nail | hook, secure |

---

[73] Kaiser, *The Messiah in the Old Testament*, 219: "Another metaphor used for the coming leader is a "peg" (יָתֵד). Elsewhere, it refers to the pegs that secured the tabernacle (Exod. 27:10; Num. 3:37), but it can also refer to a peg that is driven into a wall to hang something up (Isa. 22: 23, 25; Ezek. 15:3). Metaphorically speaking, it can also mean a secure and safe dwelling place (Ezra 9:8). … In Zechariah 10:4 the peg thus symbolizes the support for the people, the one on whom the weight of the nation's needs rests. Accordingly, the Messiah will be the nail in a sure place on whom his people can hang all their burdens, cares, and anxieties."

| | | |
|---|---|---|
| **H** - Hey | man with arms raised | behold, look, reveal |
| **Y** - Yod | outstretched arm and hand | arm, hand, work |

**INTERPRETATION FROM COMBINED MEANINGS**

Behold the man with his arms raised, hooked is the nail in his outstretched hand.

As for the third witness of the Triune Godhead, the Holy Spirit. As the author of the scriptures, the Holy Spirit planted a special watermark as verification for the truth of Jesus Christ and of the Trinity. First consider how in the Old and the New Testament, both the God of Israel and its Messiah, Jesus Christ, refer to themselves as the "first and the last," the creators of all things (ISA. 41:4; 44:6; 48:12; REV. 1:8; 17; 2:8; 21:6; 22:13). The Holy Spirit supported the truth of this statement by utilising the full breadth of its expression, the "first and the last" letters of the Bible, to spell out the word *Son* (Ben בן). Indeed, the first letter of the first word of Genesis (Bet ב from Bereshit) and the last letter of the last word of Revelation (Nun ן from Amen) form the word *Son* (Ben בן) (GEN. 1:1; REV. 22:21).

*Only Begotten Son of God*

The notion that Jesus was not the son and co-equal of God, but rather one from many of the angels, was dispelled in the first book of Hebrews:

> *[Jesus] became as much superior to the angels as the name he has inherited is superior to theirs. For to which of the angels did <u>God</u> ever say, "You are my <u>Son</u>; today I have become your <u>Father</u>"? Or again, "I will be his <u>Father</u>, and he will be my <u>Son</u>"? ... "Your throne, O <u>God</u>, will last for ever and ever; a sceptre of justice will be the sceptre of your kingdom. You have loved righteousness and hated wickedness; therefore <u>God, your God</u>, has set you above your companions by anointing you with the oil of joy" ... To which of the angels did <u>God</u> ever say, "Sit at my right hand until I make your enemies a footstool*

> *for your feet"? Are not all angels ministering spirits sent to serve those who will inherit salvation? (Heb. 1:3-9, 13 NIV).*

The author of Hebrews asked the very direct and pertinent question, when has God ever said to any angel, "you are my Son, today I have begotten you?" (HEB. 1:5). The word used for begotten in the original Greek is *monogenes,* the equivalent of the Hebrew *yachid*, and is defined as the "one and only of its kind." Throughout the Old Testament genealogy, we see the pattern of one begetting another: Adam begat Seth, and Seth begat Enos, and Enos begat Cainan, and so on. That is to say, they fathered their own kind. In this same way, God begat Jesus—he was not created, and if "the Son is 'begotten' of the Father, then he is of the same substance or essence as the Father."[74]

> *In these last days <u>God</u> has spoken to us in his <u>Son</u>, whom he appointed heir of all things, through whom he created the universe. The <u>Son</u> is the radiance of <u>God's</u> glory and the exact representation of his being, sustaining all things by his powerful <u>word</u> (Heb. 1:2-3 NIV).*

Jesus, the one and only begotten son of God, was sent to earth to truly live up to the image and likeness of God so that salvation could be made available to all (JOHN 1:14-18; 3:16; GEN. 1:26):

> *Since the children have flesh and blood, he too shared in their humanity so that by his death he might break the power of him who holds the power of death—that is, the devil—and free those who all their lives were held in slavery by their fear of death. For surely it is not angels he helps, but Abraham's descendants. For this reason, he had to be made like them, fully human in every way, in*

---

[74] Brigden, "Monogenes: "'Only Begotten' or 'One of a Kind'?" *Christian Library.* https://www.christianstudylibrary.org/article/monogenes-%E2%80%9Conly-begotten%E2%80%9D-or-%E2%80%9Cone-kind%E2%80%9D.

*order that he might become a merciful and faithful high priest in service to God, and that he might make atonement for the sins of the people (Heb. 2:14-18 NIV).*

To anoint Jesus for his divine mission on earth, God had him baptised with the Holy Spirit and declared him as His "beloved son" (MATT. 3:13-17; MARK 1:9-11; LUKE 3:21-22; ACTS 10:36-38). This marked the beginning of Jesus' ministry, and fittingly, all three members of the Trinity came together for its authentication.

**Divine Ministry of Christ**

*God anointed Jesus of Nazareth with the Holy Spirit and with power, who went about doing good and healing all who were oppressed by the devil, for God was with Him (Acts 10:36-38 NKJV).*

Once Jesus began his ministry, he performed unprecedented miraculous works which testified to his divine nature as God manifested in the flesh. One of the most striking cases which illustrated the greater priestly authority of Jesus in his ministry was his healing of the woman with menstrual issues. This woman was perpetually unclean under the law because her flow of blood was continual and she was unable to be healed by physicians (LEV. 15:19; LUKE 8:43). Having heard about Jesus, she found him among a great crowd and despite her uncleanness, touched the hem (edge) of his garment, believing that just by touching it she would be healed (MATT. 9:20-22; MARK 5:25-34; LUKE 8:43-48). For the Jewish readers of the time the implications of this action were obvious. As touched upon in the section on King David, all Jews (Jesus included) attached special tassels called *tzitzit* to each of the four corners of their outer garment, the *tallit* (NUM. 15:37-40; DEUT. 22:12).[75]

---

[75] For a deep study of the tzitzit and the tallit read the book: "The Hem of His Garment: Touching the Power in God's Word" by John D. Garr.

> *"Throughout the generations to come you are to make tassels on the corners of your garments, with a blue cord on each tassel. You will have these tassels to look at and so you will remember all the commands of the Lord, that you may obey them and not prostitute yourselves by chasing after the lusts of your own hearts and eyes. Then you will remember to obey all my commands and will be consecrated to your God" (Num. 15:38-41 NIV).*

Rabbi scholar Jacob Milgrom further explained the cultural importance of this uniform for the Jews of antiquity:

> *In antiquity, the tzitzit (and the hem) was the insignia of authority, high breeding and nobility. By adding the blue woolen cord to the tzitzit, the Torah combined nobility with priesthood: Israel is not to rule man but to serve God. Furthermore, tzitzit is not restricted to Israel's leaders, be they kings, rabbis or scholars. It is the uniform of all Israel.*[76]

The blue woolen cord affixed to the tzitziot was doubly significant. First, the mixture of wool with the linen garments. In all other circumstances this mixture was forbidden for all but the priests to wear (LEV. 19:19; DEUT. 22:11), Second, the blue dye used for the blue cord called *tekhelet* was usually reserved for the priesthood—elements of the priestly garments, the tabernacle, and the temple used this blue dye (EXOD. 26:30-37; 28; 39:1-30; NUM. 4:1-12).[77] The priesthood may have been under the temporary authority of the tribe of Levi, but by wearing the tzitzit, the hope for Israel to fulfil

---

[76] Milgrom, "The Tassel and the Tallit." The Fourth Annual Rabbi Louis Fineberg Memorial Lecture.

[77] To learn more about the purpose of the tekhelet I recommend the article "The Meaning of Tekhelet" by Baruch Sterman: https://tekhelet.com/pdf/MeaningOfTekhelet.pdf.

their priestly destiny was kept alive (Exod. 19:5-6).[78]

The gospels seem to indicate that by the time of Jesus the tzitzit had developed a messianic association. Besides the case of the unclean woman, it is said that everywhere Jesus went, people "begged him to let the sick touch the edge of his cloak, and all who touched it were healed" (Matt. 14:35-36; Mark 6:56). Lois Tverberg suggested, "this may have come from the idea that the messiah would come with 'healing in his wings' (Mal. 4:2), with 'wings,' *kanafim,* also meaning 'corners,' where the tzitzit were placed."[79] In support of this reference out of the book of Malachi, we hear in the book of Zechariah:

> *"Thus says the Lord of hosts: 'In those days ten men from every language of the nations shall grasp the sleeve [kanafim – wing of the garment] of a Jewish man, saying, "let us go with you, for we have heard that God is with you" (Zech. 8:23 NIV).*

It seems that the unclean woman acknowledged the messianic authority of Jesus because she genuinely believed that he possessed "healing in his wings." When she grasped the tzitzit and was healed, it is said that Jesus immediately knew "power had gone out of him." I think this was speaking not only of his healing power, but of the sanctity of his tzitzit, the symbol of power, which would explain why the woman was reluctant to come forth:

> *Then the woman, seeing that she could not go unnoticed, came trembling and fell at his feet. In the presence of all the people, she told why she had touched him and how*

---

[78] Currently it is those joined to Christ through faith who comprise this nation of priests, but Israel is soon to follow, as stated by Adat Hatikvat Tzion, "The Tallit and Tzitzit," https://adat.org/the-tallit-and-tzitzit/; *"The symbolism of the tallit can remind believers in Yeshua of who they are in Christ. Now not only Israel, but all humanity has the opportunity through Messiah Yeshua to become a "kingdom of priests" interceding in prayer on behalf of the world."*

[79] Tverberg, "Letting Our Tassels Show," *Our Rabbi Jesus,* https://ourrabbijesus.com/articles/letting-our-tassels-show/.

> she had been instantly healed. Then he said to her, "Daughter, your faith has healed you. Go in peace" (Luke 8:42-48 NIV).

Jesus did not scold her but praised her for the faith she possessed in him to heal her and declare her clean (PSA. 110:1-4). Unlike in other cases, Jesus simply told her to "go in peace." There was no reminder of her legal duties due to her menstrual uncleanness. Under the law it would have taken her seven days set apart to be declared clean, and on the eighth day a sacrifice offering was required in the temple for atonement (LEV. 15:19-30). Perhaps by intuition, or revelation, she saw in Jesus' tassels a messianic authority and in its blue cords a greater high priest. This would have required the faith of Abraham who honoured the priesthood of Melchisedech through faith, not the law (GEN 14:18-20). If this were the case, Jesus would have known she need not go before the priests and make an offering of sacrifice under the law, for her offering of faith was far more precious to God who "desire[s] mercy, not sacrifice, and acknowledgment ... rather than burnt offerings" (HOS. 6:6).

Another example of Jesus overcoming impurity is when he circumvented the Mosaic purity laws surrounding the deceased to resurrect the daughter of Jarius. Under the law, one would become ritually unclean for seven days if they were to enter the room of the deceased or touch them (NUM. 19:11-14). Because Jesus was the sinless and divine high priest, he could enter the girls room and take her by the hand without fear of contamination. As confirmation of this divine authority, he simply said, "little girl, I say to you, arise" and the girl was resurrected (MATT. 9:18-26; MARK 5:21-43; LUKE 8:40-56).

We see another instance where Jesus authenticated his divine nature as God incarnate when he forgave the sins of the paralytic man and healed him (MATT. 9:2-8; MARK 2:1-12).

> Some men brought to him a paralyzed man, lying on a mat. When Jesus saw their faith, he said to the man,

> "Take heart, son; your sins are forgiven." At this, some of the teachers of the law said to themselves, "This fellow is blaspheming!" Knowing their thoughts, Jesus said, "Why do you entertain evil thoughts in your hearts? Which is easier: to say, 'Your sins are forgiven,' or to say, 'Get up and walk'? But I want you to know that the Son of Man has authority on earth to forgive sins." So, he said to the paralyzed man, "Get up, take your mat and go home." Then the man got up and went home. When the crowd saw this, they were filled with awe; and they praised God, who had given such authority to man (Matt. 9:2-8 NIV).

To realise how astonishing this claim of possessing the power to forgive sins really is, let me elaborate. I can freely forgive sins someone commits against me. I cannot forgive the sins that same person commits against others unless the injured party gives me authority to do so. Jesus claimed to forgive people's sins without consulting those who had been (and will be) affected by those transgressions (MATT. 9:2; MARK 2:9; LUKE 5:20; 7:48). This seems to be because God Himself is the truly affected party. He is entitled to forgive our sins because they hurt Him more than anyone else.

The teachers of the law knew it was harder for him to forgive sins than to heal, as only God can truly forgive sin, but out of hearts unwilling to be humbled they refused to acknowledge the reality of not only the miracle they had witnessed, but of the only possible explanation for why Jesus could do it—that he was indeed God manifested in the flesh.

## Miracles of the Messiah

The religious authorities could not feign ignorance of what exactly Jesus was communicating to them. By this time, certain hopes and expectations had developed surrounding the miracles of the coming Messiah. These were largely derived from the book of Isaiah, in which the prophet described how the Messiah would resurrect the dead; heal afflictions of the body and soul, specifically the deaf, blind, lame, mute, and broken-hearted; preach good news to the poor; and liberate the oppressed (Isa. 26:19; 29:18; 35:5-6; 42:1-7; 61:1).[80] Similar sentiments are expressed in the Psalms:

> Bless the Lord ... who forgives all your iniquities, who heals all your diseases, who redeems your life from destruction, who crowns you with lovingkindness and tender mercies (Psa. 103:2-4 NKJV).

Testifying to the expectations of this period is the Dead Sea Scrolls fragment 4Q521, dating between the third-century B.C. to the time of Christ. The miraculous works of the coming Messiah are clearly outlined in this fragment, reflecting the interpretation of Isaiah of the time:

> [the heavens and the earth will listen to His Messiah ... over the poor His spirit will hover and will renew the faithful with His power. And He will glorify the pious on the throne of the eternal Kingdom. He who liberates the captives, restores sight to the blind, straightens the b[ent] ... And the Lord will accomplish glorious things which have never been as [He...] For He will heal the wounded, and revive the dead and bring good news to the poor.[81]

With these messianic expectations firmly in the minds of the people, it was clear who Jesus was claiming to be when he read these scriptures from Isaiah in the synagogue:

> "'The Spirit of the Lord is upon me, because He has anointed me to preach the gospel to the poor; He has sent

---

[80] For justification of the KJV translations inclusion of the phrase "to heal the brokenhearted" read
https://peterrodgerssite.files.wordpress.com/2016/10/luke-4.pdf.

[81] Dead Sea Scrolls fragment 4Q521 (4QMessianic Apocalypse).

*me to heal the brokenhearted, to proclaim liberty to the captives and recovery of sight to the blind, to set at liberty those who are oppressed; To proclaim the acceptable year of the Lord.' Then he closed the book, and gave it back to the attendant and sat down. And the eyes of all who were in the synagogue were fixed on him. And he began to say to them, 'Today this Scripture is fulfilled in your hearing'" (Luke 4:18-21 NKJV).*

Jesus added a clause absent from many modern translations of Isaiah 61:1-2, the "recovery of sight to the blind," but there is evidence for the inclusion of this passage well before the time of Christ, such as in the Septuagint, the Dead Sea Scrolls, and the Aramaic Targum.[82] This is significant because it provides yet another messianic prophecy which Jesus fulfilled.

Notice how Jesus referenced these prophecies of Isaiah to John the Baptiser when affirming his messiahship (MATT. 11:1-6; LUKE 7:18-23):

*When John, who was in prison, heard about the deeds of the Messiah, he sent his disciples to ask him, "Are you the one who is to come, or should we expect someone else?" Jesus replied, "Go back and report to John what you hear and see: The blind receive sight, the lame walk, those who have leprosy are cleansed, the deaf hear, the dead are raised, and the good news is proclaimed to the poor" (Matt. 11:2-5 NIV).*

John the Baptiser came to recognise that Jesus was the "one who is to come," the Messiah, once he received verbal testimony from Jesus' disciples on the miraculous acts he had performed. These same disciples later provided written testimony for us to believe as John did. They recorded thirty-seven of his many miracles so

---

[82] Wayne, "Does Luke 4:18 misquote Isaiah 61:1?" *CARM*, https://carm.org/about-the-bible/does-luke-418-misquote-isaiah-611/.

that, in the words of John, "you may believe that Jesus is the Christ, the Son of God, and that believing you may have life in His name" (JOHN 20:30-31; 21:25).[83]

I believe there were four miracles in particular which the contemporary Jewish world would have recognised as unique messianic signs. The Jewish believer Victoria Radin considered these to be the following:

> *In Jewish belief, there were four physical conditions in mankind that could only be corrected by G-d Himself. It was believed that when G-d would send His Messiah, the SIGN that would prove to the Pharisees who He was would be the performance of four specific miracles. They are known as the four messianic miracles: cleansing a leper; casting out a deaf and dumb Spirit; the healing of birth defects; raising the dead after three days.*[84]

It was commonplace to hear of great acts of healing, or of exorcisms, but the following miracles were totally unprecedented. They were truly miracles of the Messiah. The people were called as witnesses, especially the religious authorities, to judge whether Jesus was the Messiah from their scriptural understanding. The choice was upon them, would they heed the word of God, or would they dispense with it at their own peril?

### 1. Heal an Israelite from leprosy

Leprosy in the ancient Jewish world was often considered a sign of divine punishment for sin and ritual uncleanness. Lepers were isolated from their communities as a preventative measure, and

---

[83] To see all of the miracles in chronological order with references across all four synoptic gospels, consult the following table provided by the Archdiocese of Washington: http://blog.adw.org/wp-content/uploads/2018/03/37-Miracles-of-Jesus-in-Chronological-Order.pdf.

[84] Radin, "The Four Messianic Miracles," *HaDerek Ministries*, https://www.haderekministries.com/index.php/articles/62-old-testament-new-testament-typology/164-the-four-messianic-miracles.

only the high priest was authorised to inspect and restore lepers back into the community (Lev. 13:1-46; 14:1-32).

We hear in Luke how in the time of Elisha the prophet, not one Israelite was cleansed of leprosy, only Naaman the Syrian (Luke 4:27). We have no recorded cases of a high priest, nor any other person, having healed an Israelite from leprosy before or after Elisha. Not in the Tanakh (Old Testament), nor in any historical record. In fact, Naaman was only cleansed of this affliction because God Himself had worked through Elisha—it was a miracle of God (2 Kgs. 5:1-14). When God personally healed Naaman, the great and respected army commander, Naaman was required to humble himself before Elisha and obey his instructions (2 Kgs. 5:8-19). This picture of humility squares perfectly with us today. We must all come to this place of humility before Jesus to be healed of the greater disease of sin and death.

The signs of the Messiah's coming are related to the miraculous healing of the lepers, as it is written in the Babylonian Talmud tractate *Sanhedrin*:

> *In the Talmud it is written, "When will the Messiah come?" And "By what sign may I recognize him?" Elijah tells the rabbi to go to the gate of the city where he will find the Messiah sitting among the poor lepers ... "The Messiah -- what is his name?... The sages say, the Leper Scholar, as it is said, 'surely he has borne our griefs and carried our sorrows: yet we did esteem him a leper, smitten of God and afflicted.'"*[85]

In fulfilment of the messianic expectations, Jesus did what no other man could by cleansing Israelites from leprosy (Matt. 8:1-4; Mark 1:40-44; Luke 5:12-16). Normally touching a leper would render those clean unclean, but Jesus had no reason to fear contamination because he was above impurity. To the contrary, he possessed the power to wash away the leprous contamination

---

[85] B. Talmud Sanhedrin 98a-b.

upon the man so that he too could be pure and whole—the very purpose of salvation.

This divine display of authority forced the Sanhedrin to seriously consider the possibility of Jesus being the Messiah. On one occasion when Jesus cleansed a man with leprosy, he sternly warned him "See that you don't tell this to anyone. But go, show yourself to the priest and offer the sacrifices that Moses commanded for your cleansing, as a testimony to them" (MARK 1:40-44). Those healed of their leprosy began to enter the temple to be purified under the law and no doubt gave testimony of Jesus. For the priesthood there could have been no stronger signal that an authority greater than them had arrived.

Besides authenticating Jesus' messiahship, these miraculous acts of healing taught us an important lesson. In the story of Jesus cleansing the ten men with leprosy, only one showed him gratitude, and he was a Samaritan, a foreigner seen as less than a gentile in the eyes of the Jews (LUKE 17:11-19).

> *"'Were not all ten cleansed? Where are the other nine? Has no one returned to give praise to God except this foreigner?' Then he said to him, 'Rise and go; your faith has made you well'" (Luke 17:11-19 NIV).*

This fits the familiar pattern of the hardened hearts of the Jews leading them to obey the law but not embody the law. With the exception of the foreigner, the lepers went to the priest in obedience of Jesus' instruction and were healed, but only in the physical sense. It was only the foreigner whose heart was softened to the extent that spiritual transformation was possible. He threw himself at Jesus' feet and praised God in a loud voice while the nine Jews did not even return (LUKE 17:15-16). Jesus unconditionally cured the sick of their physical ailments, but spiritual ailments—the sickness of the heart—were bound to the stubbornness of man.

> *The heart is deceitful above all things and beyond cure (Jer. 17:9 NIV).*

God can do all things, but He will only renew the spirits of those who are willing. It may not be our natural disposition to humble ourselves before God, but it is the key to our salvation.

## 2. Exorcise demons from the blind and mute

It was known that one could cast out demons through speaking with them in the name of the Lord, but to perform an exorcism on the blind and mute was unheard of. There was no biblical precedent for such a thing. Without the ability to physically interface with the demon, one must have held spiritual authority over the demonic realm itself, the source of the impurity. Therefore, when Jesus performed this miraculous sign in view of the people, they all wondered if he was the son of David, the anointed one (Messiah in the singular):

> *Then they brought him a demon-possessed man who was blind and mute, and Jesus healed him, so that he could both talk and see. All the people were astonished and said, "Could this be the Son of David?" But when the Pharisees heard this, they said, "It is only by Beelzebul, the prince of demons, that this fellow drives out demons" (Matt 12:22-24 NIV).*

The Pharisees still were not satisfied with the authentic messianic nature of this healing, attributing it to Beelzebul (Satan). They asked to see another sign from Jesus, to which he answered:

> *"A wicked and adulterous generation asks for a sign! But none will be given it except the sign of the prophet Jonah. For as Jonah was three days and three nights in the belly of a huge fish, so the Son of Man will be three days and three nights in the heart of the earth" (Matt. 12:38-40 NIV).*

He was telling them that there was no sign above that of the prophet Jonah, the resurrection from the dead. This was the ultimate miracle for which he came, the one of true consequence. Jesus commonly downplayed his miraculous works, even hiding them from the public, because his legitimacy did not depend on them, but this was not the case for the sign of Jonah (MATT. 8:4; 9:30; 12:16; 16:20; 17:9; MARK 1:44; 3:12; 5:43; 7:36; 8:30; 9:9; LUKE 4:41; 5:14; 8:56; 9:21). He told his disciples not to speak of him to the world until this sign was finally fulfilled (MATT. 17:9; MARK 9:9). It was to be global in scope—reaching all mankind. His substitutionary death would atone for our sins and heal us of our afflictions, but his resurrection would do much more than heal—it would save us from death itself. This is why he warned the Pharisees that if they remained fixed in their rebellious mindset after witnessing the sign of Jonah, judgement would come upon them (LUKE 11:29-32).

## 3. Restore the sight of the blind

On several occasions Jesus restored the sight of the blind, a feat which John reported nobody had ever seen (MATT. 9:27-31; 12:22-3; 20:29-34; MARK 8:22-26; 10:46-52; LUKE 11:14-23; 18:35-43; JOHN 9):

> "Nobody has ever heard of opening the eyes of a man born blind. If this man were not from God, he could do nothing" (John 9:32-33 NIV).

In each case of healing, their faithful obedience to the power of Jesus is stressed in the text, and for good reason. For example, only after the man born blind went and washed in the pool of Siloam in simple obedience to Jesus was he able to see (JOHN 9).

Notice how in contrast to these faithful men, when the Pharisees were alerted of this miracle, they chose to remain spiritually blind to the truth. They claimed Jesus was "not from God" for performing acts of healing on the Sabbath, a day of rest (JOHN 9:16). Jesus replied, "which is lawful on the Sabbath: to do good or to do evil, to save life or to kill?" (MARK 3:4). The Pharisees remained silent because they knew they had been caught out. They placed greater importance on their position of authority than on adhering to sound biblical interpretation. If they truly lived in accordance with God's commandments, they would have recognised the virtue of Jesus. Instead, they willingly closed their eyes to biblical revelation as it unfolded before them. On the other hand, the physically blind were quick to receive Jesus. This dichotomy was encapsulated wonderfully by Jesus when he said:

> *"For judgment I have come into this world, so that the blind will see and those who see will become blind.' Some Pharisees ... asked, 'What? Are we blind too?' Jesus said, 'If you were blind, you would not be guilty of sin; but now that you claim you can see, your guilt remains"* (John 9:39-41 NIV).

### 4. Resurrect a man after three days

The final messianic miracle was performed by Jesus when he raised Lazarus from the dead after four days (JOHN 11:43-48). Previously, Elijah and Elisha had resurrected the dead, but never after three days (1 KGS. 17:17-24; 2 KGS. 4:18-27). The contemporary Jewish understanding was that "for three days after death the soul hovers over the body intending to re-enter it."[86] By the fourth day corruption was said to have truly set in and life was gone. This is the uniform view present in the earliest rabbinic texts. It is written in the Babylonian Talmud tractate *Sanhedrin* that "after three days, the soul returns to God to await the time of resurrection,"[87] and this is affirmed in the Jerusalem Talmud tractate *Moed Qatan*:

> *For the first three days after death, the soul flutters over the body, thinking that she will return to it. When she sees that the appearance of the corpse deteriorates, she leaves the body and goes her way.*[88]

---

[86] Leviticus Rabbah 18:1; B. Talmud Semachot 8:1; Midrash Tanchuma Miqetz 4.
[87] B. Talmud Sanhedrin 90b-91a.
[88] Y. Talmud Mo'ed Qatan 3:5 [I:7 E] Jacob Neusner ed.

Fitting these expectations, Jesus deliberately stayed two more days in Jordan after receiving the request from Lazarus' sisters to come and heal their brother. By the time he arrived, Lazarus had been dead four days, past the point of corruption. When Jesus raised him from the dead, many believed him to be the Messiah and word of the miracle quickly reached the religious authorities:

> *Then the chief priests and the Pharisees called a meeting of the Sanhedrin. "What shall we do? For this Man works many signs. If we let Him alone like this, everyone will believe in Him, and the Romans will come and take away both our place and nation" (John 11:46-48 NIV).*

Jesus had conquered the ultimate impurity from the human perspective, and yet the Sanhedrin still refused to acknowledge him as Messiah. In fact, they "made plans to kill Lazarus as well, for on account of him many of the Jews were going over to Jesus and believing in him" (JOHN 12:9-11).

The insistent refusal to acknowledge these messianic signs can only be explained by a deep-seated attitude for rebellion (1 SAM. 15:23). Jesus made it plain to them that he was the seed of the woman, the divine son of Man prophesied by Daniel, and the Messiah. It could not be ignored by them that these mighty miraculous acts from Jesus showed God had entrusted him with all authority. He demonstrated to them that he ruled over the impure realm which had entered into humanity because of the deception of the serpent in Eden.

## Conclusion

Jesus, in declaring he was one with the Father, was speaking in accordance with the word of God as the prophet greater than Moses (DEUT. 18:15–19). He was the long-awaited seed of the woman, God manifested in the flesh. The creator of all things and the one who sustains them. To Jesus was given the right to justly silence all accusations by the satanic realm against the Godhead, and to open the eyes and hearts of men and women who had trusted in their mighty deceptions. The ultimate messianic miracle he promised the people was to offer himself as the unblemished sacrifice for mankind and resurrect to life as a new creation. This shall be the subject of the remaining two chapters.

# 5

# Righteous Atonement

In the beginning of this book we outlined how Jesus' divinity is confirmed by his fulfilment of the appointed festivals God gave to Moses and the Israelites (Lev. 23; Exod. 12-13; 23:14-19; 34:18-26; Num. 9:1-14; 28-29; Deut. 16; 26). God sent Jesus, the prophet that Moses himself warned his people to follow, to live out these appointed festivals at their appointed time (Deut. 18:15-22):

> But when the fullness of the time had come, God sent forth His Son, born of a woman, born under the law, to redeem those who were under the law, that we might receive the adoption as sons (Gal. 4:4-5 NKJV).

Each of the seven feasts honoured the story of their salvation both historically, and prophetically—the past and the future. The entire redemptive plan of God was embedded within them. The apostle Paul, in his letter to the Colossians, affirmed that the feasts were a shadow of an even greater reality:

> Therefore, do not let anyone judge you by what you eat or drink, or with regard to a religious festival, a New Moon celebration or a Sabbath day. These are a shadow of the things that were to come; the reality, however, is found in Christ (Col. 2:16-17 NIV).

By holding the feasts, the people were simultaneously celebrating their history while rehearsing for their future as if they were acts of a play. Consider how God established each of the feasts as "holy convocations" (Hebrew *miqra qodesh*) (Lev. 23; Exod. 12; 16; Num. 28:18-26). The word *miqra* can be used as a convocation or assembly, and also as a rehearsal. The word *qodesh* denotes that the convocation or assembly is sacred. In the words of Rabbi Dr. Greg Killian, thus, "miqra defines an assembly of people for the purposes of rehearsing." Killian also noted how by celebrating the feasts, the participants, or actors in the final acts of the play, "will be in the right place, at the right time, wearing the right clothes, saying the right words, and doing the right things."[89]

*Image 5.1 – The seven feasts of the Lord in the Mosaic Law (OT)*

| FEAST | HISTORICAL SIGNIFICANCE |
|---|---|
| **SPRING** | |
| Passover | Blood of the lamb saved the firstborns of Israel from death during the tenth plague upon Egypt. |
| Unleavened Bread | God freed the Israelites from captivity in Egypt and in haste, they departed with unleavened bread. |
| Firstfruits | God parted the Red Sea for the fleeing Israelites and raised them to new life as the firstfruits. |
| Pentecost | Giving of the Law at Mount Sinai fifty days from the beginning of the Exodus. |
| **FALL** | |
| Trumpets | Sacred time for Israel to gather together and rest. |
| Day of Atonement | Day of national repentance and cleansing of the sanctuary and the people for the year. |
| Tabernacles | God provided for the Israelites during the forty years in the wilderness and dwelled with them in Tabernacles. |

The first four feasts occurred in spring (Passover, Unleavened Bread, First Fruits, and Pentecost) and the last three in the fall (Trumpets, Atonement and Tabernacles). The two clusters coincide with the first and second comings of Jesus and is when

---

[89] Killian, "HaShem's Rehearsals," *Betemunah*, https://www.betemunah.org/rehearse.html.

they find their respective fulfilments. The feasts culminate with the final great harvest of Tabernacles, and this points to the spiritual harvests of souls that Jesus shall gather into God's tabernacle. The following chapter shall deal with the last two spring feasts of First Fruits and Pentecost. These relate to the resurrection of Jesus as the first fruits of the dead, and the subsequent outpouring of the Holy Spirit upon the disciples on Pentecost which ushered in the age of the Church under the grace of the new covenant. For this chapter we shall deal with the first two spring feasts of Passover and Unleavened Bread which are celebrated by Jews every year in remembrance of their exodus from Egypt by the mighty hand of the Lord (Exod. 12-13; Deut. 16:1-8).

## Preparation for Deliverance

The spring feasts began to be directly fulfilled from the time of Jesus' triumphal entry into Jerusalem on Palm Sunday (Nisan 10), four days before the Passover (Matt. 21:1-11; Mark 11:1-11; Luke 19:28-44; John 12:1, 12-19). This was the very day when the lambs were chosen for inspection in preparation for the Passover sacrifice (Exod. 12:3-5). The lambs that were found to be without blemish were sacrificed on the 14th of Nisan to remind the Israelites of the night the blood of the lamb delivered them from bondage (Deut. 16:1-8; Lev. 23:5; Exod. 12:1-13, 21-28; Num. 9:1-4). Jesus was essentially announcing to the religious authorities that he was the ultimate purpose of the Passover. He was living out a future dimension of deliverance from a king greater than Pharaoh (John 1:29). Take note of this timeline as we continue through his final week on earth.

As he made his way through the city, the people shouted, "Hosanna! ["save" or "rescue us now"] 'Blessed is he who comes in the name of the Lord!'" in reference back to Psalm 118:25-26 (Matt. 21:9, 15; Mark 11:9-10; John 12:13). This was an exclamation of joyous hope for their Messiah, "the blessed one who saves." The idea of redemption fixed within their minds was that Jesus was about to "grant them success and prosperity" by leading them straight into the messianic kingdom. They were not aware that he was coming to them not as the conquering king (Mashiach ben David), but as the suffering servant (Mashiach ben Joseph). This was the beginning of a second Exodus, not the end. Their slave masters were not the earthly tyrant of Rome (for others had come before and would come after) but the heavenly tyrant of Lucifer (JOHN 8:34). Just as the Israelites could not come into possession of the promised land (Tabernacles) unless they were delivered out of Egypt by the Passover, the same is true for mankind enslaved by the kingdom of Satan. Jesus rode into Jerusalem upon a donkey and a colt at his first coming because he was fighting the spiritual kingdom of Satan, not Rome. This war did not call for violence or military force. He will return as a conquering king upon the clouds of heaven because the earthly powers of Antichrist must be destroyed before the messianic kingdom is established (ISA. 62:11; MATT. 21:1-7). Even the early rabbis perceived the functions of Christ's first and second comings, as recorded in the Talmudic tractate *Sanhedrin*:

> *It is written: "There came with the clouds of heaven, one like unto a son of man ... and there was given him dominion and glory and a kingdom ... his dominion is an everlasting dominion" (Dan. 7:13–14). And it is written: "Behold, your king will come to you; he is just and victorious; lowly and riding upon a donkey and upon a colt, the foal of a donkey" (Zech. 9:9). Rabbi Alexandri explains: If the Jewish people merit redemption, the Messiah will come in a miraculous manner with the clouds of heaven. If they do not merit redemption, the Messiah will come lowly and riding upon a donkey.*[90]

Fitting these expectations, Jesus did not ascend the steps to the praetorium and cast out the Romans as the Jews had hoped. Instead he entered the Temple, the most sacred and important place in Jewish life, and began to cast out those who were

---

[90] B. Talmud Sanhedrin 98a.13.

exchanging goods. Out of anger that the Temple was being desecrated by sin, Jesus exclaimed, "do not make my Father's house a house of merchandise" and "you have made it a den of thieves" (MATT. 21:12-13; MARK 11:15-18; LUKE 19:45-48; JOHN 2:13-21). Jesus took matters into his own hands to illustrate that he was, as John the Baptiser said, the "Lamb of God who takes away the sin of the world" (JOHN 1:29, 36). The purging of sin from the Temple prefigured the ultimate atonement for sin when the true Passover lamb was sacrificed four days later. Over these four days of inspection, the religious authorities tested the Lamb of God for fault but found not one blemish. Clearly frustrated, they misattributed his messianic miracles and prophetic words to Beelzebub, a pejorative used for the Canaanite god, Baal (MATT. 12:22-24; MARK 3:22). The Jewish preacher Jacob Prasch made an interesting observation on their hypocrisy in his book *The Final Words of Jesus and Satan's Lies*:

> The Sanhedrin were responsible for the purging of leaven from Jerusalem before the Passover Feast. However, when Jesus drove the moneychangers out of the Temple, it was He who performed the true purging of leaven at Passover time. Where the Sanhedrin had merely removed physical leaven, Jesus removed the actual leaven.[91]

Seeing how popular Jesus was with the people, and how dangerous he was to their power, "they schemed to arrest Jesus secretly and kill him" (MATT. 26:3-5; MARK 14:1-2; LUKE 20:22-40). But even in their efforts to frustrate prophecy they would inadvertently fulfil it.

*The Last Supper*
On the evening of Nisan 14 (the beginning of the Jewish day) Jesus was gathered with his disciples to share the Passover Seder before

---

[91] Prasch, *The Final Words of Jesus and Satan's Lies*, chap. 3.

his imminent arrest, trial, and execution (MATT. 26:17-30; MARK 14:12-26; LUKE 22:7-22; JOHN 13:1-39).[92] Known to us today as the Last Supper, the Passover Seder is the ritual feast which takes place on the eve of Passover. The proceedings of the Passover Seder are inextricably linked to the Feast of Unleavened Bread which begin the following day. Today these two feasts are synonymous, and celebrations start a day later than the biblical calendar.[93] Historically speaking, the Israelites were released from slavery in Egypt as the day of Passover turned over into the day of Unleavened Bread, and began their journey to the promised land during the night (NUM. 33:1-4). The story goes that because the Egyptians were terrified of God's wrath after the final plague they urged the Israelites to leave in haste (EXOD. 12:33). Before their dough even had time to rise, the Israelites trekked into the wilderness and subsisted on this unleavened bread until the Lord provided them with the heavenly bread called *manna* (EXOD. 12:34-39; 16). In remembrance of this momentous deliverance, at the giving of the law at Mount Sinai, the Lord established the annual feasts of Passover (Nisan 14) and Unleavened Bread (Nisan 15-21) (EXOD. 12:1-28; 23:15-18; LEV. 23:4-8; NUM. 28:16-25). During the seven-day feast of Unleavened Bread, the people were only to eat *matzah* (unleavened bread) and *maror* (bitter herbs) to commemorate their journey to physical and spiritual freedom (EXOD. 12:11-20; 13:3-10; DEUT. 16:3-4).

Besides leaven being a product of haste, the New Testament strongly associates it with impurity, sin, pride, hypocrisy, rebellion, and false doctrine (MATT. 16:5-12; MARK 8:15; LUKE 12:1). As an allusion to the pervasiveness of sin, it is said that "a little leaven

---

[92] For more on the connection between the Last Supper and the Passover Seder read the Tyndale journal 53.2 article "Passover and Last Supper" by Robin Routledge:
https://legacy.tyndalehouse.com/tynbul/Library/TynBull_2002_53_2_03_R outledge_PassoverLastSupper.pdf.

[93] The distinction between Passover and Unleavened Bread gradually blurred because with the destruction of the temple, the offering of the lamb could no longer be made. The Jews were forced to celebrate the feast differently.

leavens the whole lump" (GAL. 5:9; 1 COR. 5:6-8). You can also understand leaven as being that which puffs up bread to appear to be more than it really is:

> *See, the enemy is puffed up; his desires are not upright— but the righteous person will live by his faithfulness (Hab. 2:4 NIV).*

On the contrary, unleavened bread represents purity (free from leaven), goodness, humility, faithfulness, and sound doctrine (1 COR. 5:6-9). With this context in mind, at the Passover Seder, Jesus recontextualised the unleavened bread, the bread of affliction, as his own body, and his blood as the symbol of a new covenant:

> *"'I have eagerly desired to eat this Passover with you before I suffer. For I tell you, I will not eat it again until it finds fulfilment in the kingdom of God.' After taking the cup, he gave thanks and said, 'Take this and divide it among you. For I tell you I will not drink again from the fruit of the vine until the kingdom of God comes.' And he took bread, gave thanks and broke it, and gave it to them, saying, 'This is my body given for you; do this in remembrance of me.' In the same way, after the supper he took the cup, saying, 'This cup is the new covenant in my blood, which is poured out for you'"* (Luke 22:15-20 NIV).

The Luciferic covenant had been ratified by Adam and Eve and symbolically affirmed by eating the forbidden fruit. Jesus allowed us to cut a new covenant with God ratified by faith, and symbolically affirmed by partaking in his flesh and blood through the bread and wine (MATT. 26:26-28; LUKE 22:19-20; JOHN 6:45-59; 1 COR. 10:16-17; 11:23-26). This covenant was established in a similar fashion to the old covenant under Moses:

> *And Moses took the blood, sprinkled it on the people, and said, "This is the blood of the covenant which the LORD has made with you according to all these words" (Exod. 24:8 NKJV).*

Before the new covenant could be established however, Jesus was required to live and die a life totally free of leaven to become an acceptable Passover sacrifice. That is to say, he must remain totally unblemished and pure in heart by perfectly following the commandments of God. To this point there had yet to be found any trace of leaven within him, so he was justified in declaring himself as the ultimate Passover sacrifice. Remember that Jesus made this same declaration of himself after he fed the five thousand:

> *"I am the bread of life. Your fathers ate the manna in the wilderness, and are dead. This is the bread which comes down from heaven, that one may eat of it and not die. I am the living bread which came down from heaven. If anyone eats of this bread, he will live forever; and the bread that I shall give is My flesh, which I shall give for the life of the world" ... Then Jesus said to them, "Most assuredly, I say to you, unless you eat the flesh of the Son of Man and drink His blood, you have no life in you. Whoever eats My flesh and drinks My blood has eternal life, and I will raise him up at the last day. For My flesh is food indeed, and My blood is drink indeed. He who eats My flesh and drinks My blood abides in Me, and I in him. As the living Father sent Me, and I live because of the Father, so he who feeds on Me will live because of Me. This is the bread which came down from heaven—not as your fathers ate the manna, and are dead. He who eats this bread will live forever" (John 6:48-58 NKJV).*

This final statement that his flesh was the true bread from which we were to eat caused many to turn away from him (JOHN 6:66). For those who could accept these bitter words (symbolised by the bitter herbs, the maror), their sorrow would soon be turned to joy (JOHN 6:60-65). By celebrating Jesus in this manner through the communion, the Eucharist, believers both Jewish or gentile partake of the bread and wine in the present to remember his work of deliverance and atonement in the past in anticipation of his return in the future. Along with baptism, the Eucharist is a declaration to the Luciferic principalities that they have been separated from their domain and rule.

But his own people—the Jews—only acknowledge him to be the true unleavened bread symbolically through the Passover Seder. God said they would be His witness people to the nations even in unbelief. This happens to be one of their testimonies. As with all the feasts, they rehearse for the day their hardened minds and shrouded hearts are opened to the Lord, and they finally understand the true significance of their performance (2 COR. 3:14-15). God said of this day:

> "I will pour on the house of David and on the inhabitants of Jerusalem the Spirit of grace and supplication; then they will look on Me whom they pierced. Yes, they will mourn for Him as one mourns for his only son, and grieve for Him as one grieves for a firstborn" (Zech. 12:10 NKJV).

It is only in act that they currently accept their culpability (along with all of humanity) in preparing Jesus as the bread of affliction. They cannot truly eat it (believe in true faith) until they are circumcised in the heart (JOHN 6:47-51).

### Testimony of the Seder

The basis for contemporary Passover Seder proceedings is the Mishnaic and Talmudic period text *Pesach Haggadah*. Some of these steps would have been familiar to Jesus but others would have been added over time. There are more steps and details to the Seder than I will describe here, but the following are some of the main testaments to him.[94]

During the seder, three pieces of unleavened bread called matzah are each placed inside three separate pouches of a bag called the matzah tosh, or put on a matzah plate.[95] Later into the service the second or middle matzah is taken out and broken in half. The smaller half is returned but the larger half is wrapped in linen cloth and hidden. The hidden piece becomes the *afikomen*, known as the "dessert which comes later" because it is the sweetest part. According to the late Jewish scholar David Daube, among others, the word of origin is the Greek *afikomenos*, meaning "the coming one."[96] The children are tasked with locating the afikomen near the end of the ceremony and, according to *Haggadot*, the largest online resource for the Haggadah, it is so precious and "essential to the story of redemption" that until it is found and the child is rewarded, the service cannot conclude. After the afikomen is found, it is brought back to be "embraced, enjoyed, and celebrated." It is broken into pieces and shared by everyone as the last meal of the service. No more food or wine is allowed to be consumed after the afikomen is eaten.

The two halves of the middle matzah speak to the hypostatic union of Christ—his divinity and humanity. The smaller half which is kept inside the unity bag corresponds to Jesus' divine

---

[94] Visual infographics of the Passover Seder proceedings courtesy of NCSY: https://ncsy.org/passover-seder-cheat-sheet-infographic/.

[95] A common Jewish interpretation of the three matzos is the unity of "the three patriarchs, Abraham, Isaac, and Jacob, by whose merit [they] were redeemed from Egypt and whose covenant with God [they] were redeemed to fulfil." Would this suggest the broken middle matzah relates to the middle patriarch, Isaac? We previously discussed how the binding of Isaac alluded to the sacrifice of Jesus, but he was never sacrificed. What can we say about the two halves? Where does redemption through the afikomen fit into the story of Isaac? It seems to me there are more parallels to match to his successor, Jesus. Perhaps the ultimate picture is in the unity of the greater, spiritual patriarchs of the triune Godhead. Under this interpretation, the first matzah represents God the Father, the second Jesus the Son, and the third the Holy Spirit.

[96] Jews for Jesus, *The Passover Symbols and Their Messianic Significance*, https://jewsforjesus.org/blog/the-passover-symbols-and-their-messianic-significance/.

nature which is unseen. The afikomen symbolises his humanity stripped away for our redemption. We see this with the Passover Seder that was the Last Supper. Jesus broke bread (afikomen) and shared it between his disciples, stating: "this is my body which is given for you; do this in remembrance of Me" (MATT. 26:17–29; MARK 14:12–25; LUKE 22:7–22; 1 COR. 11:24). He became the afikomen. His sinless and unleavened body was broken in death, wrapped in cloth, hidden in the grave, and then brought back to be partaken of by his people. The afikomen is the last meal allowed to be consumed because salvation only comes from Jesus. It must be consumed before the service concludes because without Jesus we cannot be saved, nor can the end come for this world.

As we know, Jesus has yet to be fully "embraced, enjoyed, and celebrated" as the afikomen or "coming one." The gentiles have found him as the afikomen (e.g. Eucharist), but Israel have not because of the veil of unbelief which covers their eyes (ACTS 28:26-27; JOHN 12:37-41; ROM. 10:16-21; 11:7-10; 2 COR. 3:14; DEUT. 29:3-4; PSA. 69:22-23; ISA. 6:9-10). As Jesus said, "seeing they do not see, and hearing they do not hear, nor do they understand" (MATT. 13:13-15). A great example of this spiritual blindness comes from the popular Jewish Hasidic authority *Chabad*:

> *The afikomen represents our liberation from Egyptian exile. That redemption, however, was not a complete one, as we are still awaiting the final redemption with the coming of Moshiach. Setting aside or hiding the larger half of the matzah reminds us that the best, the real redemption, is yet to come, still hidden in the future.*[97]

Here it is acknowledged that the Messiah is portrayed by the afikomen, but not that the Messiah and his redemption has already come. To be clear, the gentiles are not elevated above

---

[97] Shurpin, "Why Do We Hide the Afikomen?" *Chabad*, https://www.chabad.org/holidays/passover/pesach_cdo/aid/2910434/jewish/Why-Do-We-Hide-the-Afikomen.htm.

Israel as a people who are more faithful. Paul the Apostle explained that salvation came to the gentiles through the fall of Israel, and that "blindness in part has happened to Israel until the fullness of the gentiles has come in ... so all Israel will be saved" (ROM. 11:11-27). It all is for the ultimate purpose of salvation, "for if their being cast away is the reconciling of the world, what will their acceptance be but life from the dead?" (ROM. 11:15). Salvation will come to the world again through Israel during the day of the Lord. Israel will be humbled to earnestly seek their afikomen like children, for as Jesus said: "unless you change and become like little children, you will never enter the kingdom of heaven" (MATT. 18:3-4; 19:14; MARK 10:14-15; LUKE 18:16-17).

> *"Ask, and it will be given to you; seek, and you will find; knock, and it will be opened to you. For everyone who asks receives, and he who seeks finds, and to him who knocks it will be opened" (Matt. 7:7 NKJV).*

Israel will discover the afikomen Jesus in the flesh and finally accept him into their hearts as their salvation. At last the ultimate Passover Seder of the age will be able to conclude, and Israel and the Church will be united together in the millennial kingdom and in the new heaven and earth.

## Gethsemane to Golgotha

The unlawful trial of the righteous one Jesus Christ commenced shortly after he shared the Last Supper with his apostles. One of the twelve named Judas Iscariot was aligned with the spiritual entities of darkness and handed him over to those desperate to corrupt his unleavened character (EPH. 6:12):

> *Let us lie in wait for the righteous one, because he is annoying to us; he opposes our actions, reproaches us for transgressions of the law and charges us with violations of our training. He professes to have knowledge of God and styles himself a child of the Lord. To us he is the*

> *censure of our thoughts; merely to see him is a hardship for us, because his life is not like that of others, and different are his ways. He judges us debased; he holds aloof from our paths as from things impure. He calls blest the destiny of the righteous and boasts that God is his Father. Let us see whether his words be true; let us find out what will happen to him in the end. For if the righteous one is the son of God, God will help him and deliver him from the hand of his foes. With violence and torture let us put him to the test that we may have proof of his gentleness and try his patience. Let us condemn him to a shameful death; for according to his own words, God will take care of him"* (Wisdom 2:12-20 NABRE).

This prophetic message came from the Jewish apocryphal or deuterocanonical *Book of Wisdom* from the first-century BC. What they could not foresee was that God had mandated the rejection and condemnation unto death of His own son, "the righteous one," from before the foundation of the world (1 PET. 1:18-20). In fact, the "righteous one" as the son of God had to suffer this death to uphold the righteousness of God Himself. Any righteous value that we are to receive comes through his death, but his righteousness in death is dependent on his life as a man. In other words, if he has not lived a perfectly righteous life, he has nothing of value to offer in his death. Anything less than perfection from the human incarnation of God would prove God to be less than perfect. Lucifer's accusations against him (in the heavenly realm before creation) would therefore be justified, and the push towards independence warranted. Eternal reality would fall under the authority of the serpent to shape at his own will, so the perfection of Jesus at the cross was required to prevent this reality. The mystery to be revealed was that God would deliver His son, and by him all mankind, through his death and resurrection. Death itself would be defeated, the chains of sin initiated by Satan broken, and the exacting demands of the law met perfectly (ROM. 4:20-24; 5:21; 1 COR. 15:55-56).

First the righteous one in Christ was led to the house of the high priest Caiaphas where a council of priests and elders had gathered for his interrogation (MATT. 26:45-68; MARK 14:43-65; LUKE 22:47-71; JOHN 18:3-24; PSA. 41:9; ACTS 1:16). All in attendance sought false testimony to convict him to death but came up with nothing. He was truly without fault—pure and unblemished. When he affirmatively answered that he was in fact the promised Son of Man spoken of by Daniel, the "Messiah, the Son of God" (DAN. 7:13-14; MATT. 26:62-64; MARK 14:61-62; LUKE 22:66-71), the high priest Caiaphas tore his priestly garments in rage, and condemned him for blasphemy, a crime punishable by death. The Sanhedrin was quick to concur with his judgement and all of them together demanded his death (MATT. 26:57-68; MARK 14:63:63; LUKE 22:67-71).

Early that morning they rushed to the Roman governor Pontius Pilate who wielded the authority to have Jesus executed (MATT. 26:65-66; MARK 14:64; 15:1; LUKE 23:1-2; JOHN 18:31-32). During his formal trial, Pilate found "no basis for a charge against him" and was reluctant to sentence him to death (MATT. 27:23-24; MARK 14:14; LUKE 23:4; 13-22; JOHN 18:38; 19:4-6). The Sanhedrin remained insistent that he yield to their demands and execute their hated enemy. As it was the Passover and it "was the governor's custom at the festival to release a prisoner chosen by the crowd," Pilate offered the Jews one last opportunity to save their Messiah. He put before the crowd their Messiah Jesus and a murderous insurrectionist, a false Messiah, named "Barabbas" or in some manuscripts and translations, "Jesus Barabbas" (MATT. 25:16-17; MARK 15:7; LUKE 23:18-19; JOHN 18:40).[98] The Aramaic name Bar-abba (Barabbas) means son of the Father, while Jesus *is* the son of the Father. We therefore

---

[98] Some scholars suggest that the earliest manuscripts included "Jesus Barabbas" but the "Jesus" was later omitted because it became sacred. Metzger, "a Textual Commentary on the Greek New Testament," 56: The early theologian Origen stated: "In many copies it is not stated that Barabbas was also called 'Jesus,' and perhaps [the omission] is right." Origen goes on to defend this assertion on the basis that no one in the Bible "who is a sinner [is called] Jesus."
Subsequently, many modern English translations of Matt. 27:16-17 such as the NIV, RSV, and ESV follow the ancient manuscripts which render the name "Jesus Barabbas."

have two sons of the Father named Jesus: one who loves the true God (godly), and one who rebels against Him (ungodly). One is the true Christ (Messiah) while the other is a false Christ (a type of the Antichrist). Barabbas the freedom fighter, seeking to free his people from slavery to Rome, and Jesus the freedom fighter, seeking to free his people from slavery to Satan and the associated consequence of death. The crowd remained adamant that the innocent Jesus be crucified, and the guilty Barabbas be released, so Pilate granted their wish, but not before washing his hands of his innocent blood, inadvertently declaring him unblemished and fit for sacrifice as the Passover lamb (EXOD. 12:3:14; MATT. 27:26-31; MARK 15:15-20; LUKE 23:20-25; JOHN 19:16).

Sadly, the people of Israel who demanded Barabbas be released and Jesus be condemned did so for the wrong reason. When they said to Pilate, "his blood be upon us and our children," they did not yet see his blood upon them as their salvation, they were only trying to expedite his death sentence. For this decision they have suffered great persecution and hatred from the gentiles. Even Christians (replacement theology) can be quick to assume that they would have judged differently. In reality, many of these types will join the unbelieving world in worshipping the Antichrist (Barabbas) as the Christ when he comes. The truth is that God necessitated this outcome, and wants us to rejoice in that day the Jews chose Barabbas over Jesus. In reference to this event, the apostle Peter proclaimed that by rejecting Jesus, he become the chief cornerstone of a new spiritual temple as prophesied in the Psalms (ACTS 4:8-11):

> The Lord's right hand [Jesus] has done mighty things! The Lord's right hand is lifted high ... The stone the builders rejected has become the cornerstone; the Lord has done this, and it is marvellous in our eyes. The Lord has done it this very day; let us rejoice today and be glad (Psa. 118:15-16, 22-24 NIV).

At the beginning of this section we heard the Jewish prophecy from the book of Wisdom that they would one day try and execute the "righteous one." In the book of Acts, Peter associated the "righteous one" with the unjust trial and execution of Christ. I implore you to read these two passages to see the uncanny connection:

> *The God of Abraham, Isaac and Jacob, the God of our fathers, has glorified his servant Jesus. You handed him over to be killed, and you disowned him before Pilate, though he had decided to let him go. You disowned the Holy and Righteous One and asked that a murderer be released to you. You killed the author of life, but God raised him from the dead. We are witnesses of this ... Now, fellow Israelites, I know that you acted in ignorance, as did your leaders. But this is how God fulfilled what he had foretold through all the prophets, saying that his Messiah would suffer ... For truly against Your holy Servant Jesus, whom You anointed, both Herod and Pontius Pilate, with the Gentiles and the people of Israel, were gathered together to do whatever Your hand and Your purpose determined before to be done (Acts 3:13-15, 17-18, 27-28 NIV).*

### Jesus for the Lord, Barabbas for Azazel

The outcome of the choice between Jesus and Barabbas was foreshadowed in the ceremonial sacrifice that took place every year on the Day of Atonement, the most important day of the Jewish calendar (LEV. 16; 23:26-32; EXOD. 30:9-10). While this day falls outside of the timeline of Jesus' death, it was at the same time necessary for him to become the Day of Atonement sacrifice which took place much later in the year (Tishri 10). Since man can die only once, and Jesus was himself a man, he was required to become a dual-sacrifice (HEB. 9:27-28). The Passover sacrifice would deliver us from the greater Pharaoh of Satan and sin itself, and the Day of Atonement sacrifice would permanently cleanse the sanctuary from the people's sins to make for their reconciliation with God (GAL. 3-4).[99] The Passover would be fulfilled in a literal and temporal sense, he would die as the Passover lamb on its appointed day of Nisan 14, but the Day of Atonement would be partially accomplished in a spiritual sense.[100] Its fulfilment will likewise occur on its appointed day of Tishri 10 when Jesus returns during the fall.

In the same manner as the trial, the high priest was presented with two near-identical goats taken from the flock of Israel (Jesus and Barabbas) and cast lots for them (LEV. 16:5-10).[101] The outcome of the lottery was divinely determined, as it was for Jesus and Barabbas (PROV. 16:33). Two beings were assigned for two distinct purposes. The goat cast with the white stone (in the right hand) was "for the Lord" and was sacrificed as a burnt offering to atone for the sanctuary and the people (LEV. 16:12-19).[102] The goat cast with the black stone (in the left hand) was "for Azazel" (often translated scapegoat),[103] and was driven into the wilderness with the sins of the people symbolically transferred upon its head (LEV. 16:10, 20-22).

---

[99] Parsons, "Behold the Goat of God!" *Hebrew for Christians*, https://www.hebrew4christians.com/Holidays/Fall_Holidays/Yom_Kippur/Goat_of_God/goat_of_god.html: *"Yeshua both offered Himself up as the "Lamb of God" that causes the wrath of God to (eternally) pass over those who personally trust in Him, and He also offered himself as the "Goat of God" whose blood was sprinkled in the Holy of Holies to cleanse us from sin and give us (everlasting) atonement."*

[100] Siker, "Yom Kippuring Passover: Recombinant Sacrifice in Early Christianity," chap. 5 in *Ritual and Metaphor*: *"The temporal connection between Jesus' death and Passover is inevitable since Jesus died in close proximity to this crucial festival. But John appears to import into the meaning of Jesus' death the atoning significance typically associated with the observance of Yom Kippur. John thus blurs the distinctions we might make in order to make a larger point about the unparalleled significance of the death of Jesus as the Lamb of God."*

[101] The identical nature of the goats is attested to in Mishnah Yoma 6.1, B. Talmud Chullin 11a:17, the first-century Epistle of Barnabas 7:6-10.

[102] Mishnah Yoma 5.

[103] The term "scapegoat" was coined by William Tyndale as he tried to make sense of the Hebrew term Azazel, and was later popularised in the King James translation.

Because the term "Azazel" is mentioned nowhere else in the Bible, the meaning and significance of the live goat sent to Azazel has long been argued.[104] One theory popularised by the second-century church father Origen is that two divine beings, God and Satan, are being contrasted by the two goats.[105] The most obvious sign for this in the text is the parallelism between the phrases "for the Lord" and "for Azazel." In their comprehensive commentary of the Old Testament, Keil and Delitzsch elaborated on this perspective:

> *The words, one lot for Jehovah and one for Azazel, require unconditionally that Azazel should be regarded as a personal being, in opposition to Jehovah ... the devil himself, the head of the fallen angels, who was afterwards called Satan; for no subordinate evil spirit could have been placed in antithesis to Jehovah as Azazel is here, but only the ruler or head of the kingdom of demons. The desert and desolate places are mentioned*

---

[104] Armstrong, *God's Festivals and Holy Days*, 29: "Some have seen this goat [Azazel] as a symbol of Christ, who in a sense, became the "scapegoat" for human sins though he himself was perfectly innocent. According to this explanation, Christ, in effect, carried our sins into the wilderness where the devil will be exiled. Another explanation focuses on the scapegoat as a symbol of Satan, who is ultimately responsible for human sin and who will be removed from contact with humanity at the second coming of Christ." For detailed interpretations of the ceremony and of the term Azazel see: Aron Pinker, "A Goat to Go to Azazel," *Journal of Hebrew Scriptures* 7 (2007): 3-16; Ralph D Levy, *The Symbolism of the Azazel Goat*, 26-39; Jacob Milgrom, *Leviticus 1-16*, on Lev. 16:20-22, 1010; Yaw Adu-Gyamfi, "The Live Goat Ritual in Leviticus 16," *Scriptura* 112 (2013): 1-10.

[105] Origen, *Homilies on Leviticus 1-16*, homily 9-10; Jerome, *The Homilies of Saint Jerome*, homily 93: "In the end, our he-goat will be immolated before the altar of the Lord; their buck, the Antichrist, spit upon and cursed, will be cast into the wilderness."; Heiser, "The Day of Atonement in Leviticus 16: A Goat for Azazel," *Dr. Michael Heiser*, https://drmsh.com/day-atonement-leviticus-16-goat-azazel/.

> elsewhere as the abode of evil spirits (Isa. 13:21; 34:14; Matt. 12:43; Luke 11:24; Rev. 18:2).[106]

I happen to agree with this assessment of the text, and would go even further with the dualistic theme of God versus Satan, godly versus ungodly. As I discussed in the companion book "Seed of Satan: Antichrist," the divergent destinies of the godly Abel and ungodly Cain, Shem and Canaan, Jacob and Esau, are a microcosm of the final conflict between Jesus (God) and Satan. The story of Jesus and Barabbas is no different. I do not believe that Jesus acted as both goats simultaneously. In his innocence, he substituted himself for the guilty Barabbas, becoming the sacrificial goat for the Lord, while Barabbas was released as the live goat for Azazel.[107] In the words of Origen:

> *"[A]s a type of things to come this one he-goat was sacrificed to the Lord as an offering and the other one sent away 'living.' Hear in the Gospels what Pilate said to the priests and the Jewish people: 'Which of these two do you want me to send out to you, Jesus, who is called the Christ, or Barabbas?' Then all the people cried out to release Barabbas but to hand Jesus over to be killed. Behold, you have a he-goat who was sent 'living into the wilderness,' bearing with him the sins of the people who cried out and said, 'Crucify, crucify.'"*[108]

Although it is said the two goats were taken together as a sin offering (LEV. 16:5), and indeed both were necessary for the atonement, only the goat for the Lord was a sacrificial offering.

---

[106] Keil and Delitzsch, "Biblical Commentary on the Old Testament," on Leviticus 16.6-10.

[107] Origen, "Against Celsus" in *The Ante-Nicene Fathers*, vol. 4: *"Moreover (the goat), which in the book of Leviticus is sent away (into the wilderness), and which in the Hebrew language is named Azazel, was none other than this [the devil]."*

[108] Ibid., *Homilies on Leviticus 1-16*, homily 10.2-3.

Again, two distinct beings for two distinct purposes. The guilty and sinful Barabbas had nothing to offer in his sacrifice, but the spotless and unblemished Jesus had everything. The goat intended for Azazel was corrupted by the world's filth and because it was left to roam the wilderness it forever remained in this condition. It was neither intended as a sacrifice for the Lord, nor was it eligible, and it was certainly not a sin offering for Azazel as this would be idolatrous worship (EXOD. 20:3-6; 22:20; LEV. 17:7; DEUT. 32:17; 2 CHR. 34:25; 1 COR. 10:20).[109] It was simply the vehicle to dispatch sin to its source in the wilderness, the desolate and God forsaken domain of Satan (MATT. 4:1; MARK 1:12-13; LUKE 4:1-2; 8:29).[110]

It is made clear throughout chapters 8 to 10 of Hebrews that Christ performed the Day of Atonement ceremony in the heavenly tabernacle (HEB. 8-10). He is explicitly positioned as the high priest of this "true tabernacle" and the antitype of the goat for the Lord:

> *But Christ came as High Priest of the good things to come, with the greater and more perfect tabernacle not made with hands, that is, not of this creation. Not with the blood of goats and calves, but with His own blood He entered the Most Holy Place once for all, having obtained eternal redemption ... For Christ has not entered the holy places made with hands, which are copies of the true, but into heaven itself, now to appear in the presence of God for us (Heb. 9:11-12, 23-28 NKJV).*

After the goat for Azazel was driven into the wilderness, the high priest atoned for the people by offering the goat for the Lord as a burnt offering outside the camp. Jesus as high priest likewise offered himself outside the camp at Golgotha, and was consumed as the burnt offering goat for the Lord (HEB. 13:10-13; JOHN 19:17-20;

---

[109] Mishnah Yoma 4:1; 6:6; B. Talmud Yoma 67b. At some point in time, the goat for Azazel was not just banished to the wilderness, but pushed over a cliff to its death to ensure it would not return. This, however, was not biblically sanctioned.

[110] Milgrom, *Leviticus 1-16*, on Lev. 16:20-22, 1010.

Exod. 29:7-11; Lev. 4:11-12, 21; 16:27-28). We read in Hebrews:

> *For the bodies of those animals, whose blood is brought into the sanctuary by the high priest for sin, are burned outside the camp. Therefore Jesus also, that He might sanctify the people with His own blood, suffered outside the gate. Therefore let us go forth to Him, outside the camp, bearing His reproach (Heb. 13:11-13 NKJV).*

To my knowledge, nowhere in scripture is Christ cast as the antitype of the goat for Azazel. Like I have said, I believe that is because there is a polarity between the two goats that ties into the fundamental conflict between Jesus (seed of the woman) and the Antichrist (seed of the serpent) on earth, and God and Satan in heaven. If we take the Antichrist to be the ultimate goat for Azazel (Satan) in parallel to Jesus as the goat for the Lord, what then was the purpose of Barabbas standing in as the goat for Azazel? I propose that he was a stand-in for guilty humanity. If not for the substitutionary sacrifice of Jesus, we were all destined to forever wander the wilderness of sin under the dominion of Satan (Azazel). Barabbas was a murderous insurrectionist, a false Messiah figure in the image of the Antichrist. The people who sought his release found in him a better representative than the true Christ whom they condemned to death in his place. Not only the Jews, but all mankind were guilty of his crime of rebellion— not against the Emperor of Rome, rather, the God of Creation. Israel is after all a prototype of regenerated humanity. It was for man's instruction that God set apart Israel as a nation of priests.[111] He chose this people because of Abraham, not because they were distinct from, or better than, the rest of man. In this way, the biblical story of their chequered ministry and "perpetual backsliding" is truly the story of man on the path to reconciliation

---

[111] Our discussion about the role of Israel as a nation of priests was discussed in the section "The Third Covenant with Moses" under the chapter "Living Shadows."

(Jer. 8:5; Isa. 65:2). When Christ sprinkled his own blood on the mercy seat of the Most Holy Place, *we* rejected his sacrifice, not only the Jews. When he bore the sins of the world unto death and righteously transferred them onto Satan, the author of sin and death itself, *we* denied him, and welcomed the spirit of antichrist (opposition to Christ) back into *our* camp (Acts 3:13-28; 7:51-53).

The culmination of our marriage with the spirit of antichrist will one day manifest in the greater Barabbas of the Antichrist, the ultimate insurrectionist and false Christ. At the time of the final Day of Atonement, Israel will be in hiding from the Antichrist and his armies in the wilderness of Bozrah, which is in Edom, the land of their adversary Esau (Ezek. 20:33-36; 35:1-15). This divine conflict on earth is aptly portrayed by the rival brothers Jacob and Esau, who are the archetypes of Christ as the seed of the woman and Antichrist as the seed of the serpent, and as the fathers of the rival earthly kingdoms of Israel (for the Lord) and of Edom and the Amalekites (for Azazel-Satan).[112] The goat for Azazel is led into the wilderness in parallel to Esau, the "man of the field [wilderness]," and the goat sacrificed for the Lord is in parallel to Jacob, the "plain man, living in tents [tabernacle of God]" (Gen. 25:27):

*Image 5.2 – Gematria breakdown of Jacob and Esau courtesy of Dafei Tang in the article "Toldot – Secrets of the Twins" for The Times of Israel*

| ESAU | JACOB | VALUE |
|---|---|---|
| Man of the field אִישׁ שָׂדֶה | Blameless man אִישׁ תָּם | **1371** (620 + 751) |
| Goat for Azazel הַשָּׂעִיר לַעֲזָאזֵל | Goat for Yahweh הַשָּׂעִיר לַיהוָה | **1371** (730 + 641) |

God revealed that a veil has been placed over the minds and hearts of Israel because of unbelief (Isa. 6:9-10), but a day is coming when He will remove the veil over their hearts which kept them from coming to true repentance and knowledge of Christ (2 Cor. 3:12-16;

---

[112] To understand the significance of the brothers Jacob and Esau in the context of the spiritual and earthly conflict between the forces of God and Satan (good and evil), consider reading my companion book "Seed of Satan: Antichrist."

Rom. 11:25-29). This points to the final Day of Atonement when all of Israel are gathered in the wilderness of Bozrah (meaning sheepfold in Hebrew) in Edom to evade annihilation at the hands of the Antichrist, the final animation of the Edomites and Amalekites.

> *"I will surely assemble all of you, O Jacob, I will surely gather the remnant of Israel; I will put them together like sheep of the fold, like a flock in the midst of their pasture"* (Mic. 2:12 NKJV).

As commanded on this day, Israel will afflict their souls as they never have before, praying for their Messiah to deliver them from the greater Pharaoh (Lev. 16:31; 23:27-32; Num. 29:7). They will mourn for him whom they have afflicted and for the first time see his blood upon themselves not as a curse, but the blessing of salvation (Rom. 11:25-29; Zech. 12:10). Jesus, the good shepherd, will hear the impassioned cries of his lost sheep and rush to gather them back into their fold (Gen. 49:24; Isa. 40:11; Jer. 31:10; Ezek. 34:23-24; 37:24; Mic. 5:4; Zech. 9:16; 13:7; Matt. 2:6; 25:32; 26:31; Mark 14:27; John 10:2, 11-18; Heb. 13:20; 1 Pet. 2:25; 5:4; Rev. 7:17):

> *"And I will bring you into the wilderness of the peoples, and there I will plead My case with you face to face. Just as I pleaded My case with your fathers in the wilderness of the land of Egypt, so I will plead My case with you,"* says the Lord God (Ezek. 20:35-36 NKJV).

Israel will follow their shepherd back into his fold "on the high mountains of Israel" and enter into the bond of the new covenant (Lev. 16:29-31; Isa. 63:1-6; Ezek. 20:33-44; 34:1-31; 36:12-37; 37:22-25; Mic. 2:12-13). The false shepherd they once followed, the Antichrist, will be cast out from their sight as the goat for Azazel in the wilderness.

As for the heavenly reality behind the Day of Atonement, let us consider it in light of its earthly shadow. First it should be mentioned that the primary purpose of the ceremony was to cleanse the sanctuary from the uncleanness of the people in order for God to stay among them (Lev. 16:15-17, 27, 32-34).[113] In heaven and on earth, ministers of God profaned His sacred dwelling space through acts of rebellion. To remove the sin which contaminated the holy sanctuary of God, the Day of Atonement ceremony was introduced. More specifically, it came in response to the rebellion of Nadab and Abihu, the sons of Aaron, who offered profane fire in the Most Holy Place and were thus consumed by the fire of God (Lev. 10; 16). I believe this mirrored what previously transpired in heaven. The fallen angels, namely Lucifer, likewise violated their ministerial duties in the *heavenly* tabernacle. As it was for Nadab and Abihu, the rebel angels who were cast out with Lucifer will soon be consumed by fire (the lake of fire) for profaning the sanctuary of God in rebellion (Rev. 20:7-10). Notice that blood temporarily cleansed the earthly tabernacle from Israel's impurities, but the blood of Christ *permanently* cleansed the heavenly tabernacle from the *source* of impurity (Heb. 8-10). This demanded that Satan, as the author of sin, be expelled from the heavenly sanctuary which he had defiled. Until this happened, mankind shackled by sin could never dwell in the midst of the holy God. The reconciliation promised in Genesis was contingent upon this judgement—the serpent who separated us from God had to be crushed by the seed of the woman (Christ).

In my estimation, this all suggests that Christ as high priest placed the sins of the world onto the head of Satan as the goat for Azazel, but he has yet to lead him away into the wilderness. This appears to be corroborated by the earthly analogue of Jesus soon defeating the Antichrist and casting him into the wilderness that is the lake of fire (Rev. 19-11-21). I personally contend that the fullness of the Day of Atonement will be realised when Satan is

---

[113] Wenham, *The Book of Leviticus*, 228.

finally defeated after the millennium and joins the Antichrist and false prophet in the lake of fire (Lev. 16:20-22; Rev. 19:20; 20:1-10).[114]

## Sacrificial Death on the Cross

As it was for Joseph, the suffering servant, Jesus, the Mashiach ben Joseph, was condemned to death on false charges and placed next to two criminals on the cross (Matt. 27:38-44; Mark 15:27-32; Luke 23:39-43; John 19:18; Isa. 53:12). In both cases, one criminal accepted their revelation and was saved after three days, but the other denied them and perished also after three days. In the case of Jesus, the former accepted him as the lot for the Lord for atonement and received paradise. The latter mocked him and rejected his blood of atonement, and so he remained condemned under sin like the goat for Azazel sent into the wilderness (Isa. 53:31; 1 Pet. 2:23). Joseph was released from his sentence and raised to the second-in-command of Pharaoh for his revelatory dreams. Jesus however, had to submit to death to be raised in resurrection to the second-in-command of God. For the world to be saved from death like Isaac, God had to give His only son over to death (Rom. 1:16-17; 3:23-26; 5:8-10; 6:3-5). Abraham acknowledged this by faith, for he said to the confused Isaac: "My son, God will provide for Himself the lamb for a burnt offering" (Gen. 22:8). Isaac was a willing sacrifice, and like Christ, carried the wood for his own sacrifice to the mountain, but before Abraham plunged the knife into "his only son," God intervened (Gen. 22:2, 6, 10-16). The ram sacrificed as his substitute pointed to Christ. Unlike Isaac, our Passover lamb endured dehumanising ridicule on the way to Golgotha, the place of his sacrifice, all while bearing the weight of his wooden cross (Matt. 27:32-33; Mark 15:21-22; Luke 23:26-33; John 19:17-18; 1 Cor. 5:7).

---

[114] Origen, *Homilies on Leviticus 1-16*, 184: "He [Christ] would make 'the lot of the scapegoat' the opposing powers, 'the spirits of evil and the rulers of this world of darkness' (Eph. 6:12) which, as the Apostle says, 'he led away with power triumphing over them in himself' (Col. 2:15). 'He led them away.' Where 'did he lead' them except 'to the wilderness,' to desolate places?"

> *He was oppressed and afflicted, yet He did not open His mouth; like a lamb that is led to slaughter, and like a sheep that is silent before its shearers, so He did not open His mouth (Isa. 53:7 NKJV).*

Our Passover lamb was not simply killed, he was subjected to the unspeakable torture of crucifixion. The soldiers flayed Jesus so that his bones were on display, and after piercing his hands and feet upon the cross, divided his clothes between them and cast lots for his undergarment (MATT. 27:35; MARK 15:24; LUKE 23:34; JOHN 19:23-24). This was not incidental, rather it was in meticulous fulfilment of Psalm 22, one of the clearest parallel accounts of the crucifixion of the Messiah from the Old Testament:

> *I am poured out like water, and all my bones are out of joint. My heart has turned to wax; it has melted within me. My mouth is dried up like a potsherd, and my tongue sticks to the roof of my mouth; you lay me in the dust of death. Dogs surround me, a pack of villains encircles me; they pierce my hands and my feet. All my bones are on display; people stare and gloat over me. They divide my clothes among them and cast lots for my garment (Psa. 22:14-18 NIV).*

Besides the obvious details from the above fragment that were fulfilled by the soldiers and the bystanders, medical studies on the physiological impact of crucifixion confirm that the hands and feet are pierced, the bones are pulled out of joints and the limbs stretched, blood is poured out like water prior to being nailed to the cross, and the mouth and tongue are dried up from severe dehydration.[115]

Included in John's account was a seemingly mundane description of the tunic which the soldiers cast lots over. He noted

---

[115] To understand the crucifixion from a scientific, physiological perspective, consider reading: https://www.apu.edu/articles/the-science-of-the-crucifixion/.

how it was "seamless, woven in one piece from top to bottom" (JOHN 19:23). For the Jews of the time, there would have been priestly implications of this fine and expensive one-piece garment (EXOD. 28:1-5, 31-43; 39:27-28). If not the association with the fine linen all Levitical priests were required to wear inside the temple (EZEK. 44:15-19; 1 SAM. 22:16-18), perhaps the tunic resembled that of the high priest, which according to the first-century historian Flavius Josephus, "was not composed of two pieces, nor was it sewed together upon the shoulders and the sides, but it was one long vestment so woven as to have an aperture for the neck."[116] It is said in Hebrews that the sacrifices performed by the high priest were not truly efficacious, for they were, as part of the law, only a "shadow of the good things to come" through Christ (HEB. 10:1).

> *The law is only a shadow of the good things that are coming—not the realities themselves. For this reason it can never, by the same sacrifices repeated endlessly year after year, make perfect those who draw near to worship. Otherwise, would they not have stopped being offered? For the worshipers would have been cleansed once for all, and would no longer have felt guilty for their sins. But those sacrifices are an annual reminder of sins. It is impossible for the blood of bulls and goats to take away sins (Heb. 10:1-4 NIV).*

We are told how "without shedding of blood there is no forgiveness of sins" but at the same time "it is impossible for the blood of bulls and goats to take away sins" (HEB. 9:22; 10:11; LEV. 17:11; ROM. 6:23). The sacrifices were a token of faith in the redemptive sacrifice to which they pointed. Paul explained that God covered for their sins as a reward for their salvific faith, knowing that soon all would be righteously forgiven through the redemptive sacrifice of Christ:

---

[116] Josephus, "Antiquities of the Jews," 3.159.

*Righteous Atonement*

> *God presented Christ as a sacrifice of atonement, through the shedding of his blood—to be received by faith. He did this to demonstrate his righteousness, because in his forbearance he had left the sins committed beforehand unpunished—he did it to demonstrate his righteousness at the present time, so as to be just and the one who justifies those who have faith in Jesus (Rom. 3:25-26 NIV).*

In concert with his calling as high priest and sacrifice, a darkness symbolic of the Most Holy Place covered all the land for the final three hours that Jesus hung on the cross (MATT. 27:45; MARK 15:33-34; LUKE 23:44). It was on the Day of Atonement that the high priest entered into the Most Holy Place in total darkness and blindly sprinkled the blood of the sacrificial goat onto the mercy seat to avoid the consuming presence of the holy God (LEV. 16:15; HEB. 9:1-10). Jesus entered into the Most Holy Place within heaven itself and sprinkled his own blood upon the mercy seat to cleanse us of our sins (MATT. 27:45; LUKE 23:44-45; HEB. 9:19-28; 10:19-23).[117] He was therefore permitted under God's standard of perfect righteousness to plead our case before God, being assured that those in him would not defile the heavenly sanctuary (ISA. 5:16; ROM. 3:26; 1 COR. 1:30; 2 COR. 5:21; PHIL. 3:9; EPH. 4:22-24; 1 PET. 2:24; 3:18; 1 JOHN 2:29).

> *He shall see the labor of His soul, and be satisfied. By His knowledge My righteous Servant shall justify many, for He shall bear their iniquities. Therefore I will divide Him a portion with the great, and He shall divide the spoil with the strong, because He poured out His soul unto death, and He was numbered with the transgressors,*

---

[117] As stated earlier, since Jesus can only die once, so he must perform the dual sacrifice of Passover and Atonement at the same time. Jesus mediates as the high priest and sacrifices himself as the Passover lamb and the lot for the Lord for permanent atonement of our sins.

> *and He bore the sin of many, and made intercession for the transgressors (Isa. 53:11-12 NKJV).*

After Jesus interceded on our behalf before God, the highly symbolic darkness departed. All that remained of his duties on the cross was to shoulder the sins of the world and die as our sinless and unblemished Passover lamb. Taking on the appearance of a fallen son of Adam, he experienced our own feelings of separation from God:

> *Answer me, Lord, out of the goodness of your love; in your great mercy turn to me. Do not hide your face from your servant; answer me quickly, for I am in trouble. Come near and rescue me; deliver me because of my foes. You know how I am scorned, disgraced and shamed; all my enemies are before you. Scorn has broken my heart and has left me helpless; I looked for sympathy, but there was none, for comforters, but I found none. They put gall in my food and gave me vinegar for my thirst (Psa. 69:16-21 NIV).*

In a moment of pure humanity, feeling as if God had deserted him, Jesus cried out "My God, my God, why have you forsaken me?" in reference to the first verse of Psalm 22, a prophetic chapter on his crucifixion (MATT. 27:46; MARK 15:34). We can be sure that Jesus was the subject of Psalm 22 in its totality because of his clear usage of *remez*, a common teaching method of the rabbis. This is where the rabbi (which Jesus was) would utter a single line of a familiar passage as a *remez* (hint or deeper meaning) either as a shorthand, or for the listener to consider its deeper meaning in context. As proof that Jesus intended for this statement to act as a remez (a common technique of his in the Gospels),[118] notice how he

---

[118] Doug Greenwold wrote: "the use of remezim (plural) is common in Jewish literature. It is also a common literary form used by the Gospel writers. In fact, remez words and phrases occur over 270 times in the Gospels ... Jesus

referenced not only the first line of this Psalm in relation to himself, but the last line. The final proclamation he made before he gave up his spirit was "It is finished!" (JOHN 19:30), which was in reference to the final words of this psalm: "He has done it!" (PSA. 22:31). In this case, Jesus would not be implying that God had truly forsaken him, but that he was the crucified man of Psalm 22, and the subject of all its promises.[119]

For his first-century Jewish audience who knew their Torah front to back, their minds would have been drawn to the greater context, and likely understood the deeper implications of his words. While it is certainly the case that his rejection by man was the price of our reconciliation, God the Father did not forsake or abandon His beloved son during his time of need. We read in verse 24 of this very psalm:

> *For He has not despised nor abhorred the affliction of the afflicted; nor has He hidden His face from Him; but when He cried to Him, He heard (Psa. 22:24 NKJV).*

As put by Doug Greenwold of *Preserving Bible Times*, Jesus experienced that uniquely human inclination to withdraw or hide from another in times of guilt or shame:

> *The hardest thing to do is to absorb the justifiable wrath of another being directed at you while in his or her presence. It is at those kinds of moments that we all wish*

---

used remez to signify who He was. For example, Son of Man in Luke is a messianic harkening back to the much fuller meaning of that title in Daniel 7. Daily bread in The Lord's Prayer is a remez back to daily manna in the wilderness ... walking on the water in Matthew was a remez back to Job 9:8, writing in the sand in John 8 when they brought to Jesus the woman caught in adultery is best understood as a remez back to Jeremiah 17:13 (those who turn away from you will be written in the dust)." Greenwold, "The Last Words of Jesus," *Preserving Bible Times*, https://preservingbibletimes.org/wp-content/uploads/2014/03/Story-II.Chapter2.pdf.

[119] Psalm 22 to 24 are considered the three "Shepherd Psalms" in which the first refers to his crucifixion, the second his resurrection, and the third his glorification as king.

*we could be as far away as possible from the person giving vent to that wrath!*[120]

Imagine for a moment the extent to which this applied to Jesus when he bore our sins before the righteous God in all His resplendent glory, having always known Him and never disappointed Him. Only the human incarnation of the divine Word of God could experience the feelings of separation from the curse of sin and death which plagued the first man of Adam. At the same time, only the human incarnation of the divine Word could die, and therefore atone for our sins. The divinity of the Godhead was never undermined, Jesus was never abandoned, for "only divinity could pay the perfect price God's ransom required, and being separated from the Trinity at that moment would have negated Jesus' divinity."[121]

As emphasised throughout both Old and New Testaments, God never denies those who call upon Him, although it can feel that way to us (DEUT. 4:31; 31:6-8; JOSH. 1:5; 1 SAM. 12:22; 1 KGS. 6:13; PSA. 9:9-10; 37:25-29; 71:10-11; 94:14; HEB. 13:5; ACTS 2:27). Take for example the very fall of mankind. God did not hide His face from Adam and Eve, rather He went looking for them. Why? Because *they* hid themselves from *His* presence. They recognised their own nakedness and imperfection, for the garments of light which they wore had been taken away. The juxtaposition of their mortal bodies of darkness against the light and glory of God was too difficult for them to bear. But again, despite how it may have felt for Adam and Eve, and subsequently all mankind, God never abandoned them. The reality is that we as sinners are kept from experiencing the fullness of God's presence. It is to us an "unapproachable light," and "a consuming fire" (EXOD. 24:17; DEUT. 4:24; 9:3; ISA. 33:14; HEB. 12:29; 1 TIM. 6:16). It was for this reason that God

---

[120] Greenwold, "The Last Words of Jesus," *Preserving Bible Times*, https://preservingbibletimes.org/wp-content/uploads/2014/03/Story-II.Chapter2.pdf.

[121] Ibid.

permitted Moses to see only a brief glimpse of His back from behind the cleft of a rock (EXOD. 33:12-23). Even this small partition of His light was enough to permeate through Moses' body, and his face shone so brightly that when he came down the mountain, the children of Israel became greatly afraid of him. They reacted in the same manner as Adam and Eve to the presence of God. From that point on, Moses wore a protective veil while he was in their presence (EXOD. 34:29-35), symbolic of the veil which God placed over the faces of all mankind until the time of reconciliation through Jesus Christ.

*Removal of the Veil*

This protective veil separating man from God was physically and spiritually taken away when Jesus breathed his last as our substitute. It was at that very moment that the veil or curtain covering the Most Holy Place "was torn from top to bottom" (MATT. 27:50-51; MARK 15:37-38; LUKE 23:44-46).[122] Where before only the high priest could enter the Most Holy Place, and do so blindly on one day of the year, the blood of Christ sprinkled on the mercy seat has consecrated "a new and living way" for us to enter through the veil of his body (HEB. 9:11-14; 10:9-22; EXOD. 26:31-33).[123]

> *Now all things are of God, who has reconciled us to Himself through Jesus Christ, and has given us the ministry of reconciliation, that is, that God was in Christ*

---

[122] For a deeper understanding on the significance of the temple veil see: Gurtner, "The Veil Was Torn in Two," *Desiring God*, https://www.desiringgod.org/articles/the-veil-was-torn-in-two.

[123] Ya'acov Rambsell found that by utilizing an equal distance spacing system within the Tanakh (Hebrew Bible), hidden messages can be uncovered. In Leviticus 1:10-12, which talks about the anointing of the high priest, every third letter combines to spell out "Behold! The blood of Yeshua." This fits perfectly with the reality of Jesus (Yeshua) as true high priest in the order of Melchisedech who gave his blood to seal the new covenant and enable him to anoint his servants with the Holy Spirit.

> reconciling the world to Himself, not imputing their trespasses to them, and has committed to us the word of reconciliation (2 Cor. 5:18-19 NKJV).

Now, we who minister in God's new temple, the body of Christ, enjoy unimpeded access to the Most Holy Place without fear of death (HEB. 10:19-22). The example of Nadab and Abihu is no longer applicable, and the old priesthood itself has been rendered obsolete. The sacrifices they performed on behalf of the people are no longer efficacious, for that which they merely pointed to had been fulfilled in the once-and-for-all sacrifice of Christ (HEB. 7:23-28). The veil which separated Israel from God was taken away because the old covenant was fulfilled in Christ (2 COR. 3:13-14):

> For until this day the same veil remains unlifted in the reading of the Old Testament, because the veil is taken away in Christ. Even to this day when Moses is read, a veil covers their hearts. Nevertheless when one turns to the Lord, the veil is taken away (2 Cor. 14-16 NKJV).

The veil is lifted from our faces when we accept the ministry of reconciliation preached by our high priest Jesus and allow ourselves to be gradually conformed to his perfect image:

> Now the Lord is the Spirit; and where the Spirit of the Lord is, there is liberty. But we all, with unveiled face, beholding as in a mirror the glory of the Lord, are being transformed into the same image from glory to glory, just as by the Spirit of the Lord (2 Cor. 3:15-18 NKJV).

Through him we can be delivered from certain death under the curses of the greater Egypt under Satan. Paul put it perfectly in Romans: "just as one trespass resulted in condemnation for all people, so also one righteous act resulted in justification and life for all people ... just as sin reigned in death, so also grace might reign through righteousness to bring eternal life through Jesus

Christ our Lord" (ROM. 5:18, 21). The instrument of our deliverance is our sovereign choice to accept the blood of Christ as our salvation. Nowhere is this more fittingly expressed than in the moment before our saviour gave up his life (blood) and cried out "it is finished" or *tetelestai* in Greek, meaning all debts were paid in full—perfectly perfect and completely complete:

> *Later, knowing that everything had now been finished, and so that Scripture would be fulfilled, Jesus said, "I am thirsty." A jar of wine vinegar was there, so they soaked a sponge in it, put the sponge on a stalk of the hyssop plant, and lifted it to Jesus' lips. When he had received the drink, Jesus said, "It is finished." With that, he bowed his head and gave up his spirit (John 19:28-30 NIV).*

The hyssop lifted to the lips of Christ, our Passover lamb, was yet another element of the Passover that was fulfilled. On that first Passover night, the blood of the Passover lamb was applied to the hyssop to be smeared on the doorposts (EXOD. 12:21-23). Before this final step was taken, there was no salvation for the Israelites. Christ as our Passover lamb took the hyssop branch to his lips and then said "it is finished" before he breathed his last. Until this moment there was no salvation for mankind. Just as how in the Old Testament blood and hyssop purified a defiled person, Jesus' shed blood purifies us from the defilement of sin and death.

Fifty days after the blood of the lamb secured their deliverance, the old covenant was cut between God and Israel (Pentecost). Moses dedicated the covenant by applying blood to the hyssop and sprinkling it over the book and the people (HEB. 9:18-22). Moses afterward purified the tabernacle in likewise fashion, a practice of the law which came to be used in later ceremonial rituals of purification inside the temple (LEV. 14:1-7, 49-52; NUM. 19:1-6, 18).

The old covenant brought the knowledge of sin and its necessary consequences, but it could not give life. Jesus gave his own life to complete the work of the old covenant of law and institute a new and greater covenant capable of giving life, "for the law was given by Moses, but grace and truth came by Jesus Christ" (John 1:17; Rom. 3:20 4:15). The new covenant was similarly dedicated by the blood of Christ and the hyssop. We who come under the new covenant must also take the blood of Christ from the hyssop and apply it to ourselves. We must be like the repentant King David who acknowledged the hyssop as the cleansing agent in his prayer to God: "cleanse me with hyssop, and I will be clean" (Psa. 51:7). Through this act of obedience, we acknowledge that it is because of the perfect substitutionary sacrifice of Jesus Christ that God's judgement and wrath now passes over us (Passover) and we are saved from the wrath of the greater Pharaoh in Satan (Mark 10:45; Gal. 2:16-20; 3:10-14; 1 Tim. 2:5-6; Rev. 12:9-11).

> When you were dead in your sins and in the uncircumcision of your flesh, God made you alive with Christ. He forgave us all our sins, having cancelled the charge of our legal indebtedness, which stood against us and condemned us; he has taken it away, nailing it to the cross. And having disarmed the powers and authorities, he made a public spectacle of them, triumphing over them by the cross (Col. 2:13-15 NIV).

Jesus' triumph over sin and Satan (Heb. 2:14-15; 1 John 3:8) has redeemed us from the Luciferic covenant which our mother Eve brought us under (Rom. 6:23; 8:1-4; Rev. 12:11).[124] We are now as free as Adam and Eve were to choose between the tree of life or the tree of the knowledge of good and evil. To come under the Luciferic covenant and side with the seed of the serpent, or come under the new covenant cut by Christ, the seed of the woman. To count

---

[124] The ultimate demise for Satan has been slated for the end of the millennium when all things are made subject to God, and death itself is destroyed (1 Cor. 15:20-28). Paul made this clear when he told his brothers that "the God of peace will soon crush Satan under your feet" (Rom. 16:20).

ourselves among the rebels or the ecclesia (called out ones).[125]

*Prophecy in Death*

God had promised in the Psalms that the afflicted Christ would not have a single one of his bones broken:

> *Many are the afflictions of the righteous, but the Lord delivers him out of them all. He guards all his bones; not one of them is broken (Psa. 34:20 NKJV).*

This was yet another connection point between the first and second Passovers. Back in Egypt, when God told his people the regulations for the Passover meal (EXOD. 12:43-50), He instructed them "not break any of the bones" of the Passover lamb (EXOD. 12:46; NUM. 9:10-12). The gospel of John mentioned that this was fulfilled in the death of Christ, the lamb slain from the foundation of the world (JOHN 19:36-37). It happened contrary to the wishes of the Jewish leaders who had explicitly requested of Pilate to hasten the death of the crucified by breaking their legs.[126] This was not a matter of mercy or compassion, but because they wanted the bodies down before the high sabbath of the feast of Unleavened Bread began that sunset (JOHN 19:31-33; MARK 15:42). Furthermore, this had been prophesied by the law:

> *"If a man has committed a sin deserving of death, and he is put to death, and you hang him on a tree, his body shall not remain overnight on the tree, but you shall surely bury him that day, so that you do not defile the land which the Lord your God is giving you as an inheritance;*

---

[125] Prince, "Because of the Angels: The Climax of the Conflict," *Derek Prince Ministries*, https://www.derekprince.com/teaching/01-1: this article relates our personal testimony to the power of Jesus' blood to our victory over the enemy.

[126] Those being crucified depended on their legs to push themselves up for oxygen and prevent death from asphyxiation.

> *for he who is hanged is accursed of God"* (Deut. 22-23 NKJV).

The criminals next to Jesus suffered in this manner, but because he already appeared to be dead, the soldiers simply pierced his side with a spear (John 19:34-37). John mentioned that this occurred so that the scripture be fulfilled from Zechariah 12:10, "They shall look on Him whom they pierced" (John 19:37). If we read the original scripture from Zechariah, we notice that John changed the object from "me" (God) to "Him" (Christ). What is even more remarkable is how the original context already implies this existence of the Godhead. Speaking of the coming day of salvation for Israel, God proclaimed through Zechariah:

> *"And I will pour on the house of David and on the inhabitants of Jerusalem the Spirit of grace and supplication; then they will look on Me whom they pierced. Yes, they will mourn for Him as one mourns for his only son, and grieve for Him as one grieves for a firstborn"* (Zech. 12:10 NKJV).

First, we see that Israel's revelation of God's trinitarian nature comes as a result of God pouring out the Holy Spirit upon them. Notice how God abruptly shifted the perspective from "me" to "him," as if there are two beings that are one at the same time. This was the spirited understanding of John, who recognised from this passage that God was pierced through Christ on the cross. That which immediately followed this prophecy in Zechariah was another proclamation from God bearing relationship to the pierced side of Christ:

> *"In that day a fountain shall be opened for the house of David and for the inhabitants of Jerusalem, for sin and for uncleanness"* (Zech. 13:1 NKJV).

John testified that when the soldiers pierced Jesus' side, blood and water flowed out together (JOHN 19:34-35). This fountain spoken of in Zechariah was opened from the body of Christ, whose blood cleanses our sins in the flesh (ROM. 3:25; 5:9; HEB. 9:12-14; 10:19; 13:12; EPH. 1:7; 2:13; ACTS 20:28; COL. 1:20; 1 PET. 1:17-19; 1 JOHN 1:7; 2:2; REV. 1:5; 5:9; 7:14; 12:11; 19:13), and whose water sanctifies our souls (ISA. 12:3; 44:3; JER. 2:13; 17:3; JOHN 3:5; 4:10-14; 7:38; 15:3; 1 COR. 6:11; HEB. 10:22; EPH. 5:26; ACTS 22:16; REV. 21:6; 22:1). The water and blood symbolised the duality of Christ as God and man. First is the water, his divine essence as the Word of God, the creator of all things (JOHN 1:1-4), and then is the blood, his physical incarnation when "the Word became flesh" (JOHN 1:14).

> *This is He who came by water and blood—Jesus Christ; not only by water, but by water and blood. And it is the Spirit who bears witness, because the Spirit is truth. For there are three that bear witness in heaven: the Father, the Word, and the Holy Spirit; and these three are one. And there are three that bear witness on earth: the Spirit, the water, and the blood; and these three agree as one (1 John 5:6 NKJV).*

The apostle Paul directly related water to the Word—the spiritual essence of Christ—in his message to the Ephesians on marriage:

> *Husbands, love your wives, just as Christ also loved the church and gave Himself for her, that He might sanctify and cleanse her with the washing of water by the word, that He might present her to Himself a glorious church, not having spot or wrinkle or any such thing, but that she should be holy and without blemish (Eph. 5:25-27 NKJV).*

To actuate this reconciliation between man and the divine, the Word of God became flesh and shed his own blood on the cross. Now those who live "by the blood of the Lamb and by the word [water] of their testimony" can overcome the temptations of sin and receive this reward of spiritual marriage in heaven (REV. 12:11).

> *I [Jesus] will give of the fountain of the water of life freely to him who thirsts. He who overcomes shall inherit all things, and I will be his God and he shall be My son (Rev. 21:6-7 NKJV).*

The biblical importance of the blood and the water from the side of Christ stretches back even further than these writings from the prophets, even to Genesis, the beginning of life itself. Using a similar motif, the story of the creation of woman from man foreshadowed the creation of the Church from Christ. We read how God first put Adam into a deep sleep and then, depending on our translation of *tsela*, took part of his side or one of his ribs to create Eve (GEN. 2:21-24).[127] In the case of Christ, the second Adam, he was put into a deep sleep by God on the cross (from which he would wake three days later) and from his opened side flowed the blood and water, the building blocks of the Church. We as the Church celebrate the elements of the water and blood through the sacraments of baptism and the eucharist, respectively.

The institution of marriage was introduced to us by Adam and Eve as a type of the spiritual marriage to come with Christ as our divine bridegroom in the new creation. Adam loved his wife Eve to the extent that he condemned himself to the same death she chose for herself by welcoming in the knowledge of good and evil. Prior to this, Adam was free to forever dwell in the direct presence of the loving God, but still he chose to cleave himself to his wife and eat of the fruit, knowing that to be expelled from the garden of Eden was to be deprived of eternal life (GEN. 3:6-24). God thereafter revealed to them that one of their offspring would reconcile all mankind to Himself. This came to be Jesus, who left the presence of the Father and condemned himself to death on

---

[127] The New Defender's Study Bible Notes on Gen. 2:21 claims that the "rib" was actually the "side" of Adam, because the Hebrew word tsela which occurs 35 times in the OT is nowhere else translated as "rib."

behalf of his bride of the Church, so as to reconcile us in marriage with God.

*Preparation in the Tomb*

The resting place for the condemned on the cross was the cursed valley of Hinnom (Gehenna). This was where the worshippers of Baal had previously sacrificed their children to Molech, the Phoenician god of fire, by immolation (2 KGS. 23:20; 2 CHR. 28:3-4; JER. 7:31; 19:5-6; 32:35). Written about in the Old Testament, it became associated with or explicitly translated as *hell* in the New Testament.

> *[The Valley of Hinnom] became a dump, with constant day and night burning of trash fires emitting a sulfurous stench. Another portion of the ravine became a cesspool receiving the sewage of Jerusalem ... Hinnom was a final resting place for those shamed in death. Proper burial was vital under Judaic law, both to combat the necromancy of early Semitic tribes and to show respect for the cessation of God's most precious gift. The dishonored and unclean were not entitled to a proper Jewish burial within the city. Dishonored corpses were disposed of in the reviled Valley of Hinnom.*[128]

If Jesus were leavened or sinful in any way, it would have been his fate to be thrown into Gehenna with the two other condemned criminals. Instead, Joseph of Arimathea, who had not consented to the ruling of the Sanhedrin, courageously requested for Pilate to let him be buried in his own tomb (MATT. 27:57-60; MARK 15:43-46; LUKE 23:50-54; JOHN 19:38-42). Pilate acted faithfully by consenting to his request, and Jesus was given a proper Jewish burial. As Isaiah had prophesied of this suffering Messiah, "he was assigned a grave

---

[128] Black, "Hell on Earth." *The Washington Post*, https://www.washingtonpost.com/archive/lifestyle/1999/08/29/hell-on-earth/a2777d75-cfa6-4325-814a-0a26c83086c5/.

with the wicked [two criminals], and with the rich in his death [burial by Joseph]" (Isa. 53:9).

The following day the religious leaders realised Jesus was not thrown into Gehenna, but that he was returned to his family and disciples. Because they were afraid that his disciples would steal his body and fake the resurrection he had predicted, they asked Pilate to secure the tomb with a stone seal and a guard (Matt. 27:62-66). I previously mentioned how they inadvertently played into the plan of salvation by killing Jesus. Well now they had set up the perfect conditions for Jesus to conclusively prove that he was who he said he was. The religious authorities once again attempted to frustrate the salvific plan but, as Turner and Bock noted, they only reinforced its authenticity:

> *The soldiers who were guarding Jesus' tomb became evangelists of Jesus' resurrection! Previously the leaders purported to need guards for fear that a resurrection hoax might occur, but those very guards later reported that a genuine resurrection had occurred.*[129]

As we know, the true gospel of salvation as declared by Paul the Apostle is that "Christ died for our sins ... He was buried, and that He rose again the third day" (1 Cor. 15:1-4). There could not be salvation without Jesus fulfilling each of these components, nor can we receive salvation if we preach any other gospel to this (Gal. 1:8-9). It was therefore a necessity that Jesus could resurrect from his sealed and guarded grave after three days, the point of corruption, and appear to many witnesses. Failing this, the power of sin and death would still prevail. His death would truly be for nothing. The apostle Paul acknowledged this very point in the first epistle to the Corinthians:

> *And if Christ is not risen, then our preaching is empty and your faith is also empty. Yes, and we are found false*

---

[129] Turner and Bock, *Matthew, Mark*, 11:374.

*witnesses of God, because we have testified of God that He raised up Christ, whom He did not raise up—if in fact the dead do not rise. For if the dead do not rise, then Christ is not risen. And if Christ is not risen, your faith is futile; you are still in your sins! Then also those who have fallen asleep in Christ have perished. If in this life only we have hope in Christ, we are of all men the most pitiable (1 Cor. 15:14-19 NKJV).*

It follows therefore that the primacy of the resurrection and what exactly it accomplished must be appropriately addressed. This leads us to directly into the final chapter.

# 6

# New Covenant for a New Creation

> *He was delivered over to death for our sins and was raised to life for our justification (Rom. 4:25 NIV).*

Jesus Christ, the man believed to be the seed of the woman—the son of God equal parts human and divine—was mortally wounded at the cross. The protoevangelium declared his heel would be bruised, but it appeared as if the spiritual descendants of the serpent (Satan) inflicted the crushing blow. How could a dead Jesus possibly triumph over the serpent and crush his head as prophesied? Truthfully, he could not. His only option was to do the impossible and resurrect from the dead. This was the only situation in which the protoevangelium could be fulfilled with logical precision. His heel would be bruised, but he would not be crushed. Rather, the serpent's head would be crushed, because to defeat the power of death is to defeat Satan himself. After all, his entire kingdom is built upon the enslavement of mankind to sin and death. It is therefore our task to demonstrate that "by the resurrection from the dead," Jesus was authoritatively "declared to be the Son of God" who can take the yoke of Satan from our necks (ROM. 1:4; ISA. 10:27).

### First Fruits of the Resurrection

The previous chapter demonstrated that Jesus became the atonement for mankind as the unblemished and unleavened

Passover lamb sacrifice—the fulfilment of the spring feasts of Passover and Unleavened Bread. However, for the atonement to be efficacious there must be resurrection. Christ needed to defeat death and rise as a new creation in order for us to be saved through him by sharing in his resurrection. For that reason we will now investigate the resurrection and explore its connection to the next spring feast of First Fruits.

The historical feast of First Fruits celebrated the first offering of the new barley harvest to God during the week of Unleavened Bread, always the day after the sabbath (Lev. 23:9-14). The firstfruits offering was symbolic of the Hebrew people's "spiritual journey from self-reliance to reliance on God" from bondage in Egypt to freedom in the land of Israel promised to them by God (Prov. 3:5-8).[130] It was on this very day that the Israelites were rescued from death in the Red Sea, where they were baptised into Moses (a type of Messiah) only to emerge on the other side raised to new life—or born again under God (1 Cor. 10:1-4). It was this cleansing which set them apart as His firstfruits, or His firstborn among the nations, to be blessed with abundance. To surrender the first of the harvest required immense faith for a people wholly dependent on its produce, but by acknowledging God as the source of their fortune, He promised to provide for them many times over (Prov. 3:9-10).

Because the text does not explicitly state whether First Fruits is celebrated on the day after the weekly sabbath or the high sabbath of Unleavened Bread, this matter has been hotly debated, even among the sects of Jesus's time (Lev. 23).[131] The Sadducees

---

[130] David, "First Fruits (Bikkurim)," *My Jewish Learning*, https://www.myjewishlearning.com/article/first-fruits/.

[131] The obvious assumption is that the weekly sabbath is intended. First, the chapter begins in the context of the weekly sabbath (Lev. 23:1-4), and the high sabbath is simply called a sacred assembly of no regular work, not "the Sabbath." Second, the people were told to "count the omer," or seven sabbaths, to determine the date of Pentecost, but these were all weekly sabbaths (Lev. 23:15-16). Third, if the sabbath in view was the high sabbath of Unleavened Bread, the date would be fixed, and we would therefore already know the exact date of Pentecost. If the weekly sabbath was intended, the practice of counting

understood it to refer to the weekly sabbath, while the Pharisees thought it was the high sabbath of Unleavened Bread. Because the high priest Caiaphas was a Sadducee, and this was the dominant sect, it is likely that the offering of the first fruits fell on the day after the weekly sabbath, coinciding with Christ's resurrection (ACTS 4:17). This being the case, towards the end of the weekly sabbath the priests would have been waiting in the fields for the setting of the sun, the point at which the Jewish day starts (sunset to sunset).[132] Once the sun had set and three stars were sighted together, the priests were confident the sabbath had passed and proceeded to put the sickle to the grain and reap the firstfruits of the harvest.

At this very moment Jesus reached his promised three days and three nights in the heart of the earth. He too was cut free from death's grip and lifted from the earth as the firstfruits of God's harvest (MATT. 28:1-10; MARK 16:1-9; LUKE 24:1-8; JOHN 20:1-17). This was his promised sign of Jonah which he "staked His entire claim to be the Messiah upon,"[133] the resurrection from the dead after three days (MATT. 12:38-41, 16:1-4; LUKE 11:29-32; JOHN. 2:18-22):[134]

> For as Jonah was three days and three nights in the belly of the great fish, so will the Son of Man be three days and three nights in the heart of the earth (Matt. 12:38-40 NKJV).

Just as the giant fish rejected the lifeless corpse of Jonah from its belly, death found it impossible to keep Jesus in the grave and it

---

the omer would not only be symbolic, but necessary to reach the correct date of Pentecost. This explains why a date of observation was not given as with every other feast. If God intended for firstfruits to fall on Nisan 16, he would have said as much.

[132] Mishnah Menachot 10:1-4; Shulchan Arukh Orach Chayim 293:2 (termed the most widely accepted compilation of Jewish law ever written).

[133] Jones, *Messiah and the Sign of Jonah*, chap. 1.

[134] Verses on Jesus' resurrection after three days: MATT. 16:21; 17:23; 20:17-19; 26:61; 27:40, 63-64; MARK 8:31; 9:30-31; 10:32-34; 14:58; 15:29; LUKE 9:21-22; 13:32; 18:31-33; 24:7, 21-23, 46; ACTS 10:40-41; JOHN 2:19-21.

gave him up (Jon. 1:17-2:7; Acts 2:24-32; 13:34-37).[135] He became the "Lord of both the dead and the living" by defeating death without seeing corruption (Rom. 14:9; Acts 13:26-39). "The sting of death is sin, and the power of sin is the law" but Jesus triumphed over both (1 Cor. 15:56; Acts 2:24; Heb. 2:14).

At this point Jesus had yet to ascend to the Father and be accepted before Him as the firstfruits of the new harvest. This was to take place later that morning (Sunday) when the high priest waved the prepared sheaf before the Lord in the temple alongside the unblemished lamb and wine offerings (Lev. 23:9-13). The wave sheaf represented Christ in his resurrection from out of the earth, the unblemished lamb his sinless substitutionary sacrifice, and the wine his blood poured out so we can live. Only after these offerings were made by the high priest was the new barley harvest permissible for the people to eat (Lev. 23:14). In light of this, consider what Jesus said to Mary Magdalene after she found him alive early that Sunday morning:

> "Do not hold on to me, for I have not yet ascended to the Father. Go instead to my brothers and tell them, 'I am ascending to my Father and your Father, to my God and your God'" (John 20:17 NIV).

This statement seemed to parallel how the firstfruits were not to be partaken of until they were offered up to God by the priest in the temple. It was not until later that morning that Jesus ascended to the Father and the Holy Spirit (the three stars thus mirror the trinity) and we (Mary included) became eligible to partake of him as the firstfruits of the resurrection (1 Cor. 15:20-23; Rom. 8:23, 29; James 1:18; Acts 26:23; Col. 1:15-18; 2 Thess. 2:13; James 1:18; Rev. 1:5; 14:4).

---

[135] It is important to note that Jonah was in fact dead inside the belly of the whale. He was truly resurrected from the dead. Jonah 2:1-2 records that Jonah cried out to God from Sheol, the realm of the dead, and Jonah 3:1-2 records his resurrection. God tells him to "Arise" and preach to the pagan nation of Nineveh who ends up converting for a time. After his own resurrection, Jesus gave this same task to his disciples.

> *But Christ has indeed been raised from the dead, the firstfruits of those who have fallen asleep. For since death came through a man, the resurrection of the dead comes also through a man. For as in Adam all die, so in Christ all will be made alive. But each in turn: Christ, the firstfruits; then, when he comes, those who belong to him (1 Cor. 15:20-23 NIV).*

His ultimate firstfruits offering to the Father has made permissible the harvest of God's field of souls (Hos. 6:11; Matt. 9:37-38; 13:37-43; Luke 10:2; 1 Cor. 3:9; John 15:1-11; Rev. 14:15). Henceforth, all who are in Christ, whether dead or living, have become ripening fruit in God's great harvest (Matt. 13:37; Rom. 10:9-10; 11:16; 14:8; Acts 4:11-12; 16:30-31; Rev. 3:20; John 3:13-16; 17). At the end of the age the reaper will come to reap all he has sown and God will raise from the dead all those who belong to him as he raised Christ, our firstfruits (Matt. 24:30-31; 1 Cor. 6:14; 2 Cor. 4:14; Rom. 6:4; Rev. 14:14-16). With the swing of the scythe, the fruits of his labour, whether dead (corrupted) or living (mortal), will be given bodies of incorruptibility and immortality in his image (1 Thess. 4:13-18; 1 Cor. 15:51-57; Rom. 8:10-11). God's harvest will be collected into His barn, the everlasting kingdom of peace and righteousness, to forever dwell with Him (Matt. 13:30; Rev. 21:1-7).

> *Dear friends, now we are children of God, and what we will be has not yet been made known. But we know that when Christ appears, we shall be like him, for we shall see him as he is. All who have this hope in him purify themselves, just as he is pure (1 John 3:1-3 NKJV).*

Job had foreseen this day through faith. He knew there was to come a redeemer through whom he could be resurrected in the flesh and see God:

> *I know that my redeemer lives, and that in the end he will stand on the earth. And after my skin has been destroyed,*

> yet in my flesh I will see God; I myself will see him with
> my own eyes—I, and not another. How my heart yearns
> within me (Job 19:25-27 NIV).

The disciples were fortunate to see in the flesh what Job had seen by faith. The redeemer indeed lived on earth, and through him, the firstfruits of the resurrection, we all can see God even after our skin is destroyed. Let us start with the disciples' first encounter with the resurrected son of God.

### The Tomb as the Most Holy Place

Early on the first day of the week, before the firstfruits were waved, Mary Magdalene, along with Mary the mother of James and Salome, went to the tomb and were astonished to find the stone rolled away and Jesus gone (MATT. 28:1-8; MARK 16:1-8; LUKE 24:1-12; JOHN 20:1-2). The disciples Peter and John were later alerted and rushed to see for themselves that what Mary told them was true. After they peered into the empty tomb, they noticed that Jesus' linen wrappings were left behind. His face cloth even appeared to be folded in its own place (JOHN 20:1-9). To see the linen clothes carefully wrapped and laid aside likely stopped them from assuming the worst. A would-be robber or adversary of Jesus was unlikely to go through the effort of removing the heavy oil-laden linen wrappings when time was at a premium.[136] Consider the logistical challenge of getting past the guard, rolling away the stone seal, and then unwrapping the linen from the body before stealing it, all undetected.[137]

---

[136] Grieve, *Your Verdict on the Empty Tomb*, 48.

[137] The popular dismissal of the resurrection is that the disciples stole the body, but the prospect of pulling off this feat would be no easier. Furthermore, one should consider how these disciples had failed to grasp the necessity of the resurrection, and certainly were not expecting it. Most of them had already left Jerusalem after Christ was arrested (MARK 14:50). Would these same disciples who deserted Christ suddenly transform into fearless martyrs willing to die for him if they did not believe the resurrection?

It is remarked that even at this point in time, the disciples did not understand that Jesus "must rise from the dead," but that when John saw this, he believed (JOHN 20:8-9). There was obviously serious theological significance to the linen garments that led John to finally understand that Christ resurrected as he promised. So what did he see? Okay, we talked previously about the similarities between Christ's undergarments taken from him on the cross and those of the high priest (EXOD. 28; 39:1-31). Well, the same comparison can be made for the simple linen garments of humility which the high priest wore only while in the Most Holy Place on the Day of Atonement (LEV. 16:3-4, 23-24). These bore testimony to Jesus as the heavenly high priest who performed a greater once-and-for-all atonement in the heavenly Most Holy Place (HEB. 7:24-28; 9:24-28; 10:5-14). Michael Battle pointed out how the divine God voluntarily humbled Himself by momentarily putting aside His glory to make atonement for mankind:

> *As the high priest laid aside his beautiful garments and wore only linen garments into the presence of God, so Christ left the glory of heaven and came to earth. He laid aside his heavenly majesty (not his divine nature) and clothed himself with human weakness, as he took on the likeness of men.*[138]

As the person of Jesus, He humbled himself even to death and entered the symbolic Most Holy Place, the darkness on the cross, and performed the atonement in his garments of humility (JOHN 19:23-24, 38-42, 20:5-8; MATT. 27:59; MARK 15:46; LUKE 23:53). Once his priestly duties were complete, he resurrected out of these garments and left them behind undisturbed as was commanded of the high priest (LEV. 16:23). He then exited the symbolic Most Holy Place adorned in his eternal garments of divine glory.

---

[138] Battle, "The High Priest, the Garments, and the Holy of Holies," *Rooted and Grounded in Christ*, https://rootedandgroundedinchrist.com/2016/03/31/the-high-priest-the-garments-and-the-holy-of-holies/.

This priestly reality of Christ was shown to Mary Magdalene from a different vantage point. After she followed Peter and John back to the tomb, she looked inside and "saw two angels in white, seated where Jesus' body had been, one at the head and the other at the foot" (JOHN 20:11-12). This remarkable scene must have evoked the familiar imagery of the ark of the covenant with the two cherubim on both ends of the mercy seat (EXOD. 25:10-22; 26:31-35; 37:1-9; 40:1-38; NUM. 4:1-20; 1 KGS. 6:23-28; 8:6-7; 1 CHR. 28:18; 2 CHR. 3:10-14; 5:7-8). It was from here inside the Most Holy Place that God, often referred to as He "who dwells between the cherubim," dispensed His presence on earth from the time of Moses (EXOD. 25:22; 30:6; LEV. 16:2, 13-15; NUM. 7:89; 1 SAM 4:4; 2 SAM 6:2; 2 KGS. 19:15; 1 CHR. 13:6; PSA. 80:1-2; 99:1; ISA. 37:16). Moses, as the antitype of Christ as mediator, was the only man until Christ permitted to freely commune with God above the ark. The high priest was permitted to enter the Most Holy Place only one day of the year, the Day of Atonement, and under the cover of darkness. He was there not to commune with God, but to cleanse the sanctuary of the people's sins by sprinkling the blood of the sacrifice on the mercy seat.

In the previous chapter, we explored the reality of Christ as the high priest and the sacrifice upon the mercy seat. His blood sprinkled upon the mercy seat forgave us of our sins and brought down the veil separating us from God's presence in the Most Holy Place. I believe what Mary saw confirmed that Jesus also represented the third and final component, the mercy seat.[139] Consider the words of Paul in respect to "the redemption that came by Christ":

> *God presented Christ as a sacrifice of atonement [mercy seat—hilastērion] through the shedding of his blood—to be received by faith (Rom. 3:25 NIV).*

---

[139] Zywietz, "Representing the Government of God: Christ as the Hilasterion in Romans 3:25": *"Christ is the sacrifice, killed for our sin. Christ is the priest, carrying it into the sanctuary, and Christ is the mercy seat, where sin is kept until it is cleansed."*

In the original Greek we see that God presented Christ as a "hilastērion," a mercy seat. This term is found in only one other verse in the New Testament and it refers explicitly to the mercy seat (HEB. 9:5-14). However, in Romans 3:25, hilastērion is often translated not as the object (mercy seat), but as the action of atonement or propitiation.[140] There are a contingent of scholars who argue the lexical evidence strongly supports the idea that hilastērion is used by Paul in Romans 3:25 in reference to the mercy seat itself.[141] The scholar Valentin Zywietz elaborates on this perspective of Christ as the mercy seat:

> *The mercy seat in the Old Testament is described as the locus of the divine revelation to Israel, as the center of God's divine administration, and as a place on which sin and judicial responsibility are stored during the year, so that it can be cleansed on the Day of Atonement. In all of these functions, the mercy seat parallels different aspects of the mission of Jesus: He is the pinnacle of divine revelation, he bears our guilt, and he bears the judicial responsibility God had incurred on himself by acquitting the guilty. The public display of Christ as the hilasterion in Romans 3:25 thus validates God's promise to bear the sin of his people without compromising his character.*[142]

If we follow this line of thinking, the scene of the tomb paints a beautiful picture of Christ as the new revelation of God's presence

---

[140] The third-century BC Septuagint translation of the Old Testament always used hilastērion for the mercy seat or an altar of sacrifice.

[141] Bailey, "Jesus as the Mercy Seat," *Tyndale Bulletin* 51, no. 1 (May 2000): 155-158, https://legacy.tyndalehouse.com/tynbul/Library/TynBull_2000_51_1_09_Bailey_JesusMercySeat.pdf; Talbert, Charles H. *Romans*. Macon: Smyth & Helwys Publishing, 2018, 110: Talbert considers Rom. 3:25 to speak of the two conditions required for Christ's sacrifice: *"Christ Jesus, whom God purposed as a locus of the divine presence and revelation through his faithfulness in his blood."*

[142] Zywietz, "Representing the Government of God: Christ as the Hilasterion in Romans 3:25," https://digitalcommons.andrews.edu/theses/84.

on earth. We enter the Most Holy Place through Christ as high priest to see by faith the invisible and unapproachable God through His visible and human Son (JOHN 14:9).

> *For there is one God and one mediator between God and mankind, the man Christ Jesus (1 Tim. 2:5 NIV).*

In order to substantiate this claim, let us examine the textual similarities between Christ in the tomb and the ark in the Most Holy Place. Credit for some of these findings go to the scholar Nicholas Lunn from his journal article *Jesus, the Ark, and the Day of Atonement*:[143]

Image 6.1 – Comparison of the ark of the covenant and Christ

| ARK IN MOST HOLY PLACE | CHRIST IN THE TOMB |
|---|---|
| Ark placed in the innermost chamber of the temple separated by a veil | Christ placed in a burial chamber sealed off with a large stone |
| Tearing of the veil coincides with an earthquake | Removal of the stone coincides with an earthquake |
| Tearing of the veil associated with resurrection of the saints after Christ | Removal of the stone associated with resurrection of Christ then the saints |
| Ark wrapped in the temple veil when transported | Christ wrapped in cloth for burial |
| Ark anointed with holy oil whose first and main ingredient was myrrh | Christ's body anointed with spices whose first ingredient was myrrh |
| Blood sprinkled on mercy seat for atonement of Israel for the year | Blood sprinkled on mercy seat in heaven for atonement of man |
| Two cherubim guarded both ends of the ark where invisible God dwelled | Two angels guarded both ends of the tomb where Christ once laid |

---

[143] Lunn, "Jesus, the Ark, and the Day of Atonement," *Journal of the Evangelical Theological Society* 52, no. 4 (December 2009): 731-46. https://www.etsjets.org/files/JETS-PDFs/52/52-4/JETS%2052-4%20731-746%20Lunn.pdf.

*Seed of God: Jesus Christ*

| Edenic symbolism: e.g. trees and fruit, cherubim guardians, gold and precious stones, entrance on east side[144] | Edenic symbolism: within a garden, angelic guardians, Christ mistaken for a gardener (Adam), women first to see him resurrected (Eve) |
|---|---|
| Transportation of the ark uses verbs take/carry and put/place/lay[145] | These same verbs are used for the burial and after the resurrection |

Furthermore, each of the three elements contained inside the ark bear symbolic representation of Christ (EXOD. 31:18; HEB. 9:4-5). There were the two stone tablets of the law inscribed by the finger of God, a golden pot of the heavenly manna the Hebrews subsisted on in the wilderness, and Aaron's budded rod which represented the divine authority of the Levitical priesthood (NUM. 17). Jesus came down from heaven as the true bread of life (manna) to save mankind from death in the wilderness of sin (JOHN 6:32-51). As the Word of God, he perfectly lived up to the law inscribed on stone but was denied by his own brothers (like Korah's rebellion), even unto death as the mercy seat (hilastērion). The law condemned us to death, but by virtue of Christ's blood, the mercy seat situated above the law was righteously satisfied. By his atonement and resurrection he was appointed by God to establish a new priesthood, symbolised by the budded rod of Aaron, and to inscribe a new covenantal law not upon stone, but within our hearts.

> And no man takes this honor to himself, but he who is called by God, just as Aaron was. So also Christ did not glorify Himself to become High Priest, but it was He who said to Him: "You are My Son, today I have begotten You." As He also says in another place: "You are a priest

---

[144] Ark: GEN. 2:9, 12, 15; 3:2, 24; EXOD. 25:3, 7, 18, 31-36; 27:13-15; NUM. 3:7-8; 8:25-26. Jesus: JOHN 19:41; 20:12, 15; MARK 16:9-11; LUKE 24:2-4, 22-24.

[145] Ark: take/carry (EXOD. 25:14; NUM 4:15; 10:21), put/place/lay (EXOD. 40:3, 5, 6, 22, 24, 26, 29). Jesus: take/carry (JOHN 19:38; 20:2, 13, 15), put/place/lay (JOHN 19:41-42; 20:2, 13, 15).

*forever according to the order of Melchizedek" (Heb. 5:4-6 NKJV).*

The ark of the covenant which God gave directly to Moses protected Israel through the wilderness journey into the promised land. The ark of the new covenant which God gave directly to Jesus protects us through the wilderness journey into the promised land of the millennial kingdom and then of the new heaven and earth.

*The Second Man Restored in the Garden*

As shown in the above table, the sanctuary was replete with Edenic symbolism, and so was the tomb of Christ, situated as you may know, in a garden. The priestly symbolism of the empty tomb was important enough for these two distinct witnesses to occur before the encounter with the resurrected Christ. The reason for this, I believe, goes back to the fall in the garden of Eden, the reason for the protoevangelium, God's redemptive promise to mankind. The seed of the woman in Christ was to facilitate our return into the tree of life as the mediator for our God "who dwells between the cherubim" on the mercy seat. How fitting then that Christ first appeared to women after he resurrected (MATT. 28:9-10; MARK 16:9-10; JOHN 20:11-18). Perhaps as an allusion to the grief of the woman (Eve), first the two angels, and later Jesus, both said to Mary Magdalene, "Woman, why are you weeping?" (Eve was called "woman" until after the fall) (JOHN 20:12-15; GEN. 3:20). The implication here is that the woman had no reason to weep any longer because the curse upon her was now overturned. Where before the guilty Eve hid from God in the garden, prompting Him to call out to her, "where are you?" Mary boldly searched for Jesus, prompting him to ask her, "whom are you seeking?" David Nash noted this contrast in responses:

> *Mary Magdalene stands in the garden among the angels, and rather than being driven away by them, she is met with mercy. In her pain and sorrow, she seeks to find her Lord, rather than being sought by the Lord; and, rather*

> than finding judgment, she finds compassion and forgiveness.[146]

The first man was expelled from the garden of Eden, "the way to the tree of life," and cherubim guarded the entrance (GEN. 3:24). Once the tabernacle was built during the Exodus, cherubim guarded the way to God in the Most Holy Place, the symbolic Eden (EXOD. 25:18-22; 37:7-9). When Jesus first appeared to Mary, she supposed him to be the gardener, a possible hint of his Pauline designation as the second Adam (ROM. 5:12-21; 1. COR. 15:21-22, 45), for Adam was after all the caretaker of the garden of Eden (JOHN 20:15; GEN. 2:15).[147] The garden which the second man cultivates is that of a new creation, a greater Eden. Paul said, "if anyone is in Christ, he is a new creation" and "the old things have passed away" (2 COR. 5:17). That means no more condemnation. The cherubim need not guard the entrance to the tree of life, for death and sin which came by the first man has been defeated. We hear this message from J. Lee Grady in the article aptly titled *How the Resurrection Broke Eden's Curse*:

> *Sin began in a garden. Thousands of years later, Jesus Christ stood in another garden and announced His ultimate victory. The death and resurrection of Jesus brought a great reversal. While the first man brought pain, slavery to sin and alienation from God's presence,*

---

[146] Nash, "Mary Magdalene and the Reversal of Eden," *Trinitas Blog*, https://trinitasblog.wordpress.com/2020/01/25/mary-magdalene-and-the-reversal-of-eden.

[147] Spurgeon, "Supposing Him to be the Gardener," (sermon 1699 at the Metropolitan Tabernacle, December 31, 1882): *"Behold, the church is Christ's Eden, watered by the river of life, and so fertilized that all manner of fruits are brought forth unto God; and he, our second Adam, walks in this spiritual Eden to dress it and to keep it; and so by a type we see that we are right in 'supposing him to be the gardener.'"*

*the second man of Christ brought healing, deliverance and full restoration of fellowship with the Son of God.*[148]

Paul declared on a number of occasions that we must put to death "the old man" with its fallen ways and "put on the new man" restored in the likeness of God, which is Christ, the firstborn of the resurrection (Eph. 4:22-24; Col. 3:1-11; 1 Cor. 15:20-23, 45-49; Rom. 5:12-21).

This theme of new creation is especially prevalent in the resurrection account of John, as we have touched on thus far. The gospel of John as a whole is rich in creation motifs. For example, the beginning and ending of the creation story unmistakably informs the structure of John's own gospel to point towards Christ as a new creation. John directly referenced the opening verses of Genesis at the start of his gospel to reveal how the Word, the divine essence of Christ, was the creative instrument of God, through whom, "all things were made" (John 1:1-5; Rev. 19:13; Psa. 33:6). He continued that "the Word became flesh" in the person of Christ and on three separate occasions recorded Jesus' statements on how he came to finish the works of God who was still working (John 1:9-18; 4:34; 5:17, 36; 10:25). God revealed to Isaiah these unfinished works were the creation of "new heavens and a new earth" to restore mankind to Edenic bliss (Isa. 65:17-25; 66:22).

The redemptive work of Christ which he came to complete on his first coming were the beginning of this new creation. As you would expect, confirmation of this comes from John. Twice he mentions how the resurrected Christ showed himself on "the first day of the week," first in the dawn, then in the evening, instead of using the more natural choice of the "third day" (John 20:1, 19). The emphasis of the first day over the third day appears to function as an intentional mirror of the first day of creation (Gen. 1:2-5). The Word began creation with the utterance "let there be light" and from the darkness of the void came forth light. The light was

---

[148] Grady, "How the Resurrection Broke Eden's Curse," *Charisma Magazine*, https://www.charismamag.com/blogs/fire-in-my-bones/9282-how-the-resurrection-broke-edens-curse.

separated from the darkness into day and night, morning and evening, and this was the first day of creation. The symbolic separation of the day from night, evening from morning, highlights how the light of Christ, which "shines in the darkness," overcame the darkness of the fallen creation (John 1:1-5). Firstly, it was early on the first day "while it was still dark" that Mary went to the tomb and encountered "the light of the world," the risen Christ (John 1:1-5; 8:12; 20:1). This marked the first creative act of a new creation. Secondly, it was during "the evening" that Jesus went before his disciples to restore mankind, the one aspect of God's good creation that had fallen into chaos and disorder. This referred to the sixth day of creation when God breathed into Adam's nostrils the breath of life to make him a living being (Gen. 1:26-31; 2:7; Job 33:4; Psa. 33:6; 104:29-30). The textual allusion to this from John is how Jesus breathed on his disciples the Holy Spirit to give them life under a new creation (John 20:19-23). The prophet Ezekiel described the coming of this day of recreation for Israel in the prophecy of the dry bones (Ezek. 37:1-14):

> *"Prophesy to the breath, prophesy, son of man, and say to the breath, 'Thus says the Lord God: 'Come from the four winds, O breath, and breathe on these slain, that they may live'"" (Ezek. 37:9 NKJV).*

Obviously this new heaven and earth has yet to fully materialise. The apostle Peter anticipated this day to be when Christ returns in judgement to finish the last of God's works, the destruction of the old heaven and earth to make way for the new (2 Pet. 3:10-13; Rev. 21:1-5). There in the new heaven and earth the new man shall eat again from the tree of life (Rev. 2:7; 22:2,14; Ezek. 47:12). John noted how Jesus, like the tree of life which stood "in the midst of the garden" (Gen. 2:9), was crucified "in the midst" (middle) of the two criminals on the cross (tree) (John 19:18), and after his resurrection, "stood in the midst" of his disciples when he appeared to them on the first day and again eight days later (John 20:19, 26).

## New Creation on the Eighth Day

The aforementioned detail from John that Christ appeared to the disciples on the first day of his resurrection and again eight days later was by no means incidental. The eighth day, which is the same as the first (Sunday), transcends the natural and complete seven-day cycle. In biblical thought, the eighth day is thus associated with new beginnings. For example, God consecrated the Aaronic priesthood for seven days and on the eighth day the ministry began and God bestowed His glory upon the people (LEV. 8-9). Seven days of separation are prescribed for the unclean by law before ritual cleansing or purification on the eighth day (LEV. 14-15; NUM. 19). The final feast of Tabernacles lasts eight days and the first and the eighth days are holy convocations (sabbaths) (LEV. 23:36-39; NUM. 29:33-35; NEH. 8:18). Israelite boys are brought into covenant with God through circumcision on the eighth day (LEV. 12:3; LUKE 1:59; PHIL. 3:5).

*Image 6.2 – Numerical pattern of eight as symbol of new creation*

| EXAMPLE(S) | VALUE |
|---|---|
| souls saved during the flood; days until circumcision; times God affirmed Abrahamic covenant; days in feasts of Passover and Unleavened Bread, and of Tabernacles; day of week of first fruits and Pentecost; eight sprinklings of blood in Most Holy Place; day Aaron and sons were consecrated; King David the eighth son; instances of resurrection in Bible; times Jesus showed himself alive after his resurrection | 8 |

The early church rightly appropriated the new beginnings symbolism of the eighth day to the resurrection of Christ and his new creation. The earliest surviving discourse comes from the first-century *Epistle of Barnabas*:

> *He further says to them, Your new moons and Sabbaths I disdain. Consider what he means: Not the Sabbaths of the present era are acceptable to me, but that which I have appointed to mark the end of the world and to usher in the eighth day, that is, the dawn of another world. This, by the way, is the reason why we joyfully celebrate*

> *the eighth day–the same day on which Jesus rose from the dead; after which He manifested himself and went up to heaven (Epistle of Barnabas 15:8-9).*

The early second-century church fathers Justin Martyr and Ignatius of Antioch echoed these words of Barnabas, understanding resurrection Sunday to represent the eighth day, but the first day of a "new hope."[149] Far into the future in the twentieth-century, Ivan Panin discovered that the many titles of Jesus are associated with this number eight, perhaps to authenticate his authorship of the new creation:

*Image 6.3 – Isopsephy pattern of eight in the different names of Jesus*

| NAME OR TITLE | VALUE | FORMULA |
| --- | --- | --- |
| Lord | 800 | 8 x 100 |
| Jesus | 888 | 8 x 111 |
| Christ | 1480 | 8 x 185 |
| Jesus Christ | 2368 | 8 x 296 |
| Lord Jesus Christ | 3168 | 8 x 396 |
| Saviour | 1408 | 8 x 176 |
| Emmanuel | 25600 | 8 x 3200 |
| Messiah | 656 | 8 x 82 |
| Son | 880 | 8 x 110 |
| Son of Man | 2960 | 8 x 370 |

But of course, numeric evidence must only be supplementary of

---

[149] Justin Martyr, "The First Apology," 67: *"Sunday is the day on which we all hold our common assembly, because it is the first day on which God, having wrought a change in the darkness and matter, made the world; and Jesus Christ our Saviour on the same day rose from the dead."* Ignatius of Antioch, "Epistle to the Magnesians," 9: *"Those who were brought up in the ancient order of things have come to the possession of a new hope, no longer observing the Sabbath, but living in the observance of the Lord's Day, on which also our life has sprung up again by Him and by His death."*

what is made plain in scripture. There is further justification for its use by the next example of eight as a sign of the new creation. I am speaking of the Festival of Weeks (Shavuot), better known by Christians as Pentecost (fiftieth in Greek), the final spring feast left for us to unpack. Pentecost is the only feast of the Lord in which the date is not given, but calculated. Let me explain why I believe this to be by God's brilliant design.

To determine the time of Pentecost, God instructed the people to count (by inclusive reckoning) seven sabbaths (49 days) from the firstfruits offering the day after the sabbath (Sunday, day 8) before presenting Him with the firstfruits of the wheat harvest on the fiftieth day, again the day after the sabbath (Sunday, day 8) (LEV. 23:15-16; EXOD. 23:16; 34:22; NUM. 28:26; DEUT. 16:9-11). As previously mentioned, the eighth day transcends the perfect completeness of the seven days of creation to mark a new beginning. The fiftieth day can be likened to the eighth day, not only because it always falls on the Sunday (day 8), but because it follows or transcends the seven cycles of seven days that are counted ($7^2 = 49$). These patterns are not incidental. First, consider how the "counting the omer" from firstfruits to Pentecost commemorated the transformation, or new beginning, of the Hebrew people from the Exodus to the marriage with God and receiving of Torah fifty days later on Shavuot (Pentecost).

To reinforce this from a different context, God similarly commanded the Israelites to "count seven sabbaths of years" ($7^2 = 49$) and consecrate the fiftieth year, the Jubilee, as a sabbatical year of freedom and rest (LEV. 25:8-13). In radical renewal of the natural order, all property was returned to the original owners, no agricultural work was to be done, all prisoners were released, and all debts were cancelled (LEV. 25). In this same manner, it was not until Pentecost, the equivalent of the Jubilee year (day 50 or 8), that the apostles were imputed with the fullness of the Holy Spirit to share in the new creation through the firstfruits of Christ. The new creation will be an eternal Jubilee of freedom and rest from all burdens of the flesh.

> *For God's firstfruits, Pentecost is the announcing of the Jubilee, when we reclaim dominion over the earth with Christ, are free of the world's hold on us, and receive our inheritance as kings and priests and children of the eternal God in His kingdom.*[150]

The prior period of counting the omer was for the disciples a time of spiritual maturation. As it was for the Hebrews during the Exodus, they were called to walk before God and withstand the physical and spiritual tribulations of the long walk in the wilderness. For the first forty-days Jesus educated them on the "law" of the new covenant as God had done with Moses for the forty-days after giving the Torah. A time for maturation was necessary for them to become spiritually prepared to meet the Lord at their own Mount Sinai (PSA. 90:12). It was not until Pentecost ten days after Jesus' ascension (fifty from his resurrection) that the disciples received the fullest manifestation of the Holy Spirit, the seal of God's new covenant.

During the first Pentecost God appeared to the people who waited as instructed with thunder and lightning and spoke unto them the ten commandments from a thick black cloud of smoke and fire (EXOD. 19:16-19; DEUT. 4:10-15; 5). In the same manner, while the disciples were all together as Jesus had instructed, "a sound like the blowing of a violent wind came from heaven and filled the whole house" (ACTS 2:1-2). Tongues of fire came upon each of them and they were filled with the Holy Spirit (ACTS 2:3-4). Three-thousand witnesses to the visible outpouring of the Spirit were saved and renewed to life (ACTS 1:4-5; 2:1-41; JOEL 2:28-32; LUKE 24:45-49) in reversal of the judgement which came upon three-thousand on the first Pentecost for erecting the idolatrous golden calf statue (EXOD. 32:19-28; DEUT. 9:7-29). This is an excellent illustration of the fact that the letter of the law inscribed on stone kills, but the Spirit

---

[150] Be Stirred Not Shaken, "Year of Jubilee & Pentecost — Inheritance & Freedom," https://bestirrednotshaken.com/prophecy/year-of-jubilee-pentecost-inheritance-freedom/.

inscribed on the heart gives life (2 COR. 3:3-6; JER. 31:31-34; EZEK. 11:19). No longer was circumcision of the flesh required of the Jews, for the circumcision of the heart by the Holy Spirit was superior, and it was available to everyone (ROM. 2:29; GAL. 6:15).

Similar to how the people asked Moses to commune with God privately on their behalf (EXOD. 19:5-8; 24:3), the Holy Spirit was sent to be our *paráklētos*, our advocate and mediator in place of Christ, which also instructs us in the new Torah of the new covenant (MATT. 10:17-20; MARK 13:11; LUKE 12:12; JOHN 14:16, 26; 15:26; 16:7-15; ROM. 8:26; 1 COR. 2:13). The law of the new covenant is much simpler. The fundamental law is love towards God and mankind not from instruction, but from the inner attitude of the heart (MATT. 7:8-12, 25:35-40; MARK 12:29-31; 1 JOHN 3:18-24). Jesus remarked that the law is summarised by these two commandments of love, so to love is to fulfil the law (ROM. 13:8-10; GAL. 5:13-18; 1 JOHN 3:21-24; 4:20-21; JAMES 2:8-13). This message was present throughout the Old Testament, but it was not until the Word manifested in the flesh that the hearts of all men could be turned from stone into flesh (EZEK. 11:19; 36:26; JER. 4:4; GEN. 22:18).

*Image 6.4 – Pictographic meaning of the Hebrew word ahavah (love)*

| LETTER | PICTOGRAPHIC MEANING |
|---|---|
| Aleph (א) | strong, leader |
| Hey (ה) | behold, breath |
| Bet (ב) | house, in |
| Hey (ה) | behold, breath |
| **INTERPRETATION FROM COMBINED MEANINGS** | |
| The strong leader beholds his house and breathes on those within | |

The impartation of the Holy Spirit empowered the disciples to raise up the Church, a new body of believers consecrated as new creations in Christ. The Spirit that was before reserved for the few, and under special conditions (JUDG. 3:7-11; 1 SAM. 16:13; PSA. 51:9-12), was poured out upon all who called on the name of the Lord (ROM. 10:11-13; JOEL 2:28-32; ISA. 40:5; 44:3). The two leavened loaves waved before the Lord on Pentecost signified His yearning for unity between Israel and the gentiles in a circumcised state of the heart (unleavened) (Lev. 23:17-20; Num. 28:26-31; Eph. 2:11-22). Those gathered to him unleavened in heart, whether Jew or gentile, are to comprise a "new Israel, a priestly kingdom" (Exod. 19:16; 1 Pet. 2:9). We see all throughout the Old Testament how God intended for the gentile nations to enter the blessings given to the tribes of Israel (Gen. 12:3; 17:2; Psa. 67; Isa. 2:23; 49:6; 52:15; Hos. 2:23). God commanded Adam and Eve to tend the garden, to be fruitful, and to subdue the earth, and Jesus instructed his Church to become a fruitful blessing in his name to all nations, tribes, and tongues (Rev. 5:9-10; 7:9-10).

This was first evidenced by the Holy Spirit coming upon the gentile Cornelius and his household (Acts 10). After being confronted with this new reality, the stunned apostle Peter realised that God "accepts from every nation the one who fears him and does what is right" and so he humbly ordered that they be baptised in Christ all the same (Acts 10:34-35, 44-48). The Jewish believers at the Jerusalem council agreed to extend the right hand of fellowship to the gentiles after hearing Peter's testimony and that of Paul and Barnabas who had witnessed "signs and wonders God had done among the Gentiles" (Acts 11:12-21; 15:7-11).

> *For through Him we both have access by one Spirit to the Father. Now, therefore, you are no longer strangers and foreigners, but fellow citizens with the saints and members of the household of God, having been built on the foundation of the apostles and prophets, Jesus Christ Himself being the chief cornerstone, in whom the whole building, being fitted together, grows into a holy temple in the Lord, in whom you also are being built together for a dwelling place of God in the Spirit (Eph. 2:18-22 NKJV).*

Humanity became united together by the Holy Spirit in the body of Christ, the true spiritual temple (Eph. 2:11-22; John 2:19-21). Now the true temple is wherever believers commune under Christ. They are the living stones of which it consists, the "holy priesthood" who serve God through the high priest that is Christ, the cornerstone (1 PET. 2:4-9; EPH. 2:19-22; ACTS 6:1-7).

## Succession of the Priesthood

Following Pentecost, the new spiritual temple began to be fitted together one stone at a time. The old physical temple which stood in Jerusalem was made obsolete and doomed for destruction. Jesus foretold its fate, precisely stating that not one stone would be left upon another (MATT. 24:1-2). The Most High graciously provided a forty-year grace period for the transition from the physical temple to the spiritual temple in Christ (JER. 31:31-34). The symbolism of forty in scripture is widely known for its association with a period of testing, trial, or probation (GEN. 7:12; EXOD. 24:18; DEUT. 8:2-5; 9:18, 25; JUDG. 13:1; 1 SAM. 17:16; JON. 3:4; MATT. 4:2; ACTS 1:3; 7:30). The forty years that elapsed from the death of Christ to the destruction of the temple can be described perfectly in these terms. A number of supernatural happenings occurred in the temple for these forty years, and the rabbis acknowledged them for the portends of judgement which they were, but still did not heed the signs.[151] These accounts were likely transmitted contemporaneously or close to it, but we first see them compiled in the Mishnah from 200 AD. The Jerusalem Talmud tractate *Yoma* 6:3 (or 33b) offered commentary on these historical records from the Mishnah:

---

[151] B. Talmud Sanhedrin 41a:25; Just as there was a great earthquake at the giving of the law at Mount Sinai to Moses (EXOD. 19:18-20), an earthquake occurred when the law was perfectly fulfilled at Golgotha by Jesus, and again after his resurrection. The Talmud may have provided testimony of the great earthquake, for it is said that forty years before the destruction of the temple, corresponding to the time of Christ's death, an earthquake badly damaged the Chamber of Hewn Stone where the Sanhedrin met on the Temple Mount. They were forced to move to other quarters and the huge temple doors could no longer be kept closed. This being the case, could it be that the judgement against Jesus within the Chamber of Hewn Stones was the last judgment ever given by the Sanhedrin within the temple?

> Forty years before the destruction of the Temple the western light went out, the crimson thread remained crimson, and the lot for the Lord always came up in the left hand. They would close the gates of the Temple by night and get up in the morning and find them wide open.[152]

A similar report is given in the later Babylonian Talmud tractate *Yoma* 4:1 (or 39a-b):

> [F]orty years prior to the destruction of the Second Temple, the lot for God did not arise in the High Priest's right hand at all. So too, the strip of crimson wool that was tied to the head of the goat that was sent to Azazel did not turn white, and the westernmost lamp of the candelabrum did not burn continually. And the doors of the Sanctuary opened by themselves as a sign that they would soon be opened by enemies.[153]

These sources act as crucial extra-biblical authentications for the faith because the accusation cannot be made that they are sympathetic to the testimony of Christ, or that later interpolations were made to falsely support the Christian account. Each of these signs compounded the reality that God had withdrawn His presence from the temple because the greater priesthood of Christ had replaced it. Let us briefly explain the significance of each of these elements.

### 1. Temple Lamp

According to the law of Moses, the seven lamps of the menorah in the Holy Place of the temple were required to be tended continually so their light would never be extinguished (Lev. 24:1-4; Exod. 27:21). The western-most lamp was called the servant light

---

[152] Y. Talmud Yoma 6:3 [I:4 A-B] (ed. Jacob Neusner) and 33b (ed. Sefaria).
[153] B. Talmud Yoma 4:1 (ed. Jacob Neusner) and 39a.15, b.5-6 (ed. Sefaria).

(Hebrew *shamash*), because it was used to rekindle the other branches of the menorah. By the light of the shamash the other lamps could shine, but for these forty years the shamash continuously burnt out. This deeply troubling sign strongly suggested that the temple was no longer sanctioned by God, the source of this light. His light had indeed moved away from the temple and its priesthood because the greater Church had been established by Christ. He was the light of the world prophesied by Isaiah to lead us out of darkness and into his light (Isa. 42:6-7; 49:6; Matt. 4:14-16; John 3:19; 8:12; 9:5; 12:46; Acts 26:23). By his perfect death and resurrection we may be reborn in him and become "the light of the world" to spread the gospel of his salvation (Matt. 5:14-16; Acts 13:47).

> *Then Jesus spoke to them again, saying, "I am the light of the world. He who follows Me shall not walk in darkness, but have the light of life" (John 8:12 NKJV).*

When John of Patmos walked through the new Jerusalem in Spirit he discovered there was no temple in it, rather that God and the Lamb (Christ) are its temple, and that "the glory of God gives it light, and the Lamb is its lamp" (Rev. 21:22-23). The spiritual temple menorah was elsewhere identified by Christ as being the Church by his metaphor of the seven golden lampstands as the seven churches (Rev. 1:12-13, 20). In other words, the Lamb is the *shamash*, the servant light by which we as believers in his Church are illuminated (Rev. 21:24).

## 2. Temple Doors

For the temple doors to swing open on their own was no small feat because it would take at least ten men to open them. This report was corroborated by the historian Josephus in his historical account *The Wars of the Jews*:

> *The eastern gate of the inner [court of the] temple, which was of brass, and vastly heavy, and had been with*

> *difficulty shut by twenty men, and rested upon a basis armed with iron, and had bolts fastened very deep into the firm floor, which was there made of one entire stone, was seen to be opened of its own accord about the sixth hour of the night. Now those that kept watch in the temple came hereupon running to the captain of the temple, and told him of it; who then came up thither, and not without great difficulty was able to shut the gate again.*[154]

It was therefore reasonable for the Rabbis to point to this as a portend of destruction for the temple, as recorded in the Babylonian Talmud tractate *Yoma*:

> *Sanctuary, Sanctuary, why do you frighten yourself with these signs? I know about you that you will ultimately be destroyed, and Zechariah, son of Ido, has already prophesied concerning you: "Open your doors, O Lebanon, that the fire may devour your cedars" (Zech. 11:1).*[155]

This was literally fulfilled when the temple burned down, for the cedars of Lebanon were used in its construction (Ezra 3:7). By this time it was abundantly clear to the Jews that God no longer protected them from the forces seeking their destruction. Unfortunately, they did not heed the warnings from Christ and seek refuge in the spiritual temple which cannot be destroyed (John 2:19-21; 1 Cor. 3:16; 6:16-19; Eph. 2:19-22). But for those who do demonstrate saving faith, the gates to this temple of the "Lord God Almighty and the Lamb" shall never be shut to them (Rev. 21:22-27).

### 3. Lot for the Lord

The casting of lots on the Day of Atonement rendered the same

---

[154] Josephus, "The Wars of the Jews," 6.288.
[155] B. Talmud Yoma 39b.6.

result for each of the forty years before the destruction of the temple. As mentioned previously, these lots determined which of the two goats would be sacrificed as a sin offering, and which would become the scapegoat to bear the sins of the people into a desolate place. The verdict came from God Himself, for it is said: "[t]he lot is cast into the lap, but its every decision is from the Lord" (PROV. 16:33). The statistical improbability (or impossibility) of these results would be unfathomable unless for the sovereign choice of God, because the lots were drawn in a purely random manner. The Talmud states many precautions were taken by the high priest to eliminate his influence over the lottery so he would not stand accused of manipulating the results. This was considered a real concern because "it [was] a fortuitous omen for the lot for God to arise in his right hand."[156] For one esteemed high priest named Shimon HaTzaddik it was said that the lot for the Lord always came up in his right hand as a sign of God's favour.[157]

The lot for the Lord continued to come up in the left hand of the high priest because Christ, as the lot for the Lord from the foundation of the world (REV. 13:8), had accomplished the sin offering to which the ceremony pointed. God placed no importance in these old ceremonies. Having satisfied the righteousness of God, Jesus came up from death to sit at the right hand of God, the place of supreme honour (PSA. 110:1-7; ROM. 10:12-13; HEB. 1:3; 12:2; ACTS 2:34; EPH. 1:20).

*4. Scarlet Cord*

During the Day of Atonement, a tradition developed of attaching a crimson-coloured strap to the scapegoat for Azazel and to the door of the temple. If the temple strap turned from red to white once the scapegoat reached the wilderness, it was believed that the sins of Israel had been forgiven by God. The Talmud discussed at

---

[156] Ibid. 39a.8.
[157] Ibid. 39a.15-16, 39b.5-6.

length this Second Temple period Day of Atonement ceremony:[158]

> There was a strip of crimson tied to the entrance to the Sanctuary, and when the goat reached the wilderness and the mitzva was fulfilled the strip would turn white, as it is stated: "Though your sins be as scarlet, they will become white as snow" (Isa. 1:18).[159]

It was therefore deeply troubling for the people when, according to Talmud tractate *Rosh Hoshanah*: "during the forty years before the Second Temple was destroyed the strip of crimson wool would not turn white; rather, it would turn a deeper shade of red."[160]

The deepening red strip reflected their growing need for atonement because their sins were no longer being forgiven by God during the yearly Day of Atonement. The blood of goats sprinkled in the Most Holy Place were no longer efficacious for atonement. It could no longer turn them white. Instead, as symbolised by the deepening red strip, their sins were compounding each year. This is because at the beginning of these forty years, the lot for the Lord to which these sacrifices pointed was sacrificed. Jesus' blood of atonement was effective not for a year, but for all time, but his people did not accept his sacrifice:

> Not with the blood of goats and calves, but with His own blood He entered the Most Holy Place once for all, having obtained eternal redemption (Heb. 9:12 NKJV).

Outside of the true remnant of Israel who faithfully preached the gospel, being led by the Spirit promised through Moses and the

---

[158] B. Talmud Shabbat 86a states: *"By a miracle, this crimson-colored strap turned white, thus showing the people that they were forgiven of their sins. Rabbi Ishmael says, 'Now did they not have any other sign? There was a crimson thread tied to the door of the sanctuary. When the goat had reached the wilderness, the thread would turn white...'"*

[159] Mishnah Yoma 6:8; B. Talmud Yoma 68b.9.

[160] B. Talmud Rosh Hashanah 31b:16-17.

prophets, the Jews denied the transformation altogether. Whereas the Ninevites listened to Jonah and repented to evade judgement after forty days, the Jews refused the protection of Jesus, so Rome came to destroy the temple, and thus the priesthood in 70 AD (MATT. 23:37-38; 24:1-2; LUKE 21:24). Once the temple was destroyed, they simply moved to the synagogues and worshipped by prayer and study rather than sacrifice. The priesthood was replaced by the rabbis who became the teachers and leaders of their communities. These changes culminated in the development of rabbinical Judaism, with later texts such as the Talmud reaching similar importance to the Tanakh (OT).

**The Mystery of Appearances**

From the time Jesus resurrected until his ascension forty days later, we are given no indication that he appeared to the Sanhedrin, the priests, nor the general Jewish population. We know only that he appeared to at least five hundred of his Jewish disciples (1 COR. 15:3-8; ACTS 1:3; 10:40-42).

> *God raised him from the dead on the third day and caused him to be seen. He was not seen by all the people, but by witnesses whom God had already chosen—by us who ate and drank with him after he rose from the dead. He commanded us to preach to the people and to testify that he is the one whom God appointed as judge of the living and the dead (Acts 10:40-42 NIV).*

One might wonder why Jesus did not simply present himself to the world at large in his resurrected state and preach repentance like Jonah did for the Ninevites (JON. 3:1-5; 4:1-2). Presumably, people would accept the irrefutable physical evidence of his resurrection and believe him to be who he said was. But consider what Jesus said to his disciples the day before he was crucified:

> *Before long, the world will not see me anymore, but you will see me. Because I live, you also will live. On that*

> day you will realize that I am in my Father, and you are in me, and I am in you ... Then Judas (not Judas Iscariot) said, "But, Lord, why do you intend to show yourself to us and not to the world?" Jesus replied, "Anyone who loves me will obey my teaching. My Father will love them, and we will come to them and make our home with them. Anyone who does not love me will not obey my teaching. These words you hear are not my own; they belong to the Father who sent me *(John 14:19-20, 22-24 NIV)*.

Jesus sought out those with hearts that could be softened to his message. Those he foreknew would follow him. For he said: "all those the Father gives me will come to me, and whoever comes to me I will never drive away" (JOHN 6:37; PSA. 17:6). He did not set out to forcibly convert the Sadducees or the Pharisees, or to convince the masses by his miracles. In fact, he often told the witnesses to keep it a secret. He made it clear that those who were to believe, *would* believe (MATT. 13:10-17; LUKE 16:19-31). When he brought Lazarus back from the dead, he waited four days to ensure he was past the point of corruption so that the people could believe. Notice how the religious authorities were informed of this extraordinary miracle but they denied it and even sought to kill Lazarus (JOHN 12:9-11). There was no level of evidence that would soften their hearts to the truth because they were fixated on their own power. Jesus undoubtedly foresaw the lukewarm reaction the Jews would have to his resurrection. The religious authorities heard from the guards that the sign of Jonah had been fulfilled by Christ, but yet they bribed them to spread a lie to avoid any investigation (MATT. 28:4, 11-15). These were first-hand witnesses to his death. They had every opportunity to prove or disprove the resurrection but did not. The people of Jerusalem heard the story that very day, but save for a remnant, even they did not come to believe (LUKE 24:18).

Many assume that if they just saw Jesus they would whole-heartedly believe in him and trust in his Word. Putting aside the response of his own brothers, we need only look at the case of Lucifer to know that seeing and knowing God does not preclude faithlessness and rebellion. It is not the knowledge of God which saves—it is the acceptance of God and His ways into our hearts and minds. He gives us the freedom to accept or reject that revelation of Himself.

> *You believe that there is one God. You do well. Even the demons believe—and tremble! (James 2:19 NKJV).*

Millions of people (myself included) can testify by faith that they have encountered this risen Christ by the spiritual revelation of the Holy Spirit. But how many of these witnesses (myself included) have actually put their fingers in his pierced side and hands like Thomas, or talked with him in person as a disciple for the forty days following his resurrection? (MATT. 28:6-20; MARK 16:9-20; LUKE 24:15-53; JOHN 20:24:31; 21:25; 1 COR. 15:1-8). From our point of view, spiritual testimony is secondary in value to the physical testimony which Thomas received, but in the words of Jesus, that which he values most is the spiritual testimony of those who hear and believe without seeing. The kind of love and faithfulness best developed not by physical encounter, but spiritual encounter through the Word. This requires a faith that is childlike in spirit and a devotion that yearns to hear and understand His Word (MATT. 18:3; 19:13-15; MARK 10:14-15; LUKE 18:16-17). As it is said, without faith it is impossible to please God, and "faith comes by hearing, and hearing by the word of God" (HEB. 11:6; ROM. 10:17). Consider what he said to Thomas after he reached into his pierced side and finally believed by sight after dismissing the testimony he had heard from the disciples:

> *"Because you have seen me, you have believed; blessed are those who have not seen and yet have believed" (John 20:24-31 NIV).*

This may lead one to ask the question, if faith in God by hearing is paramount, why should the God of Israel differentiate between faith in Him from faith in other gods? Or from a non-Christian perspective, what differentiates faith in the God of Israel from faith in other gods? To that I answer that the key is not the capacity for man to have faith, it being clear we can place faith in the false or objectionable, but it is the object of that faith. If the object of that faith is the ultimate transcendent truth, and the identity of this object can be repeatedly inferred from a large body of cumulative evidence (the Bible), it stands that it is a reasonable faith. The reason why the good news of the gospel *is* the good news is because it provides man with a faith that is justifiable, and by which we can be justified (ROM. 3:21-28). Besides this gospel, there are no other means of justification. Christ is the narrow gate to salvation (JOHN 10:9; 14:5-6).

> *"Enter by the narrow gate; for wide is the gate and broad is the way that leads to destruction, and there are many who go in by it. Because narrow is the gate and difficult is the way which leads to life, and there are few who find it" (Matt. 7:13-14 NKJV).*

It is not enough to simply have faith because outside of him there are no men, gods, or pursuits that can take us before the Father (JOHN 14:5-6). Nor can any number of good works replace our need for Christ, for as the prophet Isaiah remarked, "all of us have become like one who is unclean, and all our righteous deeds are like a filthy garment ... and our wrongdoings, like the wind, take us away" (ISA. 64:6). In fact, good works can often become the barrier which keeps us from our own justification. Even in pursuit of the good we are susceptible in our fallen nature to the message of self-justification from the serpent:

> *"Very truly I tell you Pharisees, anyone who does not enter the sheep pen by the gate, but climbs in by some other way, is a thief and a robber. The one who enters by the gate is the shepherd of the sheep" (John 10:1 NIV).*

It is all too easy to declare ourselves good and righteous through the good deeds we perform, but it is difficult to accept that we are sinners under judgement. We cannot enter the kingdom of God through works or self-esteem. To become part of God's flock we must enter through the gate provided by our good shepherd in Christ. We must accept the gospel by faith that Christ died for us as the testator of the new covenant so that, like with any will, we as its beneficiaries can receive our inheritance from his estate— the new creation (HEB. 9:16-17).

## Servant in the Spring, King in the Fall

Jesus became the roots of the harvest during Passover and Unleavened Bread and planted the first three thousand seeds on Pentecost, germinating them with the spring rains from the Holy Spirit. People from every nation, tribe, and tongue have since received living water from the Holy Spirit and grown fruitful in God's great harvest (DAN. 7:14; ACTS 20:28; REV. 5:9; 7:9). But eschatologically speaking, of the Three Pilgrimage festivals (Unleavened Bread, Pentecost, and Tabernacles), only the first two, or the spring rains, have so far been celebrated (EXOD. 23:14-19; 34:18-26; DEUT. 16:1-17). It is outside the scope of this book to deal with the specifics of the fall feast fulfilments, but very briefly, I believe Trumpets is associated with the second coming of Christ,[161] the Day of Atonement the subsequent binding of Satan and the repentance of Israel,[162] and Tabernacles the initial harvest of humanity for the millennial kingdom and again at the end of the millennium for the new heaven and earth.[163]

In the meantime, we find ourselves in a dry period of maturation between these spring and fall rains, the first and second comings of Christ. The apostle James exhorted us to be

---

[161] **Trumpets:** LEV. 23:23-25; NUM. 29:1-6; ISA. 27:13; JOEL 2:1; MATT. 24:29-36; 1 COR. 15:51-53; 1 THESS. 4:15-16; REV. 11:15-18.

[162] **Day of Atonement:** LEV. 16; 23:26-32; NUM. 29:7-11; REV. 20:1-3.

[163] **Tabernacles:** EXOD. 23:16-17, 22-23; LEV. 23:33-44; DEUT. 16:13-17; NUM. 29:12-40; ZECH. 12:10; 14:16-19; 16-21; JOEL 3:13; MATT. 13:24-30, 36-40; JOHN 7:37-39; REV. 19:11-21; 20:1-10; 21:3.

patient for "the coming of the Lord," just as the farmer waits patiently for "the early (fall) and latter (spring) rain" (JAMES 5:7-9). It can be disheartening to see a world in spiritual drought, with only sporadic showers to sustain God's fields, but there must be sufficient time for the field of souls to accumulate. This is the purpose of the long season. Jesus told us to leave the judgement and separation of the godly wheat from the ungodly tares to him (MATT. 13:24-43). Both must "grow together until the harvest" at the end of the age because it is not for us to judge the "sons of the kingdom" from the "sons of the wicked one." Our task is to send the gospel forth and help sow "good seed" for the Holy Spirit to germinate with living water (MATT. 4:19; 13:24). We must remember to work God's fields with the guidance and backing of the Holy Spirit. As soon as we decide to control or misuse the Spirit, no sooner it will depart from us, leaving only its counterfeit behind. We have seen extraordinary spiritual revivals throughout history such as the reformation in Europe, the great revival in Wales, and the Azusa Street revival in Los Angeles, but for one reason or another the rains cease and by consequence so does the movement's vitality and influence.

> *Repent therefore and be converted, that your sins may be blotted out, so that times of refreshing may come from the presence of the Lord, whom heaven must receive until the period of restoration of all things about which God spoke by the mouth of His holy prophets from ancient time (Acts 3:20-21 NJKV).*

God has promised to His own people, the Jews, that although they have received the least of the rain from the Holy Spirit throughout history, soon they shall experience it unceasingly (HOS. 6:3; JER. 5:24; JOEL 2:23; 3:17-18). He will not depend on the Church to spark a spiritual revival like all other nations. He will seek them out directly. Israel, being the firstfruits of God, must—and will—be planted with the gentiles to bring the harvest to its fullness. The actualisation of the new covenant is contingent upon the entrance of national Israel to whom the covenant was initially promised (JER. 31:31-34).[164] The apostle Paul made it clear in Romans 11 that as much as the world was blessed through the stumbling of Israel, even more this shall be so when Israel is reconciled to God. In his commentary of this chapter, the second-century church father Origen elaborated on these words of Paul:

> *At the present time, while all the Gentiles are [still] coming to salvation, the riches of God are being gathered from the multitude of believers. But as long as Israel persists in unbelief, the fullness of the Lord's portion will not be said to be completed; for the people of Israel are missing from the whole. Yet when the fullness of the Gentiles enters in and Israel comes to salvation through faith in the end time, it will be that the very people which had been first would, in coming last, somehow complete that fullness of the inheritance and portion of God.*[165]

We do not yet see the visible reign of Christ as the Davidic "King of kings and Lord of lords" (PHIL. 2:5-11; REV. 19:16) but rest assured that he is working. The late Ivan Panin summed up the current and future duties of Christ perfectly:

> *As prophet He was sent to the Jews alone, and in a body in likeness of sinful flesh, and was visible to all and accessible to all. He became Priest, High Priest, when after being slain as the Lamb of God, and His blood is shed for the sins of the whole world, He enters the Holy of Holies and there presents the blood shed ... As prophet and priest, He is away from earth, His abode is in the*

---

[164] Master, John R, and Wesley R. Willis, *Issues in Dispensationalism*, 108: "The new covenant has been cut. The actualization of the new covenant in the lives of believers, however, is yet future, when Christ returns and the house of Israel and the house of Judah are transformed by God's grace to obey completely the commands of God."

[165] Origen, *Commentary on the Epistle to the Romans, Book 6-10*, 170.

> *heavens and He is not visible to all. The prophet is seen by saint and sinner alike, by everyone in fact, the priest is no longer seen by sinners. If seen at all it is only by the saint, and this too only on special occasions, and by the few. But as king He is again to be seen by all ... but in the body of His priesthood. As prophet the Jews as a nation would not have Him. As the priest the world would not have Him. As the king both the Jews and the World shall have Him.*[166]

Israel may have rejected Jesus as the Mashiach ben Joseph (messianic suffering servant) in the spring, but they shall accept him in the fall. In these days, the Holy Spirit will pour out the fall rains upon Israel to soften their hearts to the understanding of Jesus as Messiah (2 Sam. 7:12-13; Ezek. 37:24-28). On that final Day of Atonement, Israel shall look upon Jesus in the same way as the Ninevites who repented in ashes and sackcloth and mourned over their rejection of the servant of God (Zech. 12:1-14). Hearing that his people have finally accepted him, Christ will return to them as the Mashiach ben David (messianic king):

> *"See! Your house is left to you desolate; for I say to you, you shall see Me no more till you say, 'Blessed is He who comes in the name of the Lord!'" (Matt. 23:38-39 NKJV).*

When Jesus made his triumphal entry into Jerusalem at his first coming, the faithful among the Jews laid palm branches before him and sung "Hosanna!' Blessed is he who comes in the name of the Lord! Blessed is the king of Israel!" (John 12:12-13; Psa. 118:24-26). The whole nation will sing his praises when he returns and, fitting their expectations at his first coming, will be gathered into the messianic kingdom to celebrate the feast of Tabernacles with God and the resurrected saints:

---

[166] Panin, *Bible Chronology Restored*, IX Canon VI.

> *So shout for joy, you sons of Zion, and rejoice in the Lord your God; for He has given you the early rain for your vindication. And He has brought down for you the rain, the early and latter rain as before. The threshing floors will be full of grain, and the vats will overflow with the new wine and oil (Joel 2:23-24 NASB).*

The glory which Adam and Eve possessed before the judgement will pale in comparison to the glory we shall receive after we are released from the shackles of sin which plague our beings (1 JOHN 1:5-7; 8-10). Our leavened earthly bodies of corruptibility will be replaced with unleavened heavenly bodies of incorruptibility in the image of Christ (1 JOHN 3:2; PHIL. 3:20-21; 1 COR. 15:42-53; 2 COR. 3:17-18). The familiar pattern of God's dealings with humanity where judgement is followed by even greater mercy will be brought to its climax after Jesus' reign during the millennial kingdom:

> *Then comes the end, when He delivers the kingdom to God the Father, when He puts an end to all rule and all authority and power. For He must reign till He has put all enemies under His feet. The last enemy that will be destroyed is death. For "He has put all things under His feet." But when He says "all things are put under Him," it is evident that He who put all things under Him is excepted. Now when all things are made subject to Him, then the Son Himself will also be subject to Him who put all things under Him, that God may be all in all (1 Cor. 15:24-28 NKJV).*

## Conclusion

The foundational argument laid out in this book has been that the protoevangelium—God's promise to the woman (Eve) of a descendant to defeat the deceiving serpent—found its fulfilment in the person of Jesus Christ (GEN. 3:15). God triumphed over Satan—the great architect of rebellion and sin—by personally manifesting in the flesh and conquering both sin and death through his resurrection (GAL. 3:13-14; ROM. 4:25; 1 COR. 15:20-28; JOHN 10:17-18; 1 JOHN 3:5). The serpent may have bruised his heel in the process, but this was the very means by which he bruised the serpent's head.

The accusations Satan makes against us before God he cannot make against Christ. For this reason, God can now righteously judge and punish Satan without putting those in Christ under the same condemnation. God extends the blamelessness and righteousness of Christ to everyone who accepts him. Not only the Jews, but all "those who have the faith of Abraham" are reckoned among his Seed, namely Jesus Christ, so they too may become a second Adam, and be restored to the tree of life in the new creation (HEB. 4:16; GAL. 3:16).

By the same token, just as God allowed the rebellious serpent into the garden, God affords us the same freedom to disobey and choose our own path. We can all choose to remain as gods in our own eyes like the serpent in the garden of Eden. The aim of the companion book "Seed of Satan: Antichrist" is to understand the spiritual calling of this opposing seed of the serpent, and ultimately, to discover the possible identity of the false Christ, the Antichrist. This is important to understand because although Jesus dealt the deathblow to the Satanic powers through his death and resurrection, they have not yet been cast out. It can be likened to how the battle of Normandy during World War Two marked the beginning of the end of the war and the liberation of Western Europe from Nazi Germany. Rest assured, Jesus is justified as king to tread underfoot all principalities and powers that conspired against his Father, and ultimately, to crush the head of the serpent's seed, the Antichrist, but this will happen after the millennium when Satan is cast into the lake of fire.

Once again, I remind you, we are presented with two opposing sons, each claiming to be the light of mankind and the spiritual authority over the earth. To one of these two men alone shall mankind submit to in the days to come. I sincerely hope this book has helped you on your spiritual journey, whether you are reading as a Christian, as a follower of another faith, or as an atheist.

*If you enjoyed this book, please consider leaving a rating or a review on Amazon at the store page "Seed of God: Jesus Christ."*

*I have also published a companion to this book called "Seed of Satan: Antichrist" and written free articles on the website beholdmessiah.com which further explore these topics.*

# Appendix

**Jesus as the Word of Creation**

The numerical pattern called gematria encoded within the Bible simultaneously tells and validates interconnected stories. Gematria is the process of computing numeric values of letters, words, or phrases for the purpose of finding correspondence between words or concepts. Gematria was used by the Hebrews contemporaneous with the writing of the Bible, so it is likely that it was more widely understood at the time. That was certainly the case for early Jewish scholars, called the soferim (counters), who would copy the Torah by calculating the gematria of each verse, chapter, and book. If the numerical value of the original scroll did not match with their copy, they would discard it and start again. This process ensured the integrity of the text from generation to generation, and the spiritual currency was left intact. This same process was used in the writing and interpretation of the Greek New Testament but it is called isosephy rather than gematria.

*Biblical Significance of Seven*

Before we tackle the gematria that lies under the surface, I will highlight some patterns that appear plainly in the Bible to illustrate this concept more simply. You might have wondered about the significance of certain numbers that feature prominently in scripture. Undoubtedly, you have encountered the number seven—and for good reason. Seven is the most significant number in scripture, symbolizing divine perfection and rest. Remember that God rested on the seventh day of creation, seeing that it was perfect (Gen. 2:1-3). Here are some examples:

*Appendix*

*Image A.1 – Biblical significance of number seven*

| EXAMPLE(S) | FORMULA |
|---|---|
| God resting day after creation; days in week; sabbath year; feasts; trumpets; many metaphors in book of Revelation; spirits of God; times the Word is purified | 7 x 1 |
| Jubilee year; days from firstfruits to Pentecost | 7 x 7 |
| Seventy sevens prophecy of Daniel; times Jesus said to forgive; Lamech's vengeance | 7 x 70 |

As you can see here, the pattern of seven that exists from beginning to end in scripture is not arbitrary—in fact, it ties into the numbers meaning as the divine stamp of God's complete word. Gematria takes this one step further by embedding another layer of meaning under the surface as a hidden seal. This works to corroborate the scripture and further highlight the significance of the plain pattern of seven.

## Patterns of Seven in Genesis

Credit for the following findings go to the great Russian mathematician, Ivan Panin. One of his spectacular findings from the Genesis 1:1 relates to this pattern of seven which verifies God's authorship of this pattern and His creative works:

> In the beginning God created the heavens and the earth. Bereshit bara Elohim et hashamayim ve'et ha'aretz.
> בְּרֵאשִׁית בָּרָא אֱלֹהִים אֵת הַשָּׁמַיִם וְאֵת הָאָרֶץ

*Image A.2 – Gematria pattern of seven in Genesis 1:1*

| EXAMPLE(S) | VALUE | FORMULA |
|---|---|---|
| number of words; letters in middle and left word; letters in middle and right word; letters in the two objects "heaven," "earth"; first letter of first and last word | 7 | 7 x 1 |
| number of letters in the nouns | 14 | 7 x 2 |
| number of letters | 28 | 7 x 4 |
| sum of first and last letters of the first half | 42 | 7 x 6 |
| sum of first and last letters of the second half | 91 | 7 x 13 |

*Seed of God: Jesus Christ*

| | | |
|---|---|---|
| sum of first, middle, and last letters | 133 | 7 x 19 |
| value of the one verb "created" | 203 | 7 x 29 |
| sum of last letters of first and last words | 490 | 7 x 70 |
| sum of first and last letters of first and last words | 497 | 7 x 71 |
| sum of all three nouns "God," "heaven," "earth" | 777 | 7 x 111 |
| sum of first and last words | 1393 | 7 x 199 |

In the overall creation account these features are found:

*Image A.3 – Gematria pattern of seven in the creation account*

| WORD(S) | INSTANCES | FORMULA |
|---|---|---|
| on the earth; heaven(s) sky; good; waters; flying; fly; birds; crawls; walks; land animals; day; days | 7 | 7 x 1 |
| earth; land | 21 | 7 x 3 |
| God | 35 | 7 x 5 |

For Moses (or anyone for that matter) to have written the creation account with this signature watermark, let alone the entire Torah as is attributed to him, would require a supernatural mathematical intelligence. Panin came to this same conclusion. Moreover, in both the Old and New Testament revelations, we have another forty odd authors spanning roughly 1500 years with this same unique ability. Did they all possess this supernatural talent by sheer coincidence, or were they divinely instructed?

*Patterns of Seven in Christ's Genealogy*

This pattern of seven runs all through the genealogy of Christ up to Adam as given by Matthew. This highlights how the same author of the first creation is at work on a new creation which began after Christ's resurrection. Because the New Testament is written in Greek, the process of finding these patterns is slightly different, called isosephy instead of gematria.

*Isosephy pattern of seven in the genealogy of Christ given by Matthew (vv. 1-17).*

*Appendix*

| EXAMPLE(S) | VALUE | FORMULA |
|---|---|---|
| words in more than one form; compound nouns | 7 | 7 x 1 |
| words appearing only once | 14 | 7 x 2 |
| words appearing more than once | 35 | 7 x 5 |
| words in only one form | 42 | 7 x 6 |
| nouns | 56 | 7 x 8 |

*Image A.4 – Isosephy pattern of seven in the first section of the genealogy of Jesus given by Matthew (vv. 1-11)*

| EXAMPLE(S) | VALUE | FORMULA |
|---|---|---|
| words that are not nouns; words ending with a vowel | 7 | 7 x 1 |
| words beginning with a consonant | 21 | 7 x 3 |
| words beginning with a vowel | 28 | 7 x 4 |
| nouns that are proper names | 35 | 7 x 5 |
| words ending with a consonant; nouns | 42 | 7 x 6 |
| words | 49 | 7 x 7 |
| consonants | 126 | 7 x 18 |
| vowels | 140 | 7 x 20 |
| letters | 266 | 7 x 38 |

Panin found that the account of the virgin birth of Jesus in Matthew 1:18-25 was packed with dozens of seals of seven. Furthermore, the resurrection testimony of Jesus and his commission to his disciples had at least 75 seals of seven carefully embedded in the text of Mark 16:9-21. It should also be noted that Jesus was crucified at Golgotha which is elevated 777 metres above sea level. This seal of seven is consistent throughout the Hebrew Old Testament and Greek New Testament.

# References

Adat Hatikvat Tzion. "The Tallit and Tzitzit." https://adat.org/the-tallit-and-tzitzit/.

Adu-Gyamfi, Yaw. "The Live Goat Ritual in Leviticus 16." *Scriptura 112* (January 2013): 1-10.

Armstrong, Herbert W. *God's Festivals and Holy Days*. Pasadena: Worldwide Church of God, 1992.

———. *Pagan Holidays or God's Holy Days—Which?* Pasadena: Worldwide Church of God, 1974.

Barrick, William. "The Mosaic Covenant." *Journal of The Master's Seminary* 10, no. 2 (Fall 1999).

Battle, Michael. "The High Priest, the Garments, and the Holy of Holies." *Rooted and Grounded in Christ*, March 31, 2016. https://rootedandgroundedinchrist.com/2016/03/31/the-high-priest-the-garments-and-the-holy-of-holies/.

Be Stirred Not Shaken. "Year of Jubilee & Pentecost — Inheritance & Freedom." May 16, 2015. https://bestirrednotshaken.com/prophecy/year-of-jubilee-pentecost-inheritance-freedom/.

Black, Edwin. "Hell on Earth." *The Washington Post*, August 29, 1999. https://www.washingtonpost.com/archive/lifestyle/1999/08/29/hell-on-earth/a2777d75-cfa6-4325-814a-0a26c83086c5/.

Brigden, Larry. "Monogenes: 'Only Begotten' or 'One of a Kind'?" *Christian Library*. https://www.christianstudylibrary.org/article/monogenes-%E2%80%9Conly-begotten%E2%80%9D-or-%E2%80%9Cone-kind%E2%80%9D.

Brown, Michael L. *Answering Jewish Objections to Jesus, Vol. 4: New Testament Objections*. Ada: Baker Publishing Group, 2006.

*References*

Carson, D. A. *The Gospel According to John*. Grand Rapids: Eerdmans, 1991.

Chisholm, Robert B. "Evidence from Genesis." Chap. 1 in *A Case for Premillennialism: A New Consensus*. Edited by Donald K. Campbell and Jeffrey L. Townsend. Chicago: Moody Press, 1992.

David, Leiba Chaya. "First Fruits (Bikkurim)." *My Jewish Learning*. https://www.myjewishlearning.com/article/first-fruits/.

Dean, David Andrew. "Covenant, Conditionality, and Consequence: New Terminology and a Case Study in the Abrahamic Covenant." *Journal of the Evangelical Theological Society* 57, no. 2 (2014): 281-308. https://www.etsjets.org/files/JETS-PDFs/57/57-2/JETS_57-2_281-308_Dean.pdf.

Delitzsch, Franz, and Carl Friedrich Keil. *Biblical Commentary on the Old Testament*. Edinburgh: T. & T. Clark, 1857.

Einsiedler, David. "Can We Prove Descent from King David?" *Avotaynu: The International Review of Jewish Genealogy* 9, no. 2, (1993): 29-34.

Fisher, Edward. *The Marrow of Modern Divinity*. Fearn: Christian Focus Publications, 2009.

Shurpin, Yehuda, and Tzvi Freeman. "Why Is Jewishness Matrilineal?" *Chabad*. https://www.chabad.org/library/article_cdo/aid/601092/jewish/Why-Is-Jewishness-Matrilineal.htm.

Grady, J. Lee. "How the Resurrection Broke Eden's Curse." *Charisma Magazine*, 2010. https://www.charismamag.com/blogs/fire-in-my-bones/9282-how-the-resurrection-broke-edens-curse.

Greenwold, Doug. "The Last Words of Jesus – What Did He Really Say and Mean?" *Preserving Bible Times*, March 9, 2014. https://preservingbibletimes.org/wp-content/uploads/2014/03/Story-II.Chapter2.pdf.

Grieve, Val. *Your Verdict on the Empty Tomb*. Welwyn Garden City: Evangelical Press, 2017.

Grisanti, Michael A. "The Davidic Covenant." *Journal of The Master's Seminary* 10, no. 2 (Fall 1999): 233-250. https://www.tms.edu/m/tmsj10p.pdf.

Gurtner, Daniel M. "The Veil Was Torn in Two." *Desiring God*, April 19, 2019. https://www.desiringgod.org/articles/the-veil-was-torn-in-two.

Heiser, Michael S. "The Day of Atonement in Leviticus 16: A Goat for Azazel." *Dr. Michael Heiser*, November 7, 2013. https://drmsh.com/day-atonement-leviticus-16-goat-azazel/.

Hunter, Sam. "Did God Turn His Back on Jesus?" *The Putting Green Devotional*, April 17, 2019. https://www.puttinggreenblog.com/2019/04/17/did-god-turn-his-back-on-jesus/.

Jerome. *The Homilies of Saint Jerome*. Translated by Marie Liguori Ewald. Washington D.C.; Catholic University of America, 1964-1966.

Jews for Jesus. *The Passover Symbols and Their Messianic Significance*. March 1, 2021. https://jewsforjesus.org/blog/the-passover-symbols-and-their-messianic-significance/.

Jones, Christopher. *Messiah and the Sign of Jonah: Blueprint for Messiah's Ministry*. Scotts Valley: CreateSpace, 2013.

Josephus, Flavius. *The Works of Flavius Josephus*. Translated by William Whiston. Auburn and Buffalo: John E. Beardsley, 1895.

Kahn, Ari. "It Never Crossed my Mind - Rabbi Ari Kahn on Parsha." *OU Torah*. https://outorah.org/p/21996/.

Kaiser, Walter C. "God's Promise Plan and His Gracious Law." *Journal of the Evangelical Theological Society* 33, no. 3 (September 1990): 289-302. https://www.etsjets.org/files/JETS-PDFs/33/33-3/33-3-pp289-302_JETS.pdf.

———. *The Messiah in the Old Testament*. Grand Rapids: Zondervan, 1995.

———. *Toward an Old Testament Theology*. Grand Rapids: Zondervan, 1978.

Kalisher, Meno. *Jesus in the Hebrew Scriptures: the Identity of the Messiah*. Jerusalem: Jerusalem Assembly House of Redemption, 2010.

Killian, Greg. "HaShem's Rehearsals." *Betemunah*. https://www.betemunah.org/rehearse.html.

Kingsbury, Jack Dean. "The Title 'Son of David' in Matthew's Gospel." *Journal of Biblical Literature* 95, no. 4 (December 1976): 591-602.

Kirk, David R. "Heaven Opened: Intertextuality and Meaning in John 1:51." *Tyndale Bulletin 63*, no. 2 (2012): 237-256. https://legacy.tyndalehouse.com/Bulletin/63=2012/05_Kirk-20.pdf.

Lee, Witness. *The Economy of God*. 6th ed. Anaheim: Living Stream Ministry, 1968.

Lewis, C.S. *Mere Christianity*. New York City: HarperCollins, 1952.

Ligonier Ministries. "The Covenant Fulfilled." June 30, 2004. https://www.ligonier.org/learn/devotionals/covenant-fulfilled.

Lunn, Nicholas P. "Jesus, the Ark, and the Day of Atonement: Intertextual Echoes in John 19:38—20:18." *Journal of the Evangelical Theological Society* 52, no. 4 (December 2009): 731-46. https://www.etsjets.org/files/JETS-PDFs/52/52-4/JETS%2052-4%20731-746%20Lunn.pdf.

Maimonides, Moses. *Mishneh Torah, Kings and Wars*. Translated by Reuven Brauner. Raanana: R. Brauner, 2002.

McDowell, Josh. *The New Evidence That Demands a Verdict*. Nashville: Thomas Nelson, 1999.

McDowell, Josh, and Bill Wilson. *Evidence for the Historical Jesus: A Compelling Case for His Life and His Claims*. Eugene: Harvest House Publishers, 2011.

McHugh, John F. *John 1-4: A Critical and Exegetical Commentary*. Edinburgh: T&T Clark, 2009.

McLaughlin, Ra. "Jesus and Jeconiah." *Biblical Perspectives Magazine* 1, no. 1 (March 1999).

Meier, John P. *A Marginal Jew: Rethinking the Historical Jesus.* New York: Doubleday, 1991.

Merrill, Eugene H. *Kingdom of Priests: A History of Old Testament Israel.* Ada Township: Baker Academic, 2008.

Milgrom, Jacob. *Leviticus 1-16.* New York: Anchor Bible, 1991.

———. "The Tassel and the Tallit." The Fourth Annual Rabbi Louis Fineberg Memorial Lecture. University of Cincinnati, 1981.

Nash, David. "Mary Magdalene and the Reversal of Eden." *Trinitas Blog*, January 25, 2020. https://trinitasblog.wordpress.com/2020/01/25/mary-magdalene-and-the-reversal-of-eden/.

Neusner, Jacob. *The Jerusalem Talmud: A Translation and Commentary.* Carol Stream: Tyndale House Publishers, 2010.

———. *The Talmud of Babylonia: An American Translation, Vol. 5 - Yoma, Part B: Chapters 3-5.* Tampa: University Of South Florida, 1994.

Nickelsburg, George W. E. *Jewish Literature Between the Bible and the Mishnah.* Minneapolis: Fortress Press, 2005.

Origen. "Against Celsus." In *The Ante-Nicene Fathers.* Edited by Alexander Roberts. Grand Rapids: Eerdmans, 1985.

———. *Commentary on the Epistle to the Romans, Book 6-10.* The Fathers of the Church: A New Translation vol. 104. Translated by Thomas P. Scheck. Washington, D.C.: Catholic University of America Press, 2002.

———. *Homilies on Leviticus, 1-16.* Translated by Gary Wayne Barkley. Washington, D.C.: Catholic University of America Press, 1990.

Panin, Ivan. *Bible Chronology Restored.* Kennebec County: New England Bible Sales, 2018.

Parsons, John J. "Behold the Goat of God!" *Hebrew for Christians.* https://www.hebrew4christians.com/Holidays/Fall_Holidays/Yom_Kippur/Goat_of_God/goat_of_god.html.

*References*

Payne, Zachary. "The Trinity and Marriage." *WISEN*, March 12, 2018. https://www.wisensda.org/blog/2018/3/12/the-trinity-and-marriage.

Prasch, Jacob. *The Final Words of Jesus and Satan's Lies*. Pittsburgh: Moriel Ministries, 1999.

Prince, Derek. "Because of the Angels: The Climax of the Conflict." *Derek Prince Ministries*. https://www.derekprince.com/teaching/01-1.

Radin, Victoria. "The Four Messianic Miracles." *HaDerek Ministries*. https://www.haderekministries.com/index.php/articles/62-old-testament-new-testament-typology/164-the-four-messianic-miracles.

Resnik, Russell. *Gateways to Torah: Joining the Ancient Conversation on the Weekly Portion*. Baltimore: Messianic Jewish Publishers, 2000.

Ross, Lesli Koppelman. "What Is Matzah?" *My Jewish Learning*. https://www.myjewishlearning.com/article/matzah/.

Shurpin, Yehuda. "Why Do We Hide the Afikomen?" *Chabad*. https://www.chabad.org/holidays/passover/pesach_cdo/aid/2910434/jewish/Why-Do-We-Hide-the-Afikomen.htm.

Siker, Jeffrey S. "Yom Kippuring Passover: Recombinant Sacrifice in Early Christianity." Chap. 5 in *Ritual and Metaphor: Sacrifice in the Bible*. Atlanta: Society of Biblical Literature, 2011.

Smith, David C. "The Exodus and Christian Baptism." *The Village Church Resources*, February 2, 2017. https://www.tvcresources.net/resource-library/articles/the-exodus-and-christian-baptism.

Smith, Ralph Allan. "Barabbas." *Theopolis Institute*, September 1, 2020. https://theopolisinstitute.com/barabbas/.

Spurgeon, Charles. "Supposing Him to be the Gardener." Sermon 1699 at the Metropolitan Tabernacle, Newington, December 31, 1882.

Stanke, Caroline. "The Motif of the Messiah in Zechariah 9-14." MA theses, Andrews University, 2018. https://dx.doi.org/10.32597/theses/128.

Strawn, Brent A. "Focus On Tower of Babel." *Oxford University Press*. https://global.oup.com/obso/focus/focus_on_towerbabel.

Strong, James. "3173. יָחִיד (yachid)." In *The Exhaustive Concordance of the Bible*. Nashville: Thomas Nelson, 2009. https://biblehub.com/hebrew/strongs_3173.htm.

Torrey, R.A. "Luke 3:23." In *The Treasury of Scripture Knowledge*. Sacred Texts. https://www.sacred-texts.com/bib/cmt/tsk/luk003.htm.

Turner, David and Darrell Bock. *Matthew, Mark*. Vol. 11 of *Cornerstone Biblical Commentary*. Carol Stream: Tyndale House Publishers, 2005.

Tverberg, Lois. "Letting Our Tassels Show." *Our Rabbi Jesus*, August 25, 2013. https://ourrabbijesus.com/articles/letting-our-tassels-show/.

Watch Tower Bible and Tract Society. "Genealogy of Jesus Christ." In vol. 1 of *Insight on the Scriptures*. New York: Watchtower Bible and Tract Society, 1988.

Wayne, Luke. "Does Luke 4:18 misquote Isaiah 61:1?" *CARM*, September 9, 2019. https://carm.org/about-the-bible/does-luke-418-misquote-isaiah-611/.

Wenham, Gordon J. *The Book of Leviticus*. Grand Rapids: William B. Eerdmans Publishing Co., 1979.

Woodring, Hoyt Chester. "Grace Under the Mosaic Covenant." PhD diss., Dallas Theological Seminary, 1956.

Youssef, Michael. "6 Covenants Fulfilled in Christ." *Leading the Way*, April 1, 2020. https://au.ltw.org/read/articles/2020/04/6-covenants-fulfilled-in-christ.

Zywietz, Valentin. "Representing the Government of God: Christ as the Hilasterion in Romans 3:25." MA theses, Andrews University, 2016. https://digitalcommons.andrews.edu/theses/84.

www.ingramcontent.com/pod-product-compliance
Lightning Source LLC
Chambersburg PA
CBHW022052290426
44109CB00014B/1072